Commonsense
Bidding

Commonsense Bidding

♣ ♦ ♥ ♠ ♣ ♦ ♥ ♠

WILLIAM S. ROOT

CROWN PUBLISHERS, INC. New York

Published by Crown Publishers, Inc., 225 Park Avenue
South, New York, New York 10003 and represented in
Canada by the Canadian MANDA Group
CROWN is a trademark of Crown Publishers, Inc.
Manufactured in the United States of America
Library of Congress Cataloging-in-Publication Data
Root, William S.
    Commonsense bidding.

    1. Contract bridge—Bidding. I. Title.
GV1282.4.R66 1986   795.41'52   85-29992
ISBN 0-517-56130-1
    0-517-56129-8 (pbk.)
10 9 8 7 6

Contents

Foreword

♣ ♦ ♥ ♠ ♣ ♦ ♥ ♠

In the forties and fifties the gap in bidding methods used by the home player and the expert was relatively narrow. The home player or club player who wished to improve his bidding did not have far to go: A few hours of theoretical instruction was sufficient.

This gap has grown steadily wider. Today a player who wishes to improve his understanding of bidding needs much more than a few hours of study. He needs a book.

Bill Root has provided the book, this one, and it covers a great deal of ground. It is not for beginners, and it stops short of some of the sophisticated artificial conventions devised by would-be world champions. But for 90% of the players between those extremes the author offers many words of wisdom.

His clear presentation and simplified approach make his book a pleasure to read. Not only will you learn how to value your hand, and modify the value as the bidding continues, but you will also learn the language of bidding— a language that, like American speech, is constantly in flux. The reader is taken through the appropriate thought processes and taught to use good judgment.

Bill Root brings remarkable credentials to the task. For more than a quarter of a century he has been an outstanding teacher with thousands of students in Florida and in the New York area. He has also been an active player of the highest class. He has twice represented the United States in the world team championship, just missing a world title both times. And in a 13-month period in 1982–83 he won three major national team titles, a record that has rarely been matched in the history of a game that began when Bill Root was a baby. This book is his baby, and I am sure enthusiasts of all levels will read it with pleasure and profit.

Alan Truscott
New York Times

1

How to Value Your Hand

♣ ♦ ♥ ♠ ♣ ♦ ♥ ♠

THE POINT-COUNT SYSTEM

Bidding is an attempt by two partners to predict the number of tricks their combined hands can win in the play. To do this efficiently, you need a guideline to place a value on your hand. The best method, used by virtually all of the bridge players in the world, is *point count*. There are many different point-count systems. The following is the one I recommend because of its simplicity. If you adopt this system and play bridge with others who use a different point-count system, you will have no difficulty.

Tricks are won in three ways:

> High cards
> Long suits
> Trumps (short suits)

Since there are three ways to win tricks, points must be counted for each as follows:

1. High cards count:
> *Each ace* = 4 points
> *Each king* = 3 points
> *Each queen* = 2 points
> *Each jack* = 1 point

Note that each suit has 10 high-card points and a deck has 40. A hand with 10 points is an "average hand."

2. Long suits count:

> *Each five-card suit* = 1 point
> *Each six-card suit* = 2 points
> *Each seven-card suit* = 3 points

In other words, count 1 point for each additional card over four in every suit. For example:

a. ♠ A Q 10 9	b. ♠ K 7 6 4 2	c. ♠ 6
♡ K J 2	♡ 5	♡ 8 7 6 4 3
◊ 9 6 3	◊ A 7 5 3	◊ K Q 9 7 4 2
♣ A J 2	♣ K Q 8	♣ 2

Hand (a) is worth 15 points, all in high cards. Hand (b) is worth 13 points, 12 for high cards and 1 for the fifth spade. Hand (c) is worth 8 points, 5 for high cards, 1 for the fifth heart and 2 for the fifth and sixth diamonds.

3. Short suits count (but only when revaluing your hand after a good trump suit has been found):

> *Each doubleton* = 1 point
> *Each singleton* = 2 points
> *Each void suit* = 3 points

Do not count points for short suits unless a good trump suit has been found. In other words, count points for short suits when: (1) Your partner has bid a suit that you intend to raise. Four cards or more is considered good trump support. With only three trumps, count points for any short suits and subtract 1 point from the total. (2) Your partner has just indicated good trump support by raising your suit. For example:

	WEST	EAST
	♠ A Q 10 8 3 2	♠ K J 9 7
	♡ A 5 2	♡ 7
	◊ A Q	◊ 8 7 3 2
	♣ 8 7	♣ 10 6 5 4
The bidding:	WEST	EAST
	1 ♠	2 ♠
	4 ♠	

When East picked up his hand he counted only 4 points for high cards. After West opened the bidding with 1 ♠, he *revalues* his hand by counting 2 points for the singleton heart to give him a total of 6.

When West picked up his hand, he counted 18 points, 16 for high cards and 2 for the six-card spade suit. After East raised him to 2 ♠, he *revalues* his hand by adding 2 points for the two doubletons to give him a total of 20.

QUICK TRICKS

High cards that have the potential to win tricks the first or second time a suit is led are called "quick tricks." In certain auctions (for example, when responding to partner's preemptive bid), counting quick tricks is a better way to value your hand than counting points for high cards. The occasions when you should count your quick tricks (instead of your high-card points) will be explained in the appropriate chapters throughout the book. For now, here is the quick-trick table:

> *An ace and a king in the same suit* = two quick tricks
> *An ace and a queen in the same suit* = one and one-half quick tricks
> *A king and a queen in the same suit* = one quick trick
> *An ace* = one quick trick
> *A king guarded by one or more smaller cards* = one-half quick trick

THE POINT-COUNT REQUIREMENTS TO BID GAMES AND SLAMS

To bid the following games and slams, you need in the combined hands:

> *Three notrump, four hearts, or four spades* ....26 points
> *Five clubs or five diamonds* ....29 points
> *Any small slam (six-bid)* ....33 points
> *Any grand slam (seven-bid)* ....37 points

The objectives of bidding are to decide how high to bid (whether to bid a part-score, a game, or a slam) and to decide which suit to play or whether to play notrump. Note that minor-suit games require more points in the combined hands than notrump and major-suit games. This suggests that you should seek a game contract of 3 NT, 4 ♡, or 4 ♠ before rushing into 5 ♣ or 5 ◇. The point-count requirements to bid slams—whether notrump, major suit, or minor suit—are the same. However, it is usually safer to bid a slam in a good trump suit—major or minor—rather than in notrump.

The numbers that should be foremost in your mind during the bidding are 26 and 33. When you find out that the combined total is below 26, stop bidding in a part-score; when the total is between 26 and 32, bid a game; and when the total is 33 or more, consider bidding a slam.

USING YOUR JUDGMENT

As Terence Reese, the great English bridge writer and player, once said: "Make point count your servant, not your master." Point count is a barometer to help you place a value on your hand; it is not entirely accurate on its own. If, after counting points as prescribed by your point-count system, you have a close decision whether to bid aggressively or conservatively, take into account any bidding that may have taken place and reexamine your points. If you like the quality of your points, add a point or two and bid accordingly. If you dislike the quality of your points, subtract a point or two and bid accordingly. To do this well you must exercise good judgment. Throughout the book you will find numerous examples showing how to use your judgment to get a truer value of your hand, but the features in a hand that may make it worth more or less are listed here:

1. An ace is slightly undervalued at 4 points. When you have a close decision, bid aggressively with three or four aces, but bid conservatively with no aces.
2. It is potentially better to have honor cards in the same suit rather than in different suits. For example: A-K versus K-X, the king in the same suit with

the ace is better; A-Q-X versus Q-X-X, the queen in the same suit with the ace is better; A-K-J versus J-X-X, the jack in the same suit with the ace and king is better; Q-J-X versus J-X-X, the jack in the same suit with the queen is better.

3. Honor cards in your long suit (or suits) increase the chances of winning tricks with the low cards. For example: ♠ A-K-X-X-X ♡ X-X is better than ♠ X-X-X-X-X ♡ A-K. When defending against a suit contract, the reverse is true; it is better when your honor cards are in your short suit (or suits).

4. The presence of several "body cards" (tens and nines) should sometimes influence you to take an aggressive action, especially when the body cards are in the same suit with other honor cards. For example: K-10-9-8 is better than K-4-3-2.

5. Unguarded or poorly guarded honor cards, such as a singleton king, queen, or jack or a doubleton Q-J, Q-X, or J-X, will be worthless if partner has no honors in that suit. However, these holdings figure to be useful if they are in a suit that your partner has bid, or if partner has shown a strong balanced hand.

6. An honor card, especially a king or queen, in a suit bid naturally by your partner figures to be of greater value than an honor card in a suit he did not bid. When partner's bidding indicates he has one very long suit, or two long suits, he is unlikely to have more than one or two cards in a side suit. In the side suits, only "quick tricks" (A-K, A-Q, A, K-Q, K-X) are apt to be of value; stray queens and jacks will be useless.

7. Honor combinations such as A-Q, K-J-X, and K-X should be promoted in value when your right-hand opponent bids that suit, and demoted in value when your left-hand opponent bids it.

8. Distributional points vanish when there is an indication of a misfit. Do not count points for long suits when there is an apparent misfit unless your long suit (or suits) is very strong.

2

Opening Notrump Bids

♣ ♦ ♥ ♠ ♣ ♦ ♥ ♠

This chapter deals with opening bids of 1 NT, 2 NT, and 3 NT. A notrump opening bid indicates a "balanced hand" with a specific range of high-card points.

BALANCED HANDS

Hands with approximately the same number of cards in each suit are called balanced hands and are desirable for notrump opening bids. The possible distributions for a balanced hand are 4-3-3-3, 4-4-3-2, and 5-3-3-2. Note that none of these distributions contains a singleton, or more than one doubleton. Here are a few examples; since we are not concerned with high cards for the moment, X is used to represent any card in that suit:

♠ X X X X ♡ X X X ◇ X X X ♣ X X X	4-3-3-3 distribution
♠ X X X X ♡ X X ◇ X X X X ♣ X X X	4-4-3-2 distribution
♠ X X ♡ X X X X X ◇ X X X ♣ X X X	5-3-3-2 distribution

POINT-COUNT REQUIREMENTS

The point-count requirements for opening notrump bids are:

1 NT = 16, 17, ~~or 18~~ high-card points   *15-17*
2 NT = 21, ~~22,~~ or 23 high-card points   *20 -21*
3 NT = 24, 25, or 26 high-card points

   The zone of strength for all opening notrump bids is 3 points; do not violate this principle. Giving such a precise picture of your hand is important, as it makes it easy for your partner to judge the combined strength.

   When you have a balanced hand and 13, 14, or 15 points you are too weak to open the bidding with 1 NT, and when you have 19 or 20 points you are too strong to open 1 NT and too weak to open 2 NT. The proper procedure with these point ranges is to open the bidding with a suit bid of one, planning to bid notrump at your next turn (see page 44 for a detailed explanation).

   The requirements for opening notrump bids are always stated in *high-card* points. Since only 1 distributional point is possible when you have a balanced hand (for the five-card suit when you have 5-3-3-2), the only two cases that would make any difference are when you have 15 high-card points and a five-card suit, or 18 high-card points and a five-card suit. For example:

♠ K 4 2	♠ K 4	Technically, both hands have
♡ A Q 10	♡ A Q 10	only 15 high-card points and
◊ K 10 8 7	◊ K 10 8 7 2	should be opened with 1 ◊. But
♣ Q J 3	♣ Q J 3	a five-card suit is a potential as-
		set (it may take an extra trick).
		So with a five-card suit a 1 NT
		opening bid is recommended
		with the hand on the right.
♠ A 10 2	♠ A 10	Here both hands have 18 high-
♡ K 9 5	♡ K 9 5	card points and could be opened
◊ K J 9	◊ K J 9	with 1 NT. But with a five-card
♣ A Q J 7	♣ A Q J 7 2	suit you should open the hand on
		the right with 1 ♣; it is slightly
		too strong for an opening 1 NT
		bid.

   When you pick up a balanced hand with 27 or more points you must use your judgment to open with 3 NT (an underbid) or with a strong two-bid. The old-fashioned idea of opening the bidding with 4 NT to show a hand too strong to open with 3 NT is not recommended; an opening 4 NT bid should be used as Blackwood (to ask for aces).

   NOTE: If you elect to play the Strong Artificial Two-Club Opening Bid (and its sister convention, the Weak Two-Bid), all balanced hands with 23 or more high-card points are opened with 2 ♣; so the point range for a 2 NT opening is lowered to 20 to 22 and a 3 NT opening is no longer needed to show a balanced hand. See pages 91–92. Also, there is a modern trend toward changing the requirement for an opening 1 NT bid to 15, 16, or 17 high-card points. When you think you are ready I recommend that you make these changes to improve your bidding. Throughout Chapters 2 and 3 the point ranges for opening notrump bids will be 16-18 for 1 NT, 21-23 for 2 NT, and 24-26 for 3 NT, but all of this information is applicable to any range for opening notrump bids; the responder simply adjusts his bidding to the agreed point range for the opening notrump bid.

STOPPERS

A *stopper* is a combination of cards that will prevent the opponents from winning all of the tricks in a suit before giving up the lead. For practical purposes in bidding, a suit is considered stopped when it contains at least A, K-X, Q-X-X, or J-X-X-X. Note that high cards and length, together, form stoppers. Holdings such as Q-X and J-X-X are not stoppers, although they are considered "partial stoppers." Stoppers in all four suits are not required for an opening notrump bid. You may open 1 NT with a worthless doubleton. Although some authorities recommend that you need all four suits stopped to open 2 NT or 3 NT, a more sensible minimum is Q-X or X-X-X when no other opening is attractive. For example:

♠ 7 2   Open 1 NT with a worthless doubleton in spades.
♡ K 10 8
♢ A Q 5 3
♣ A K 9 4

♠ 9 6 4   Open 2 NT with no spade stopper.
♡ A K 7 2
♢ A K 8
♣ A K J

NOTRUMP OPENING BIDS WITH A FIVE-CARD MAJOR SUIT

It is often right to open the bidding with notrump when holding a five-card major suit (especially a five-card heart suit) to avoid rebidding problems. However, with a very strong five-card major and/or a worthless doubleton, it is usually better to bid the major suit. For example:

♠ K 10   Open 1 NT. If you open 1 ♡ and your partner responds
♡ K 9 8 7 3   1 ♠, you have an awkward rebidding problem.
♢ A Q 8
♣ K Q 4

♠ K 10 6 4 3   Open 2 NT. The five-card spade suit is no deterrent.
♡ A Q
♢ A K J
♣ K Q 2

♠ A K Q 9 5   Open 1 ♠. With such a strong five-card suit and a
♡ A 10 3   worthless doubleton, 1 ♠ is a better opening bid than
♢ K J 2   1 NT.
♣ 9 7

SEMIBALANCED HANDS

The semibalanced distributions are 5-4-2-2 and 6-3-2-2. In other words, your hand includes two doubletons, but no singletons or void suits. It is sometimes best to open the bidding with 1 NT, 2 NT, or 3 NT with a semibalanced hand, provided you do not have a four-card or longer major suit and you have no worthless doubletons. The high-card point requirement should be lowered a point or two with a very strong six-card suit. For example:

♠ K 2 ♡ A Q ◊ A 10 7 5 ♣ K 10 9 4 2	Open the bidding with 1 NT.
♠ A 10 7 5 ♡ A Q ◊ K 2 ♣ K 10 9 4 2	Open 1 ♣. With a four-card major and a semibalanced hand, a one-of-a-suit opening is wiser than 1 NT.
♠ Q 10 2 ♡ A 8 ◊ A K Q 10 7 3 ♣ A 10	Open 2 NT. You have only 19 high-card points, but the powerful diamond suit compensates.

RESPONSES TO OPENING NOTRUMP BIDS

An opening bid of 1 NT, 2 NT, or 3 NT describes the strength of a balanced hand within 3 points. With such a precise picture of his partner's hand, the responder is the captain—he is in charge of the subsequent bidding.

As responder, add the number of points in your hand to the number of points your partner has shown by his opening notrump bid. If the total is definitely below 26, stop bidding at the lowest safe part-score. If the total is between 26 and 32, bid a game. If the total is 33 or higher, bid a slam.

If, when you add the totals, you find the sum may be more or less than 26 (or more or less than 33), depending on whether partner has a *minimum* or *maximum* notrump opening, *invite* a game (or a slam).

In addition to deciding how high to bid, the responder must figure out whether to play the hand in notrump or in a suit:

> With a *balanced hand* (and no interest in major-suit play), stick with notrump; pass or raise notrump according to strength.
>
> With an *unbalanced hand,* you almost always bid a suit, or use the "Stayman Convention." You may, of course, end up in a notrump contract.

(NOTE: The Stayman Convention is indispensable to good bidding, and it is covered thoroughly in the next chapter. In order to simplify the presentation, bidding clubs—whether as the Stayman Convention or as a natural bid—is ignored in this chapter.)

RESPONSES TO 1 NT OPENING BIDS WITH BALANCED HANDS

If an opening 1 NT bid shows 16, 17, or 18 points, the responder should always pass with a balanced hand and 7 points or fewer. Even 7 added to 18 is only 25, and you need at least 26 points in the combined hands to bid 3 NT. Suppose your partner opens the bidding with 1 NT and you hold:

♠ 4 2	Pass and let partner play 1 NT. You should also pass
♡ K 10 3	with any lower point count.
◇ Q 7 6 4	
♣ Q 9 8 5	

With 8 or 9 points and a balanced hand, raise partner's opening 1 NT bid to 2 NT. This *invites* game. Partner should pass 2 NT with only 16 points and bid 3 NT with 17 or 18. It is true that 17 added to 8 is only 25, but bidding is not an exact science and this is about as accurate as it can get. Suppose partner opens the bidding with 1 NT and you hold:

♠ 9 5 2	Bid 2 NT with 9 points, 8 in high cards and 1 for the
♡ Q 10 8	five-card diamond suit. *(Note that points are counted for*
◇ A Q 9 8 4	*long suits when responding to opening notrump bids.)*
♣ 6 3	You should make the same bid with 8 points; for example, you should bid 2 NT if the diamond suit was A-J-9-8-4.

With from 10 to 14 points and a balanced hand, raise partner from 1 NT to 3 NT. When you know the combined total is between 26 and 32 (not enough for slam), you should bid 3 NT and your partner *must* pass. Suppose your partner opens the bidding with 1 NT and you hold:

♠ A J 9	Bid 3 NT with 10 points. You would make the same bid
♡ 6 3	with 11, 12, 13, or 14 points. ~~15~~
◇ K Q 8 4	
♣ 7 6 3 2	

or 17

If your partner opens the bidding with 1 NT and you have ~~15 or~~ 16 points and a balanced hand, you should invite slam; with 17 points or more you should bid a slam. See **Chapter 17, Slam Bidding**, especially "The Quantitative Notrump Raise."

RESPONSES TO 1 NT OPENING BIDS WITH UNBALANCED HANDS

When your partner opens the bidding with 1 NT and you have an unbalanced hand (or in some cases a balanced hand that shows promise to play in a major suit contract), bid as follows:

Bid 2 ◇, 2 ♡, or 2 ♠ to show 7 points or fewer and at least a five-card suit. The purpose of bidding with such a weak hand is to get to a better part-score contract than 1 NT. For example:

♠ 9 7 5 4 3 2	Answer your partner's 1 NT opening with 2 ♠. He
♡ 3	should then pass (he knows you have at most 7 points),
◊ 7 6 4	and 2 ♠ is bound to be a better contract than 1 NT.
♣ 8 6 2	

♠ 4 3	Bid 2 ♡. This time it would be reasonable to pass
♡ Q J 10 9 7	1 NT—you do have a balanced hand—but in most cases
◊ Q 7 4	two of your five-card suit will make a better contract.
♣ 8 3 2	

Bid 3 ◊, 3 ♡, or 3 ♠ to show 10 or more points and at least five cards in the bid suit. These bids are forcing to game and are often the beginning of a slam auction. For example, your partner opens 1 NT and you hold:

♠ 7 2	Bid 3 ♡ with 12 points. Your partner should then bid
♡ A J 8 6 3	3 NT or 4 ♡, depending on his hand; you should pass
◊ K 9 8 7	either bid.
♣ K 5	

♠ A Q J 6 4	Bid 3 ♠ with 18 points. Your plan is to bid a slam before
♡ 7	you are through bidding.
◊ K 10	
♣ A Q 9 5 2	

Bid 4 ♡ or 4 ♠ to show 9 to 14 points and at least a six-card suit. When you are convinced that four of a major will make the best contract, bid it directly. For example, your partner opens 1 NT and you hold:

♠ K 10 9 6 4 3	Bid 4 ♠ with 10 points. It should be clear that 4 ♠ is the
♡ 2	best contract. Bidding 3 ♠, or any other bid, is a waste
◊ A J 8 7	of time. Your partner must pass 4 ♠.
♣ 6 4	

With a strong five- or six-card minor suit, it is usually better to raise notrump rather than to bid your suit. For example, your partner opens 1 NT and you hold:

♠ 9 4	Bid 3 NT with 10 points. This is a gambling bid, but a
♡ 10 7 2	good one. With a similar hand and only 8 or 9 points,
◊ A K J 8 6 2	you should bid 2 NT.
♣ 7 3	

REBIDS AFTER OPENING 1 NT BIDS

When your partner answers your 1 NT opening by bidding 2 ◊, 2 ♡, or 2 ♠, he shows at most 7 points; he has judged that there is no possible game and he expects you to pass. For example:

	You	Partner
♠ A Q 10	*You*	*Partner*
♡ A J 9	1 NT	2 ♠
◊ K J 7 2	P	
♣ Q J 3		

In spite of your 18-point maximum, you should pass 2 ♠.

These two-level suit responses to 1 NT are sign-off bids (sometimes called "drop-dead bids," to emphasize to the opening bidder that he must pass). However, there are very rare exceptions (maybe one time in a hundred) when you should bid again. With 18 high-card points of top quality, very good trump support, and a doubleton, you should raise your partner's suit to the three-level; no other bid should be considered. For example:

♠ A 9	*You*	*Partner*
♡ K Q 8 2	1 NT	2 ♡
♢ A J 10 3	3 ♡	
♣ A 6 4		

This hand is worth more than 18 points after your partner bids hearts, and that is what your 3 ♡ bid implies. After your raise, your partner should revalue his hand by adding extra points for short suits; if he counts 6, 7, or 8 points, he should bid game. For example, your partner holds:

You	*Partner*	♠ 7 5 3
1 NT	2 ♡	♡ J 10 9 4 3
3 ♡	4 ♡	♢ 2
		♣ K J 8 2

After your heart raise, your partner should add 2 extra points for his singleton diamond to give him 8 points. Note that these two hands will almost surely make a game in hearts. If you change your partner's club holding to J-X-X-X, 2 ♡ would still be his proper response, but then (with only 5 points) he should pass 3 ♡.

When your partner responds 3 ♢, 3 ♡, or 3 ♠, he has at least 10 points and his bid is forcing to game. After a 3 ♡ or 3 ♠ response, the general rule is to bid 3 NT with a doubleton in partner's major suit, or to bid four of his major with three or more trumps. After a 3 ♢ response you should be less inclined to raise partner's suit: Do not bid beyond 3 NT unless you judge 5 ♢ to be a safer contract than 3 NT and wish to encourage your partner to bid a slam (you should have good diamond support and a doubleton, and most of your high cards in the side suits should be quick tricks). Here are two examples:

♠ A Q 7	*You*	*Partner*
♡ K 8 2	1 NT	3 ♡
♢ Q J 10 3	4 ♡	
♣ A 9 4		

If you take away the ♡ 2 and add the ♠ 2, then 3 NT would be a better bid than 4 ♡.

♠ K 10 2	*You*	*Partner*
♡ K J 10	1 NT	3 ♢
♢ A J 6	3 NT	
♣ A J 9 3		

With 4-3-3-3 distribution and stoppers in the three unbid suits, 3 NT is the logical bid. If you change the hand by removing the ♠ 2 and adding the ♢ 2, then 4 ♢ would be a good bid. A 4 ♢ bid would be encouraging and may influence the responder to bid a makable slam.

Before leaving this section on rebids after an opening 1 NT bid, note the responsibility of the opening bidder:

1. If the responder raises a 1 NT opening to 2 NT, the opener is *invited* to bid again; he should pass with 16 points and bid 3 NT with 17 or 18 points.
2. If the responder jumps the bidding to 3 ◊, 3 ♡, or 3 ♠, the opener is *forced* to bid again; he is expected to choose between raising the responder's suit and bidding 3 NT.
3. If the responder at any time in the auction bids a game (3 NT, 4 ♡, 4 ♠, 5 ♣, or 5 ◊), the opening 1 NT bidder is *not* entitled to make any bid that takes the auction beyond the game level; if there is any chance for a slam, the responder must make the first bid beyond game.

RESPONSES TO 2 NT OPENING BIDS

If an opening 2 NT bid shows 21, 22, or 23 points, the responder should always pass with a balanced hand and 0 to 3 points; bid 3 NT with a balanced hand, no interest in the major suits, and 4 to 9 points; and invite or bid a slam with a balanced hand and 10 points or more (see "The Quantitative Notrump Raise," page 201). Here is one example:

♠ J 10 9	Pass partner's opening 2 NT bid with 3 points. You need
♡ 8 7 5 3	1 more point to venture a 3 NT bid.
◊ 9 4 2	
♣ Q 6 4	

If your partner opens the bidding with 2 NT and you have an unbalanced hand, bid 3 ◊, 3 ♡, or 3 ♠ with at least five cards in the bid suit and 4 points or more. It is also right to bid three of a six-card *major* suit with fewer than 4 points, even though the bid is forcing. For example, partner opens 2 NT and you hold:

♠ Q 10 7 5 2	Bid 3 ♠, a forcing bid. Your partner is expected to bid
♡ 6 3	4 ♠ with three or more spades, or 3 NT with a
◊ A 9 8 4	doubleton spade. You will pass either bid.
♣ 7 6	

♠ A Q 9 7 5	Bid 3 ♠. This is the beginning of a slam auction. You
♡ 4	should bid a slam as soon as you decide where to play it.
◊ A Q 6 3	
♣ 7 4 2	

♠ 10 9 7 6 4 3	Answer partner's 2 NT opening with 3 ♠. If partner's
♡ 2	next bid is 3 NT, bid 4 ♠. There is no way to stop
◊ 7 5 3 2	bidding at 3 ♠, and 4 ♠ figures to be a better contract
♣ 8 6	than 2 NT; you may even make it.

A direct 4 ♡ or 4 ♠ response to an opening 2 NT bid has no universal meaning, and most bridge teachers and writers ignore the subject entirely, so you might be wise to ignore it too and avoid a bidding disaster. One old-fashioned idea was to play that the jump to 4 ♡ or 4 ♠ showed a six-card major headed by two of the top honors (A-K, A-Q, or K-Q) and about 7 to 9 high-card points; since the bid rarely comes up and few players would understand it, it would be impractical for you to adopt this method. Some players like to use the jump to 4 ♡

or 4 ♠ as a sign-off bid (showing a hand with a long major suit but no hope for slam)—the same meaning as a 4 ♡ or 4 ♠ response to an opening 1 NT bid. Unless you and your partner have a clear understanding as to its meaning, you are asking for trouble if you bid 4 ♡ or 4 ♠ in response to a 2 NT opening bid.

RESPONSES TO 3 NT OPENING BIDS

If an opening bid of 3 NT shows a balanced hand with 24, 25, or 26 points, the responder should always pass with a balanced hand and 0 to 6 points; with 7 points or more he should consider a slam (see "The Quantitative Notrump Raise," page 201).

When your partner opens the bidding with 3 NT and you have an unbalanced hand, bid as follows:

Bid 4 ♡ or 4 ♠ with at least six cards in the bid suit and a maximum of 6 (or possibly 7) points. For example, partner opens the bidding with 3 NT and you hold:

♠ 9 ♡ J 9 8 5 4 3 ◇ 6 3 2 ♣ 7 6 4	Bid 4 ♡. Your hand will produce several tricks if the hand is played in hearts, and possibly no tricks in notrump. The opening bidder should generally pass 4 ♡, but he may bid 5 ♡ with 25 or 26 points of excellent quality and very good trump support. With this hand you should pass a 5 ♡ bid by partner, but change the ♡ J to the ♡ K and you should bid 6 ♡.
♠ Q 7 6 4 2 ♡ 9 8 6 ◇ J ♣ 10 5 4 3	Pass, with only a five-card spade suit. Although 4 ♠ could be the only makable game contract, 3 NT should succeed more often.

If your partner has opened 3 NT and you have 7 points or more, you may have a slam. You may bid 4 ♣ (the Stayman Convention; see next chapter) to learn more about your partner's hand, bid 4 ◇ with a five-card or longer suit, or bid a slam directly with 9 or more points if you know where to play it.

RESPONSES TO 1 NT AFTER AN ENEMY OVERCALL

If your partner opens the bidding with 1 NT and your right-hand opponent overcalls, bid any five-card or longer suit at the *two-level* with about 5 to 8 points. For example:

Partner	Opp.	You	♠ K 4 2
1 NT	2 ◇	2 ♡	♡ J 10 9 7 3
			◇ 6
			♣ 9 7 5 2

You have 5 points. Your partner should usually pass your 2 ♡ bid, but he may raise to 3 ♡ with good trump support and a maximum. The high cards figure to be pretty evenly divided between the two sides, about 20 high-card points each. Each side should be able to win a majority of the tricks if the contract is played in its long suit. Based on this reasoning, you should bid 2 ♡ and will probably make your bid, while if you pass your opponent could probably make his bid.

With fewer than 5 points and a long suit, you should pass. For example:

Partner	Opp.	You	
1 NT	2 ◊	P	♠ 7 4 2
			♡ J 9 8 7 3
			◊ 6
			♣ 9 7 5 2

With only 2 points, you must pass. However, if your right-hand opponent had passed, you should bid 2 ♡.

You may bid a very strong five-card suit, or any six-card or longer suit, at the *three-level* (a nonjump bid) with 5 to 8 points. For example:

Partner	Opp.	You	
1 NT	2 ♠	3 ◊	♠ 7 2
			♡ A 10 5
			◊ J 9 8 6 4 3
			♣ 8 4

You have 7 points. The 3 ◊ bid is natural and meant to discourage your partner from bidding further. Although your partner should generally pass when you bid a new suit at the three-level (your bid shows a maximum of 8 points), he may bid 3 NT with a good fit in your *minor suit*, a maximum 1 NT opening, and the opponent's suit securely stopped. If your response were 3 ♡, he may raise to 4 ♡ with a good trump fit and a maximum.

With a five-card or longer suit and at least 9 or 10 points, you should jump the bidding. For example:

Partner	Opp.	You	
1 NT	2 ♡	3 ♠	♠ K J 10 6 2
			♡ 6 4
			◊ A 9 7 3
			♣ 9 8

You have 9 points and your hand is too good to bid 2 ♠. Your 3 ♠ bid is forcing. Your partner should bid 4 ♠ with three or more trumps, or bid 3 NT with only two trumps; you should pass either bid.

With a balanced hand, or with an unbalanced hand if you have a strong five- or six-card minor suit, raise your partner to 2 NT with 8 or 9 points and raise him to 3 NT with 10 to 14 points. For example:

Partner	Opp.	You	
1 NT	2 ♠	3 NT	♠ 7 4
			♡ K 8
			◊ A Q J 6 2
			♣ 10 7 5 4

You have 11 points. If you take away the ♡ K, leaving only 8 points, you should bid 2 NT. Note that it is not necessary to have a stopper in the opponent's suit when you raise notrump; you must gamble that partner has a stopper.

Another possible action when an opponent overcalls your partner's opening 1 NT bid is to double. The requirements to double, with an illustration, can be found on page 133.

RESPONSES TO 1 NT AFTER AN ENEMY DOUBLE

If your right-hand opponent doubles your partner's opening 1 NT, it is a *penalty double* (see page 134). With a weak hand and no five-card or longer suits, you must pass and hope for the best. For example:

Partner	*Opp.*	*You*	
1 NT	DBL	P	♠ 10 7 4 3
			♡ 7 3
			◊ J 9 8 2
			♣ 9 8 5

Your partner may be set two or three tricks in 1 NT doubled, but there is nothing sensible you can do about it; you have no place to go.

If you have a poor hand that includes a five-card or longer suit, bid two of your long suit. This is a "rescue bid." For example:

Partner	*Opp.*	*You*	
1 NT	DBL	2 ♡	♠ 8 7 4
			♡ J 9 8 4 3
			◊ 7
			♣ 6 5 3 2

You are unlikely to make your contract, but if you get doubled in 2 ♡ you should fare better than your partner would if you left him to play 1 NT doubled.

If you have 7 or more high-card points, you should redouble; this is the only strong action. For example:

Partner	*Opp.*	*You*	
1 NT	DBL	RDBL	♠ A 9 8 6
			♡ 9 7
			◊ K 10 8 3
			♣ 7 5 2

If everyone passes, your partner should have no difficulty making 1 NT redoubled. If the opponents bid 2 ◊ or 2 ♠, you should double them; if they bid 2 ♣ or 2 ♡, maybe partner can double. The opponents may be in trouble, so you must try not to let them off the hook.

3

The Stayman Convention

♣   ♦   ♥   ♠   ♣   ♦   ♥   ♠

This convention is used when your partner opens the bidding with 1 NT, 2 NT, or 3 NT and *your right-hand opponent passes*. The Stayman bid in response to 1 NT is 2 ♣, to 2 NT it is 3 ♣, and to 3 NT it is 4 ♣. These club bids are all artificial, which means you may or may not have length in the club suit and you are not suggesting clubs as the trump suit. A Stayman response asks the opening notrump bidder to bid a four-card (or five-card) major suit if he has one, or to bid diamonds if he does not.

Using Stayman is essential to good bidding. Along with the "takeout double" and "Blackwood," it is one of the three most popular bidding conventions played. Here are the reasons you should use Stayman:

1. It is the way to reach a major-suit contract when the trump suit is divided 4-4. Remember, you should *never* bid a four-card (or shorter) suit in response to an opening notrump bid.
2. When your partner opens the bidding with specifically 1 NT, you can bid accurately with 8- or 9-point hands that include a five- or six-card major suit. You learned in Chapter 2 that a suit response at the two-level shows at most 7 points and a suit response at the three-level shows at least 10 points. With 8 or 9 points and a five- or six-card major, the first step is to bid 2 ♣.
3. It is a way to get more detailed information about your partner's opening notrump bid to help you decide whether or not to bid a slam, or which slam to bid.

STAYMAN AFTER 1 NT OPENING BIDS

In response to an opening 1 NT bid, you should use Stayman on any hand that has 8 or more points and four cards in one or both major suits. Exception: Do not use Stayman with 4-3-3-3 distribution. For example, your partner opens the bidding with 1 NT and you hold:

♠ K 10 6 2
♡ K 10 5 4
◇ 7 5
♣ A 8 2

Bid 2 ♣. This hand is ideal for Stayman. You have two four-card majors (although only one is required) and more than enough points.

♠ Q 9 8 5
♡ J 9 7 3
◇ 2
♣ Q 7 4 3

Pass. Although your distribution is great for Stayman, with only 5 points your hand is too weak.

♠ K 8 6 3
♡ A J 6
◇ Q 10 4
♣ 5 3 2

Bid 3 NT with 10 points, even though you have a four-card major suit. Using Stayman is not recommended with 4-3-3-3 distribution.

Stayman is customarily used with a four-card major suit, but it also comes in handy with a five-card major and 8 or 9 points. Suppose your partner opens 1 NT and you hold:

♠ K 10 9 8 7
♡ A 2
◇ 6 3
♣ 10 7 5 4

Bid 2 ♣ with 8 points. Your hand is too good to bid 2 ♠ and too weak to bid 3 ♠. If you bid 2 ♣ and follow with 2 ♠, you show 8 or 9 points and a five- or six-card major suit.

THE OPENING 1 NT BIDDER'S REPLY TO STAYMAN

A 2 ♣ Stayman response asks the opening bidder to bid a four-card major suit if he has one, or else *he must bid 2 ◇; he may not make any bid except 2 ♡, 2 ♠, or 2 ◇*. For example:

♠ A Q 2	*You*	*Partner*
♡ K J 10	1 NT	2 ♣
◇ 6 4 3	2 ◇	
♣ A Q J 9		

The 2 ◇ bid is artificial. It simply tells your partner that you do not have a four-card (or five-card) major suit.

♠ 10 7 5 4	*You*	*Partner*
♡ A J	1 NT	2 ♣
◇ A 6 2	2 ♠	
♣ A K 8 2		

Note that any four-card major suit is biddable.

♠ K 2	*You*	*Partner*
♡ A J 8 6 4	1 NT	2 ♣
◇ A Q 3	2 ♡	
♣ Q 10 9		

Your 2♡ bid promises only four hearts. There is no way to tell your partner right away that you have five, but you may get a chance to rebid the suit.

If you open the bidding with 1 NT and have two four-card majors, I recommend that you bid the *stronger first.* Some authorities suggest always bidding spades first, while others suggest always bidding hearts first. Obviously, this is a debatable area of bidding and no one method is outstanding. Here is one example:

♠ 9 7 6 3	*You*	*Partner*
♡ A Q J 8	1 NT	2 ♣
◇ K 2	2 ♡	
♣ A Q 10		

It is when one four-card major is much stronger than the other that bidding the stronger first is apt to work out better.

USING STAYMAN WITH WEAK HANDS

Stayman is an *asking bid,* not a *telling bid.* Although you usually have at least 8 points when you bid 2 ♣ in response to 1 NT, it is not a requirement. The fact that the opening 1 NT bidder must bid 2 ♡, 2 ♠, or 2 ◇ allows you to bid 2 ♣ with little or no strength, but you must be prepared to pass his next bid; *to bid again you must have a good hand,* at least 8 points. The only time that bidding 2 ♣ with a weak hand would be sensible is with length in spades, hearts, and diamonds. Suppose your partner opens the bidding with 1 NT and you hold:

♠ 10 7 4 2	Bid 2 ♣, then pass partner's next bid, which must be
♡ J 9 6 3	2 ♡, 2 ♠, or 2 ◇. This bidding should get you to the
◇ J 8 6 5 2	best contract. Although a 2 ◇ reply does not show a
♣ —	four-card suit, partner will usually have at least three
	diamonds, since he denied more than three cards in
	either major suit.

REBIDS BY THE 2 ♣ BIDDER

After using Stayman and finding out about your partner's major-suit holding, you may (1) raise his major suit to the three- or four-level; (2) bid 2 NT or 3 NT; (3) bid 2 ♡, 2 ♠, or a nonjump bid of 3 ♡ (these bids are not forcing); or (4) bid 3 ♣ or 3 ◇, or jump the bidding to 3 ♡ or 3 ♠ (these bids are forcing). Here are several examples:

Raise partner's major suit to the three-level with 8 or 9 points and at least four-card trump support. This bid is invitational; partner should pass with a minimum 1 NT opening, or bid game in the major with a maximum.

Partner	*You*	
1 NT	2 ♣	♠ A 9 7 2
2 ♠	3 ♠	♡ K 8 5 3
		◇ 6 4
		♣ J 7 2

The value of your hand increased from 8 to 9 points after your partner bid 2 ♠, but 3 ♠ is still the right bid.

Raise partner's major suit to game with 10 to 14 points and at least four-card trump support.

Partner	You	
		♠ 7
1 NT	2 ♣	♡ K 9 8 5
2 ♡	4 ♡	◇ A J 10 4
		♣ 7 6 3 2

After partner's 2 ♡ bid, the value of your hand increased from 8 to 10 points, so the hand qualifies for a jump to 4 ♡. Partner must pass 4 ♡.

If your partner rebids 2 ◇, or two of the "wrong" major suit, invite game by bidding 2 NT with 8 or 9 points.

Partner	You	
		♠ K 10 8
1 NT	2 ♣	♡ A J 10 2
2 ♠	2 NT	◇ 7 3
		♣ 6 5 4 2

Note that you must not raise spades with only three-card support. Partner should pass 2 NT with 16 points, or bid on to game with 17 or 18.

If partner bids 2 ◇ or the wrong major suit, bid 3 NT with 10 to 14 points.

Partner	You	
		♠ A Q 10 6
1 NT	2 ♣	♡ A 8 6 2
2 ◇	3 NT	◇ 9 8 7 3
		♣ 7

You have 10 points and 3 NT is the only sensible bid. You must not bid a major suit or "raise" diamonds unless you have at least a five-card suit; partner's 2 ◇ bid is artificial.

You may bid a five- or six-card major suit at the cheapest level with 8 or 9 points. This is not a forcing bid, it is invitational.

Partner	You	
		♠ A 10 2
1 NT	2 ♣	♡ Q 10 9 8 5 4
2 ◇	2 ♡	◇ 3
		♣ 9 7 4

You have 8 points and 2 ♡ describes your hand perfectly. Note that if partner had rebid 2 ♠ instead of 2 ◇, you would bid 3 ♡ to invite him to game.

If, after using Stayman, you jump the bidding to 3 ♡ or 3 ♠, or bid 3 ♣ or 3 ◇, your bid is forcing to game.

Partner	You	
		♠ A Q 9 7 4
1 NT	2 ♣	♡ A 10 6 3
2 ◇	3 ♠	◇ 7
		♣ 7 5 2

Your 3 ♠ bid shows a five-card or longer suit and at least 10 points. Note that 2 ♣ was a better bid than a direct response of 3 ♠, because a good 4 ♡ contract would be reached if partner had four hearts.

Partner	You	♠ 7
1 NT	2 ♣	♡ A 9 7 6
2 ◊	3 ◊	◊ A Q 10 9 2
		♣ 8 5 3

Your first bid of 2 ♣ was to find out if partner could bid 2 ♡, in which case you would raise to 4 ♡. Over your 3 ◊ bid, your partner must bid again; he may bid 3 NT, raise diamonds, or bid a new suit, depending on his hand. His next bid is the key to deciding whether to play 3 NT or 5 ◊.

THE OPENING 1 NT BIDDER'S THIRD BID

If your partner rebids 2 ♡ or 2 ♠ (or 3 ♡ without jumping), showing a five- or six-card suit and 8 or 9 points, you should pass with a minimum 1 NT opening and bid again with a maximum. This sometimes requires good judgment. For example:

♠ A 7 5	You	Partner
♡ K J 6 2	1 NT	2 ♣
◊ Q J 10	2 ♡	2 ♠
♣ K Q 3	P	

With only 16 points and 4-3-3-3 distribution, you should reject your partner's invitation to game.

♠ Q 6 4	You	Partner
♡ A 9 8 7	1 NT	2 ♣
◊ A K 7 2	2 ♡	2 ♠
♣ A 3	4 ♠	

This hand is far superior to the preceding one. You have 17 points (top-quality), three-card spade support, and a doubleton club.

♠ A Q 8	You	Partner
♡ K 2	1 NT	2 ♣
◊ Q J 10 6	2 ◊	2 ♡
♣ A Q 9 5	3 NT	

You have 18 points and should accept partner's game invitation by bidding 3 NT; you need at least three trumps to raise partner's major.

When your partner rebids a minor suit at the three-level, his bid is forcing to game and he may be looking for a slam. Your next bid will help him decide which game or slam to play. For example:

♠ Q J 2	You	Partner
♡ A Q 9	1 NT	2 ♣
◊ K 10 5	2 ◊	3 ◊
♣ K J 7 3	3 NT	

With 16 points (some of them pretty junky) and 4-3-3-3 distribution, 3 NT figures to be the best game contract. Also, your bid warns your partner that you have a poor-quality 1 NT opening bid for a slam.

	You	Partner
♠ A 5		
♡ A Q 7 2	1 NT	2 ♣
♦ Q J 6 4	2 ♡	3 ♦
♣ A 10 8	4 ♦	

This hand could not be better to play in diamonds; all your points in the side suits are quick tricks, and you have a doubleton spade and four-card trump support. The 4 ♦ bid may encourage your partner to bid a slam. If he does, he will be very happy with this dummy.

If your partner follows his 2 ♣ bid with 2 NT or 3 NT, he must have a four-card major suit; or else why Stayman? For example:

	You	Partner
♠ A Q 6 3		
♡ K 9 7 2	1 NT	2 ♣
♦ K 10	2 ♠	3 NT
♣ A 5 4	4 ♡	

Since your partner did not raise your spades, he must have four hearts. Otherwise he would have bid 3 NT directly over 1 NT. Hence the 4 ♡ bid.

HOW TO BID WHEN YOU HAVE A REAL CLUB SUIT

Opposite a 1 NT opening bid, there are two ways to show your partner that you have a real club suit:

1. Partner	You		2. Partner	You
1 NT	2 ♣		1 NT	3 ♣
2 ♦/♡/♠	3 ♣			

In the original version of Stayman, bidding sequence #1 was used to show a six- or seven-card club suit and a maximum of 7 (or 8) points; this is commonly called a "club bust" and the opening 1 NT bidder would always pass the 3 ♣ bid. Bidding sequence #2 was used to show a five-card or longer club suit and a strong hand; the 3 ♣ bid was forcing to game.

The above method is used by a vast majority of bridge players, and it is still recommended in many bridge books and taught by many teachers. On that basis you will certainly encounter players who play this way.

However, it is far superior to reverse this procedure; use the bidding in sequence #1 to show the strong hand (the 3 ♣ bid is forcing to game), and use the bidding in sequence #2 to show the weak hand (the direct jump to 3 ♣ shows a "club bust"). Virtually every expert would agree with this, and I recommend that you play this way. Since this is one of the most controversial areas of bidding, *be sure to make an agreement with your favorite partners as to which method you will use;* otherwise you are very apt to encounter a bidding disaster.

The following assumes that the direct jump to 3 ♣ shows the weak hand, and a bid of 2 ♣ followed by 3 ♣ shows the strong hand:

Partner	*You*	♠ 8
1 NT	3 ♣	♡ 7 4 2
		◊ 9 4 3
		♣ Q J 8 6 5 3

Since your 3 ♣ bid shows a maximum of 7 points, your partner must pass. Note that the opponents have about 20 high-card points and are likely to fare well in a spade contract; your jump to 3 ♣ may persuade them not to enter the bidding.

Partner	*You*	♠ 7 6 2
1 NT	P	♡ 3
		◊ 7 6 5 4
		♣ Q 10 8 6 5

Your partner is not likely to make 1 NT, but it figures to be a better contract than 3 ♣. You need a better suit than this one to venture a bid at the three-level.

There is no bid to describe a hand with long clubs and 8 or 9 points; you may have to overbid or underbid slightly, but the solution is often to bid 2 NT with a strong club suit. For example:

Partner	*You*	♠ 10 8 7
1 NT	2 NT	♡ 3
		◊ 7 6 5 4
		♣ A Q J 9 2

With 8 points your hand is too strong to pass and too weak to force to game. So the least of evils is to bid 2 NT and invite game, in spite of your singleton heart.

With a five-card or longer club suit and a hand strong enough to insist on reaching game, bid as follows:

Partner	*You*	♠ A J 9 4
1 NT	2 ♣	♡ 2
2 ◊	3 ♣	◊ K 7 3
		♣ A Q 10 8 5

You have 15 points and are interested in bidding a slam; your partner's next bid will help you decide. If partner had bid 2 ♠, instead of 2 ◊, it is likely that you could make a slam in spades. Note the advantage of playing this sequence as forcing; if you play that 2 ♣ followed by 3 ♣ is weak, there is no intelligent way to bid this hand.

Partner	*You*	♠ 3
1 NT	2 ♣	♡ K 8 3
2 ♠	3 ♣	◊ K 9 5
		♣ A K J 7 4 2

You have 16 points and it is still unclear whether you should play this hand in clubs or notrump, and whether you should bid a slam or just a game. Note that it is useful to use Stayman without a four-card major suit when you have a strong hand and a long minor suit.

Partner	You	♠ A 5
1 NT	2 ♣	♡ K J 4 2
2 ♠	3 ♣	◇ 7
		♣ Q 10 9 8 5 3

This 12-point hand with exciting distribution belongs in game in notrump, hearts, or clubs, and if your partner has the "right hand" you may even have a slam. If partner's next bid is 3 NT he is advertising the wrong hand and you should pass 3 NT. If he bids 4 ♣ he says he has the right hand and you would be justified in bidding 6 ♣.

STAYMAN AFTER 2 NT AND 3 NT OPENING BIDS

A 3 ♣ response to a 2 NT opening bid is Stayman, normally showing 4 points or more, and asks the opening bidder to bid 3 ♡ or 3 ♠ to show a four-card (or five-card) major suit, or to bid 3 ◇ to deny one. For example:

Partner	You	♠ J 10 6 3
2 NT	3 ♣	♡ J
		◇ Q 9 8 7 2
		♣ 9 8 5

If your partner's next bid is 3 ♠, you will bid 4 ♠. If his next bid is 3 ◇ or 3 ♡, you will bid 3 NT.

To show a real club suit opposite a 2 NT opening bid, simply rebid the suit. For example:

Partner	You	♠ A Q 2
2 NT	3 ♣	♡ 7
3 ♠	4 ♣	◇ 10 9 5 4
		♣ K Q 8 6 4

You have 12 points and probably have a slam somewhere. Partner's next bid should help you decide. Note that you could not jump to 4 ♣ directly, as that would ask for aces; see "The Gerber Convention," page 199.

It is risky to use Stayman opposite a 3 NT opening bid unless you have a slam in mind; at least 7 points. However, if you do bid 4 ♣, your partner must bid 4 ♡ or 4 ♠ to show a four-card (or five-card) major suit, or bid 4 ◇ to deny one. For example:

Partner	You	♠ A J 9 3
3 NT	4 ♣	♡ K J 10 6
		◇ 7 2
		♣ 10 5 4

You have 9 points and should be planning to bid a slam. If partner rebids 4 ♡ or 4 ♠, you should bid six of his suit. If he rebids 4 ◇, to deny a four-card major suit, you should bid 6 NT.

Partner	You
3 NT	P

♠ Q 7 6 2
♡ 10 8 5 4
◇ 7
♣ 8 5 4 2

Although 4 ♡ or 4 ♠ would make a beautiful contract if partner has a four-card major, you dare not bid 4 ♣ for fear that partner will bid 4 ◇.

STAYMAN AFTER ENEMY INTERFERENCE

If your partner opens the bidding with 1 NT and your right-hand opponent overcalls or doubles, Stayman is off altogether—although if your opponent has made an overcall, you may cue-bid his suit to inquire about a major suit. For example:

Partner	Opp.	You
1 NT	DBL	2 ♣

♠ 8 5 4 2
♡ 3
◇ 9 8 6
♣ J 10 7 5 3

You are unlikely to make your contract, but if you get doubled in 2 ♣, you should fare better than your partner would if you left him to play 1 NT doubled.

Partner	Opp.	You
1 NT	2 ◇	3 ◇

♠ K 10 7 2
♡ 9 8 7 3
◇ 4
♣ A Q 10 5

Your 3 ◇ bid is a cue-bid and it is forcing to game. It shows support for the unbid suits, especially the unbid major suits, and at least 9 or 10 points. Your partner must bid a four-card major suit if he has one; if not, he should usually bid 3 NT.

So, you may never use Stayman unless your right-hand opponent passes. However, we must still contend with interference *after* you or your partner have used Stayman.

If, after you have opened the bidding with 1 NT, your right-hand opponent overcalls your partner's 2 ♣ response, you may bid a four-card major suit at the *two-level*, double the opponent's bid with a strong four-card holding in his suit, or else you must pass; do not bid at the three-level. For example:

♠ A 6
♡ K J 10 5
◇ A Q 9
♣ K 8 3 2

You	Opp.	Partner	Opp.
1 NT	P	2 ♣	2 ♠
P			

Your pass gives partner a chance to double 2 ♠, or to pass if he had bid 2 ♣ with a weak hand. If he makes another bid he can be counted on for a good hand—at least 8 points—so you should bid hearts at your next turn.

If your right-hand opponent had bid 2 ◇ instead of 2 ♠, then you should bid 2 ♡; if his bid were 2 ♡, you should double.

If, after you have opened the bidding with 1 NT, your right-hand opponent doubles your partner's 2 ♣ response (a "lead-directing double"; see page 136), you should make your normal bid if you have a four-card major suit, bid 2 ◊ if that is your longest suit, pass if clubs is your longest suit, or redouble with exceptionally strong clubs (A-J-9-X, or better). For example:

♠ A Q 10	*You*	*Opp.*	*Partner*	*Opp.*
♡ K 7 2	1 NT	P	2 ♣	DBL
◊ A J 9	P			
♣ Q 8 6 3				

Your pass indicates that clubs is your only four-card or longer suit. If you had a different long suit, you would bid two of that suit. With a long and strong club suit, you would redouble. In any case, the additional information this gives your partner may help him to decide the best contract.

4

Opening Suit
Bids of One

♣ ♦ ♥ ♠ ♣ ♦ ♥ ♠

The most common opening bid is in a suit at the one-level. When you pick up your cards you must judge whether or not your hand qualifies for an opening bid, and if it does, you must then decide which suit to bid. The first step is to decide whether or not to open the bidding at all.

POINT-COUNT REQUIREMENTS

The *minimum* requirement for an opening suit bid of one is 12 or 13 points, counting points for high cards and long suits. With 12 points you should pass more often than not; with 13 points you should rarely pass; and with 14 points or more you should always open the bidding. Note that the only time there is a problem is when you have 12 or 13 points, and that is when you must use your judgment.

The features that should encourage you to open a borderline hand are: Most of your high-card points are made up of quick tricks, especially aces; most of your high cards are in your long suit (or suits); you have length in the major suits; you have an abundance of body cards (tens and nines).

The features that should discourage you from opening a borderline hand are: You have unguarded honor cards (such as K, Q-J, Q-X, J-X); you have high cards in your short suits (such as a doubleton K-Q or K-J); you have stray queens and jacks (such as Q-X-X or J-X-X-X); you are short in the major suits; you lack body cards.

Here are several examples:

♠ A Q 2   Open this 12-point hand with three quick tricks.
♡ 7 6 4
◊ 8 5 2
♣ A Q 10 9

♠ Q 9
♡ J 8 5 4
♢ Q 7 2
♣ A K 6 3

Pass with 12 points. The spade queen, heart jack, and diamond queen are all doubtful values.

♠ A K 10 9 8
♡ A 9 8 7
♢ 6 2
♣ 7 4

Open with 12 points. You have nine cards in the major suits, three quick tricks, and good body cards in your long suits.

♠ Q 2
♡ K J
♢ Q 10 8 5
♣ K J 7 6 3

Pass with 13 points. Your 12 high-card points are of the "junky" variety and half of them are in your short major suits.

♠ K Q 10 9 2
♡ A J 10 9 2
♢ 6 4
♣ 2

Open with 12 points. You have two gorgeous five-card major suits.

♠ 6 4
♡ 7
♢ K Q 10 7 3
♣ K Q 10 9 2

Pass this 12-point hand with no aces and shortness in the major suits. This is a close decision, as you do have two very good minor suits.

♠ K Q
♡ Q J 7
♢ Q J 8 2
♣ Q 10 9 4

Open with 13 points. It is my recommendation that you never pass 13 *high-card* points, not even with this pile of junk. There are those, even in expert circles, who would recommend a pass.

The *maximum* requirement for an opening suit bid of one ranges up to the minimum requirement for a *strong* opening suit bid of two, about 22 points. For example:

♠ A K 7 4
♡ A
♢ K Q 8
♣ A J 9 7 2

This 22-point hand (1 point for the five-card club suit) should be opened with a suit bid of one. If you change the ♣ J to the ♣ Q, the hand just barely qualifies for an opening bid of 2 ♣. (For more illustrations, see page 83.)

So the point-count requirement to open the bidding with a suit bid of one is roughly from 13 to 22 points, counting points for high cards and long suits.

FIVE-CARD MAJORS AND THE SHORT MINOR

Once you have decided your hand qualifies for an opening suit bid of one, you must choose which suit to bid from among your *biddable suits*. The requirements to bid a major suit—hearts or spades—are quite different from the requirements to bid a minor suit—clubs or diamonds.

Major Suits

An opening bid of 1 ♡ or 1 ♠ promises at least a five-card suit, but any five-card suit is biddable (even 6-5-4-3-2). A few authorities approve of opening the bidding with a strong four-card major suit (such as K-J-10-X or A-J-X-X), but five-card majors have become increasingly popular through the years with the experts as well as the average player. I strongly recommend that you play five-card majors because they minimize your bidding problems and improve your results. I practice what I teach. (NOTE: In third or fourth seat, or if your side has a part-score, it is sometimes right to open the bidding with a *strong* four-card major suit. See pages 30 and 206.)

Minor Suits

Any four-card or longer minor suit is biddable (even 5-4-3-2). Provided you have no five-card or longer major suit and no four-card or longer minor suit, then, and only then, you may open the bidding with a three-card minor suit. This procedure is an everyday part of standard bidding, even for those who play four-card majors, and it is misleadingly referred to as the "short club." Since you may open the bidding with a three-card diamond suit as well, it is more appropriate to call it the "short minor." On rare occasions it may be necessary to open the bidding with a worthless three-card minor suit (such as 4-3-2), but never open the bidding with a two-card (or shorter) suit.

WHICH SUIT TO BID FIRST

When two or more biddable suits are available, you must decide which suit to bid first. One of the secrets of good bidding is to ask yourself before you make a bid, "What am I going to bid next?" If you choose the right suit to bid first you will have a convenient rebid, while if you choose the wrong suit you may have an awkward rebidding problem. So this section is important. The logic behind the following rules, and exceptions to the rules, is explained in detail in Chapter 6, Rebids by the Opening Bidder; note the portion about "reverse bidding."

With only one five-card or longer suit: Bid that suit. For example:

> ♠ A K J 2   Bid 1 ◊, your only five-card or longer suit.
> ♡ A 9 5
> ◊ Q 6 4 3 2
> ♣ 7

There is a rare exception to this rule when you have specifically four *strong* diamonds and five clubs: With a minimum-range opening bid (at most 16 points), bid the four-card diamond suit first. For example:

> ♠ 7   Bid 1 ◊ with only 14 points. But if you held 17 points or
> ♡ J 9 2   more, 1 ♣ would be the right bid.
> ◊ A K Q 10
> ♣ K 8 6 5 3

With two five-card suits, or two six-card suits: Bid the *higher-ranking* suit first, whether it is stronger or not. For example:

♠ K 9 7 5 3   Bid 1 ♠, the higher-ranking suit. If you bid hearts first
♡ A K Q J 9   and spades later, you would imply greater length in
♢ 8   hearts.
♣ 6 4

There is one exception to this rule when you have specifically five clubs and five spades: With a very weak opening bid (at most 14 points) and a weak spade suit, bid clubs first. For example:

♠ J 8 6 3 2   Bid 1 ♣ with only 13 points. If you had 15 points or
♡ 4   more, 1 ♠ would be the right opening even with this
♢ A 10   weak spade suit. If the spade suit were a good one (say
♣ A Q 10 9 7   Q-J-10-X-X or better), 1 ♠ would be the right opening
                 even though you held fewer than 15 points.

With six-five distribution: Always bid the six-card suit first if it is the higher-ranking.

If the five-card suit is the higher-ranking and you have 17 points or more, bid the six-card suit first.

If the five-card suit is the higher-ranking and you have a minimum opening bid (at most 16 points), bid the five-card suit first. (Bid the hand as though you had two five-card suits.) *Exception:* With specifically six clubs and five spades, always bid the clubs first.

♠ K Q 10 6 4   Bid 1 ♠ with only 14 points. If you held 17 points or
♡ A Q 9 8 6 2 more, 1 ♡ would be the better opening bid.
♢ 7
♣ 5

When your longest suit is only four cards long, the choice is automatically between clubs and diamonds (assuming your hand does not qualify for an opening notrump bid): With two four-card minors, bid 1 ♢; with two three-card minors, bid 1 ♣; with a three-card minor and a two-card minor—and four of each major—bid the three-card minor (never open the bidding with a two-card or shorter suit). Here are a few examples:

♠ A Q 6 5   Bid 1 ♢, with four diamonds and only three clubs.
♡ K 10
♢ 7 5 3 2
♣ A J 6

♠ A Q 7 5   Bid 1 ♢, with four of each minor.
♡ 6
♢ K J 9 2
♣ A Q J 3

♠ K 9 6   Bid 1 ♣, with three of each minor.
♡ K 7 4 3
♢ A Q 8
♣ Q 7 2

♠ K 8 5 3   Bid 1 ♢, with three diamonds and only two clubs. It is
♡ A 8 6 2   unattractive to open the bidding with a worthless three-
♢ 9 7 5   card suit, but here you have no choice; you must not
♣ A Q   pass with 13 high-card points and it is wrong to open the
                 bidding with a two-card minor suit or a four-card major
                 suit.

THIRD- AND FOURTH-SEAT OPENING BIDS

When you have a full opening bid (as described in the preceding pages), you should open the bidding the same way in third or fourth seat as you would in first or second seat. However, it is sometimes right to open the bidding in third or fourth seat with subminimum opening bid strength—10, 11, or 12 points. Before looking into the requirements, let me explain the strategical differences between third-seat and fourth-seat opening bids.

When you're in the third seat, the logical reasons to open light are as follows: (1) Your partner may have passed a near opening bid and you may be able to bid and make a part-score, or even a game. (2) You may have a good sacrifice, or you may push the opponents too high. (3) If you are outbid, it may help your partner to make the winning opening lead. (4) In general, it makes life more difficult for your opponents when you open the bidding against them.

When you are in fourth seat: You will notice that some of the reasons for opening light in third seat involve cutting your losses, as opposed to making a profit. In fourth seat you can break even by passing the hand out, so it would be foolish to open unless you expect a profit.

If the other three players have passed and you have 10 or 11 high-card points, it is reasonable to assume that the high cards are evenly divided between the two sides (about 20 high-card points each) and each side can win a majority of the tricks if it plays the hand in its long trump suit. Therefore, the side that has the spade suit has the advantage, because in a competitive auction it can bid over any suit bid by the opponents at the same level of bidding, while the opponents must go to the next higher level to bid over spades. For example:

♠ K 10 9 4 2 ♡ A 9 3 2 ◊ K 5 ♣ 8 6	Open the bidding with 1 ♠ in third or fourth seat. Since you have the spade suit, you are a favorite to get a plus score.
♠ 8 6 ♡ A 9 3 2 ◊ K 5 ♣ K 10 9 4 2	Open the bidding with 1 ♣ in third seat, but pass in fourth seat. Since you are short in spades you are a favorite to be outbid, but you should still open the bidding in third seat to indicate a good lead to your partner and harass the opposition.

Note that the "spade-suit theory" for fourth-seat openings may keep the opponents out of the bidding altogether, even when they have the best of it: They must go to the two-level to bid their suit over 1 ♠, while they can bid at the one-level over 1 ♣. It boils down to this: Do not open the bidding light in fourth seat if you are short in spades.

It is especially desirable to open the bidding light in third and fourth seat when you have a strong suit to bid, because you are often outbid and partner will lead your suit. You should even open the bidding with a four-card major suit, provided you have a *strong* suit and 13 points or fewer. For example:

♠ K J 10 9 ♡ 9 7 6 ◊ A K ♣ 8 7 3 2	Open the bidding with 1 ♠ in third or fourth seat. In case you are outbid, a spade lead from partner should work out best.
♠ A Q J 10 ♡ 9 7 6 ◊ A K ♣ 8 7 3 2	Open the bidding with 1 ♣ in any position. When you have 14 points or more, open the bidding in third and fourth seat in the same way as you would in first or second seat.

Light opening bids in third or fourth seat do not require any preparation for rebidding, because your partner has already passed—his hand is limited to about 12 points—and you should be planning to pass any response he makes. In general, do not bid again after you have opened the bidding with subminimum values.

Since your plan is not to bid again, it is risky to open light unless you have a convenient pass. If you open light with a singleton and your partner bids that suit, you must either bid again to indicate a full opening bid, or pass and endure the wrath of your partner, who will be obliged to play a miserable contract. However, there is much to be gained by these light opening bids, and some chance-taking is in order. For example:

♠ K J 8 4 3
♡ 9 8 7
♢ A Q 10 5
♣ 2

Open the bidding with 1 ♠ in third or fourth seat and hope that partner raises spades, or bids diamonds or hearts. If he bids 1 NT or 2 ♣, grit your teeth and bid 2 ♢. If partner bids again over 2 ♢, pass his next bid and hope for the best. It is true that you can escape the possibility of an uncomfortable auction if you do not open the bidding, but look what you might miss. Suppose your partner holds the following hand:

♠ A Q 5 2
♡ 5
♢ K J 6 4 2
♣ 9 7 3

Note that these two hands can make game in spades with an overtrick. Furthermore, the opponents have the same holding in clubs and hearts that you have in diamonds and spades, so they may make a game too. If your side fails to open the bidding in fourth seat, you miss a game. If your side fails to open the bidding in third seat you not only miss a game, your opponents may open the bidding in fourth seat and score a game their way; then there is a double swing against you.

5

Responses to Opening Suit Bids of One

♣　　♦　　♥　　♠　　♣　　♦　　♥　　♠

Some bids are *limit bids*—they describe the strength and distribution of a hand within narrow limits. A perfect example is an opening notrump bid; it describes the strength of a balanced hand within 3 points. When a player makes a limit bid, his partner can often calculate the best final contract right away.

An opening suit bid of one is almost *unlimited,* since the strength may range from 12 or 13 to 22 points and the distribution may be a balanced hand or some extraordinary holding such as 6-6-1-0. With such a vague picture of the opening bidder's hand, it is impossible for the responder to figure out the best final contract right away; so the only thing for him to do is make a bid to begin describing his own hand, as follows.

WHEN TO PASS

When your partner opens the bidding with 1 ♣, 1 ♦, 1 ♡, or 1 ♠, the general rule is to pass with 5 points or fewer, or bid with 6 points or more. However, experienced players sometimes bend this rule a bit and bid with 5 points (in their daring moments maybe even with 4 points) if they have a reasonable suit that they can bid at the one-level. For example, your partner opens the bidding with 1 ♣ and you hold:

♠ J 8 4	Pass, before the roof caves in. Do not fear passing a 1 ♣
♡ 9 6 4 3 2	opening when you are short in clubs. If partner is left to
◇ 8 7 6 5	play the 1 ♣ contract he will probably be set a few tricks
♣ 7	for a small loss (although he may have a good club suit
	and make it), while if you bid over 1 ♣ it may lead to a
	complete disaster.

♠ 7 4
♡ K 10 9 3 2
◊ J 7 5 2
♣ 6 3

Answer partner's 1 ♣ opening with 1 ♡, even though you have only 5 points. Your good heart suit turns the odds in favor of bidding. If partner's opening bid were 1 ♠, instead of 1 ♣, you should pass.

WEAK RESPONSES

When your partner opens the bidding with a suit bid of one, *you must keep the bidding open with 6 high-card points or more.* However, when you do bid with a weak hand you must keep the bidding low. Unless you have 11 points or more, the only acceptable responses are to bid a new suit at the *one-level,* bid 1 NT, or raise the opener's suit to the two-level. The responses of 1 NT and raising partner's suit to the two-level show 6 to 10 points; they are the "weak responses." A new-suit response at the one-level—called "one-over-one"—shows 6 or more points (no upper limit); it will be explained in detail after we have covered the weak responses.

A minor-suit raise to the two-level shows 6 to 10 points and at least four-card trump support, and it denies possession of a four-card or longer major suit. (NOTE: The minor-suit raise is usually at least five-card support, not so much because you are afraid of a four-three fit, but because you probably have something else to bid with only four-card support.) For example:

Partner	You	
1 ◊	2 ◊	♠ A Q 3
		♡ 7
		◊ 8 7 5 4 2
		♣ 10 6 4 2

You have 9 points—6 in high cards, 1 for the five-card suit, and 2 for the singleton. If partner's opening bid were 1 ♣, you could bid 2 ♣, but 1 ◊ would be a better bid.

A major-suit raise to the two-level shows 6 to 10 points and at least three-card trump support. However, with a balanced hand and three weak trumps for your partner, it is better to respond 1 NT with only 6 or 7 points, but raise the major with 8, 9, or 10 points. For example:

Partner	You	
1 ♠	1 NT	♠ 10 5 3
		♡ A J
		◊ J 9 6 2
		♣ 10 9 7 4

If you choose to bid 2 ♠ your partner would revalue his hand by adding extra points for his short suits. He is more apt to bid again (than he would be over 1 NT), and your hand will be a disappointment. If he is not strong enough to bid again over 1 NT, you will not miss a game. If you change the ◊ J to the ◊ K, then 2 ♠ would be the recommended bid rather than 1 NT.

A 1 NT response shows 6 to 10 points and denies possession of a four-card or longer major suit that could be bid at the one-level. (NOTE: The requirement to respond 1 NT to specifically a 1 ♣ opening bid is controversial. Some authorities say it shows 9 to 11 points, while others recommend 8 to 10, as I did in my last book. This alteration has little merit, if any, and complicates the memory work for the aspiring player. I suggest that you treat a 1 NT response to 1 ♣ the same as to any other suit, 6 to 10 points.) Here are two examples:

Partner	You	♠ K 10 2
1 ◇	1 NT	♡ Q J 7
		◇ J 10 9
		♣ 8 6 5 3

This is a typical hand for the 1 NT response. You should also respond 1 NT to an opening bid of 1 ♣.

Partner	You	♠ 7
1 ♠	1 NT	♡ A Q J 10 9
		◇ 9 7 5 4 2
		♣ 8 2

You have only 9 points (2 for the two five-card suits) and your bids are restricted to the one-level unless you can raise your partner's suit. You need at least 11 points to bid 2 ♡, a "two-over-one" response. Responding 1 NT with an unbalanced hand is not uncommon; it is necessary anytime your point range is 6 to 10 and your only long suit (or suits) ranks below the opening bidder's suit.

SUIT RESPONSES AT THE ONE-LEVEL

When your partner opens the bidding with a suit bid of one and you respond in another suit at the one-level, your bid is called "one-over-one" and shows 6 points or more—no upper limit—and any four-card or longer suit is biddable. A new suit bid by the responder is *forcing for one round;* the opening bidder must bid again. Logically, any bid by the responder which might include 13 or more points should never be passed; you may miss a game, or a slam. Although the opener is forced to bid again, he should strive to keep the bidding low if he has a minimum opening; the responder may have only 6 points. Here are two examples of one-over-one bids:

Partner	You	♠ 10 6 5 2
1 ◇	1 ♠	♡ K 9
		◇ A 9 8 7
		♣ 8 7 3

It may be tempting to bid 2 ◇ or 1 NT, but either of those bids denies possession of a four-card or longer major suit.

Partner	You	♠ K Q 10 8
1 ♡	1 ♠	♡ 7 6
		◇ A K 4
		♣ K 9 3 2

Here you have 15 points and it is tempting to jump the bidding, but the forcing 1 ♠ bid is best. You will have a chance to show your strong hand later in the bidding.

SUIT RESPONSES AT THE TWO-LEVEL

When your partner opens the bidding with a suit bid of one and you respond in another suit at the two-level, your bid is called "two-over-one" and shows 11 points or more (including distributional points), no upper limit. You may bid any four-card or longer *minor* suit at the two-level, but if you answer your partner's opening 1 ♠ bid with 2 ♡ he should assume that you have at least a five-card heart suit. Do not confuse a two-over-one response with a jump response; for example, if partner opens the bidding with 1 ♣ and you respond 2 ◊ it is a jump response, while if partner opens with 1 ♡ and you respond 2 ◊ it is a two-over-one response. Here is one example:

Partner	You	
1 ♡	2 ♣	♠ 9 7 5
		♡ K 2
		◊ A 10 2
		♣ A 10 9 6 4

With 12 points, your hand qualifies for a two-over-one response. Take **away the** ♡ K, leaving only 9 points, and the proper response would be 1 NT.

STRONG RESPONSES

When your partner opens the bidding with a suit bid of one and you have 13 points or more you should be thinking of bidding at least a game, so be sure that any bid you make below game is forcing. You have already found out that new-suit responses are forcing for one round and it is not necessary to jump the bidding every time you have a strong hand. The right time to jump the bidding immediately is when your hand qualifies for a jump-raise to the three-level, a jump to 2 NT or 3 NT, or a jump bid in a new suit. All of these jump bids are forcing to game, and the requirements for each is described as follows:

A jump raise from one to three in any suit shows 13 to 16 points and at least four trumps. However, do not jump-raise a minor suit if you have a four-card or longer major suit. For example:

Partner	You	
1 ♠	3 ♠	♠ K 10 6 2
		♡ 7
		◊ K Q 4 3
		♣ A 8 7 3

Your hand is worth 14 points after you add 2 for the singleton; it is ideal for a jump raise. If partner's opening bid were 1 ◊, your proper bid would be 1 ♠; although you have the proper point count and trump support for a 3 ◊ bid, you should not jump-raise a minor suit when you have a four-card or longer major suit.

A 2 NT response shows 13 to 15 high-card points, a balanced hand, stoppers in all three unbid suits, and no four-card or longer major suits that can be bid at the one-level. For example:

Partner	You	
1 ♡	2 NT	♠ A Q 7
		♡ K J 8
		◊ J 10 5 2
		♣ K 6 4

This hand meets all of the qualifications for the 2 NT response. It might seem right to bid 3 ♡, but that would show four-card heart support.

A 3 NT response shows 16 to 18 high-card points, a balanced hand, stoppers in all three unbid suits, and no four-card or longer major suits that can be bid at the one-level. Experienced players tend to avoid this bid—especially when they have 18 points—as it takes away bidding room to exchange information for slam purposes. Here is one example:

Partner	You	♠ K 7 4
1 ♡	3 NT	♡ Q 2
		◊ A J 10 8
		♣ A Q 9 5

Note that this 16-point hand qualifies for an opening 1 NT bid, as well as a 3 NT response to an opening bid of 1 ♡.

A jump bid in a new suit (skipping exactly one level of bidding) is called a "jump shift." For example, if your partner opens the bidding with 1 ♡, the only jump-shift responses are 2 ♠, 3 ♣, and 3 ◊.

The appropriate point count for a jump shift is 17, 18, or 19, because your hand is not quite strong enough to bid a slam and there is no way to find out whether your partner has a bare opening bid or the little extra you need to make a slam. In other words, you will make your partner the captain and yourself the buck private; you will tell him that you have 17 to 19 points and let him decide whether or not to bid a slam.

In addition to 17 to 19 points, you should have a reasonable knowledge of which trump suit to play when you jump-shift; when there is a potential misfit, simply bid a new suit and the bidding space you save will increase your chances of getting to the right contract. Note the following four examples:

Partner	You	♠ A J 7 2
1 ♠	3 ◊	♡ J 3 2
		◊ A J 9 5
		♣ A Q

With 18 points and good trump support for your partner's suit, this hand is ideal for a jump shift to 3 ◊. You will raise spades at your next turn and leave the decision whether or not to bid a slam up to your partner.

Partner	You	♠ 7
1 ♠	3 ♡	♡ A K J 10 9 7 2
		◊ K J
		♣ Q J 2

You have 18 points and a jump shift is desirable here because you have an *independent* trump suit. Your plan is to rebid 4 ♡ at your next turn and, once again, let your partner decide whether or not to bid a slam.

Partner	You	♠ 8 2
1 ♠	3 ♣	♡ A Q 7
		◊ K 9 3
		♣ A K J 5 4

You have 18 points. If partner's next bid is 3 ◊, 3 ♡, or 3 ♠, you will rebid 3 NT. This bidding describes a hand with 17 to 19 points, a club suit, and a balanced (or semibalanced) hand with stoppers in the unbid suits.

Partner	You	♠ A Q
1 ◇	1 ♡	♡ A J 7 3 2
		◇ 7
		♣ A J 9 6 2

You have 18 points. It is wrong to jump-shift with a two-suited hand, even when you have 17 to 19 points. You need the extra level of bidding to bid both of your suits and still be able to play 3 NT if partner has a minimum opening bid and cannot support either of your suits. Do not jump-shift unless you have good support for your partner's suit, an independent suit of your own, or a notrump-type hand with all unbid suits stopped.

When you have 20 points or more, it is wrong to jump-shift, because it would serve no purpose. You know the combined hands have at least 33 points, so all slam-bidding decisions are yours. You must organize your bidding to extract information from your partner, not tell him what you have: Make yourself the captain and your partner the buck private. In most cases the best approach is simply to bid a new suit. For example:

Partner	You	♠ A J 7
1 ♠	2 ♣	♡ A 2
		◇ A Q J
		♣ K J 9 5 2

You should be planning to bid a small slam, probably 6 ♠, even if partner gives no further encouragement. If his subsequent bidding is to your liking (for example, he bids 3 ♠ over your 2 ♣ response), you should bid a grand slam. The 2 ♣ response is much better than 3 ♣, 4 NT, or any other bid, because it may enable you to find out something more about your partner's hand.

RESPONSES WITH 11 OR 12 POINTS

The standard point-count requirements to raise the opening bidder's suit and bid notrump are: A raise to the two-level shows 6 to 10 and a jump raise to the three-level shows 13 to 16; a response of 1 NT shows 6 to 10 and a jump response to 2 NT shows 13 to 15. So when the responder has 11 or 12 points he should not raise his partner or bid notrump; his first step must be to bid a new suit. For example:

Partner	You	♠ K 10 6 3
1 ♠	2 ♣	♡ 4 2
		◇ 9 8 6
		♣ A K 10 7

After adding 1 point for the doubleton heart you have 11 points, so your hand is too strong to bid 2 ♠ and too weak to bid 3 ♠. After partner's next bid you will support spades. When you have 11 or 12 points, it takes two bids to get your message across.

Partner	You	♠ 6 3
1 ♠	2 ◇	♡ K 9 6 3
		◇ A 8 4 2
		♣ A J 7

It is tempting to bid notrump, but your 12-point hand is too strong for 1 NT and too weak for 2 NT. Your next bid will depend on partner's rebid. For example, if he rebids 2 ♡ you will raise hearts; if he rebids 2 ♠ you will bid 2 NT; if he rebids 2 NT you will bid 3 NT; etc.

WHICH SUIT TO BID FIRST

It should be apparent from what you have read so far that when responding to an opening suit bid of one, four-card and longer suits are biddable and three-card and shorter suits are not. Sometimes there are two biddable suits, and it may be important to bid the right one first. Here is the way to do it.

With one suit longer than any other, bid it first, provided you have the point count to do so; remember, you need at least 11 points to bid a new suit at the two-level. For example:

Partner	You	♠ K Q 10 8
1 ♡	2 ◇	♡ 7 4
		◇ A Q 9 7 2
		♣ 6 3

With 12 points, you have sufficient strength to bid at the two-level. Your plan is to bid spades at your next turn. If partner opened the bidding with 1 ♣, the proper response would be 1 ◇.

Partner	You	♠ J 8 5 2
1 ♡	1 ♠	♡ 7 4
		◇ A Q 9 7 2
		♣ 6 3

This hand has only 8 points, so you must keep the bidding at the one-level. If partner opened the bidding with 1 ♣, the proper response would be 1 ◇.

With two five-card suits, or two six-card suits, bid the higher-ranking suit first whether it is stronger or not. For example:

Partner	You	♠ Q 7 5 3 2
1 ♣	1 ♠	♡ A K J 9 5
		◇ 6
		♣ 8 4

Your plan is to bid hearts at your next turn.

With two or three four-card suits, the general rule is to bid up the line; disregard the strength of the suits and bid the cheapest one first.

There is one controversial case. That is when your partner opens the bidding with 1 ♣ and you hold four diamonds and a four-card major. My suggestion is that you bid 1 ◇ with all good hands (11 points or more) and bid the major with all weak hands (10 points or fewer); with a weak hand, it is also okay to bid a four-card major ahead of a weak five-card diamond suit. (NOTE: Not all authorities agree with this; some say always bid the major first, while others say always bid up the line.)

For example:

Partner	You	♠ A Q 6 4
1 ◊	1 ♡	♡ J 6 5 2
		◊ 7
		♣ K Q 10 8

A bid of 1 ♡ is lower than 1 ♠ or 2 ♣. Note the complete disregard for the strength of the suits.

Partner	You	♠ 8
1 ♠	2 ♣	♡ A Q 10 6
		◊ A 10 7 2
		♣ J 9 8 3

A bid of 2 ♣ is lower than 2 ◊ or 2 ♡.

Partner	You	♠ 7 4
1 ♣	1 ♡	♡ K 10 8 3
		◊ A 9 6 2
		♣ J 7 5

With only 8 points, it is important to bid the major right away. Add 3 points or more to this hand and 1 ◊ would be a better response. *A 1 ◊ response to 1 ♣ does not deny possession of a four-card major suit.*

WEAK JUMP RESPONSES

Some jump bids show weak hands, and this is a cross to bear for aspiring bridge players. However, it is not difficult if you understand the concept that jump bids that skip exactly one level of bidding are strong and *jump bids in a suit that skip two or three levels of bidding are weak.* There are two categories for weak jump responses: raising your partner's suit, or bidding a new suit.

A leaping raise of partner's suit (as partner 1 ♠, you 4 ♠; or partner 1 ♣, you 4 ♣ or 5 ♣, etc.) shows excellent trump support—usually five trumps—a highly distributional hand—such as 5-5-2-1, or 6-5-1-1, etc.—and a poor hand in high cards, usually 4, 5, or 6 high-card points, but it could be slightly more or less. For example:

Partner	You	♠ 7 2
1 ♡	4 ♡	♡ K 10 9 5 4
		◊ 7
		♣ J 10 8 6 2

Your 4 ♡ bid is "preemptive." Its chief purpose is to keep the opponents out of the bidding (they may do very well in another trump suit), but at the same time, there is a high hope that partner will make his contract. Notice that I ignored counting points with this hand. The point-count system is inaccurate on these good-fitting and highly distributional hands. When you have such a hand, leap to game and hope for the best.

A leaping bid in a new suit (as partner 1 ◊, you 3 ♡, 4 ♡, 4 ♣, or 5 ♣, etc.) shows a substantial seven-card or longer suit and about 4, 5, 6 high-card points; the high cards should be concentrated in your long suit. The length and strength of your long suit determines how high you should bid, similar to the requirements for opening preemptive bids (see page 76). For example:

Partner	You	
1 ◊	3 ♡	♠ 7
		♡ K J 10 9 8 6 2
		◊ 4 3
		♣ 7 5 3

Your partner should pass 3 ♡, or bid 4 ♡ if he thinks you can make it. He should be very reluctant to bid another suit or 3 NT; you have advertised a hand that will be useless unless your long suit is the trump suit. A jump to the four-level would require a better suit. For example, if your partner opens 1 ◊, you should bid 4 ♣, 4 ♡, or 4 ♠ with a suit such as K-Q-10-9-7-5-3-2, eight cards long.

RESPONSES TO THIRD- AND FOURTH-SEAT OPENING BIDS

When your partner opens the bidding in third or fourth seat (you are a "passed hand"), he knows your hand is limited to about 12 points. However, if you have good support for your partner's bid suit you must revalue your hand by adding extra points for short suits; you may wind up with 13, 14, or even 15 points.

When you have from 6 to 10 points, the requirements to respond to partner's third- or fourth-seat opening bids are exactly the same as the requirements to respond to his first- or second-seat openings; the only available bids are to bid a new suit at the one-level, bid 1 NT, or raise partner's suit to the two-level. These subjects are covered earlier in this chapter and will be ignored here.

It is when you have 11 points or more that being a passed hand may affect your response. The usual responses with 11 points and up are: Bid a new suit at the one-level, bid a new suit at the two-level, jump to 2 NT, jump-raise your partner's suit to the three-level, and jump the bidding in a new suit (jump-shift). The requirements for these responses are explained in the analysis of the following examples:

	You	Partner
♠ A Q J 3	You	Partner
♡ 7 4	P	1 ♡
◊ Q 10 5	1 ♠	
♣ K 8 3 2		

Some players are under the illusion that if you have passed with 11 or 12 points, you must jump the bidding to tell your partner you have a near opening bid. A popular bid with this hand would be 2 NT, which is inferior to 1 ♠. If your partner has a full opening bid, he will bid again over 1 ♠ just as readily as he would over 2 NT; you will not miss a game.

	You	Partner
♠ J 6	You	Partner
♡ 8 5	P	1 ♡
◊ K Q 10 9 6	2 ◊	
♣ A J 10 2		

Even when you are a passed hand you need at least 11 points to bid a new suit at the two-level, but you also need a reasonably good five-card or longer suit.

When you are a passed hand, *never bid a four-card suit at the two-level.* Your bid is not forcing and your partner may pass with little or no trump support.

♠ J 10	*You*	*Partner*
♡ Q 4 3 2	P	1 ♠
◇ A 10 4	2 NT	
♣ K J 10 8		

A 2 NT response by a passed hand shows 12 high-card points, or 11 high-card points and good "body cards." Take away the three ten-spots and a slight underbid of 1 NT is recommended. Note that if you were not a passed hand your first response would be 2 ♣ with this hand, but you should not introduce a four-card suit at the two-level after you have passed.

♠ K J 7	*You*	*Partner*
♡ 9 2	P	1 ♠
◇ K 10 6 4	3 ♠	
♣ A 8 7 2		

The jump raise of a major suit shows 11 to 13 points and is sometimes necessary with only three-card trump support, but they should be good ones. Note that if you were not a passed hand your first response would be 2 ♣, intending to raise spades later.

A jump raise of a minor suit by a passed hand also shows 11 to 13 points, but you need at least four-card trump support. If partner's opening bid in this hand were 1 ◇, a 3 ◇ response would be correct.

The traditional procedure among inexperienced players is to play that a jump-shift response by a passed hand is not a forcing bid. If the responder, after passing, jumps the bidding in a new suit (for example, opener 1 ♡, responder 2 ♠, 3 ♣, or 3 ◇), he shows a hand with 11 or 12 points and a good five-card or longer suit; the opener should pass if he has a subminimum opening, or bid again with a full opening bid. This is not putting the jump-shift response to its best use, because if the opener has a full opening bid, he will bid again over a nonjump suit response just as readily as he will over a jump shift.

My recommendation is that you make an agreement with your favorite partners to play that a jump shift by a passed hand is forcing, showing a very good fit in the opener's suit and 13, 14, or 15 points. For example:

♠ Q 8 7 5 2	*You*	*Partner*
♡ 5	P	1 ♠
◇ K J	3 ♣	
♣ A 10 6 4 3		

When you passed this hand you had only 12 points, but after partner's opening 1 ♠ bid you add 2 points for the singleton heart and 1 point for the doubleton diamond, to give you 15 points. You certainly want to reach game even if partner has a subminimum opening, so 3 ♣ is the correct bid only if you and your partner have agreed to play it forcing.

If you have no agreement with your partner to play the jump shift forcing, the correct response here would be 4 ♠, instead of 3 ♣. But you would also bid 4 ♠ with a much weaker hand; for example, if you exchange the ♣ A for the ♣ 2, you should respond 4 ♠. The advantage of playing that the jump shift is forcing is that the leaping raise to game is always weak; this will enable the opening bidder to figure out whether or not to bid a slam when he has a strong opening bid.

6

Rebids by the Opening Bidder

♣   ♦   ♥   ♠   ♣   ♦   ♥   ♠

An opening suit bid of one shows a hand with from 13 to 22 points, a very vague picture of the opening bidder's strength. At his second turn to bid, his rebid, the opening bidder must describe his strength more accurately. He does this by indicating that his point count is in one of the three following ranges:

> 13 to 16 points, the minimum range
> 17 to 19 points, the invitational range
> 20 to 22 points, the game range

In addition to showing his point range, the opening bidder must try to give a better picture of his distribution by either raising the responder's suit, rebidding his original suit, bidding notrump, or bidding a new suit. The requirements for these rebids depend on the responder's first bid and are explained as follows.

RAISING THE RESPONDER'S SUIT

When your partner responds by bidding a new suit at the one-level, raise him to the two-level with 13 to 16 points and at least four trumps; or, on rare occasions, it may be necessary to raise him with three strong trumps. For example:

♠ Q 8 7	*You*	*Partner*
♡ Q 9 6 2	1 ◇	1 ♡
◇ A Q 10 9	2 ♡	
♣ K 6		

You have 14 points after you add 1 for the doubleton club, so the 2 ♡ bid describes this hand perfectly.

If partner's response were 1 ♠ instead of 1 ♡, you should not raise to 2 ♠; a rebid of 1 NT would be far superior.

♠ K Q 2	*You*	*Partner*
♡ A 9 5 3	1 ♣	1 ♠
◊ 7 6	2 ♠	
♣ A Q 8 4		

You have 15 points of good quality and a strong three-card spade holding, so rebidding 2 ♠ is better than 1 NT, the only alternative. Raising a one-level suit response with only three trumps is always a doubtful maneuver, so avoid it unless all other bids seem less attractive.

You should jump-raise your partner's one-level suit response to the three-level with 17 to 19 points and at least four trumps. For example:

♠ A K 8 3	*You*	*Partner*
♡ 7 6 4 2	1 ♣	1 ♡
◊ 7	3 ♡	
♣ A K J 9		

After adding 2 points for the singleton you have 17 and must jump the bidding to show your invitational-range hand. Note that you may raise your partner with any four trumps.

Jump-raise your partner's one-level major-suit response to game with 20 to 22 points and at least four trumps. For example:

♠ A Q 7	*You*	*Partner*
♡ K Q 9 5	1 ♣	1 ♡
◊ 8 6	4 ♡	
♣ A K J 2		

You have 20 points and partner has shown a minimum of 6, so the combined total is at least 26, enough to bid game.

REBIDDING YOUR OWN SUIT

You may rebid your own suit at the two-level with 13 to 16 points and any six-card or longer suit, or a five-card suit *provided no other reasonable bid is available*. In general, rebidding a five-card suit is an undesirable action and should be avoided whenever possible. For example:

♣ A Q 2	*You*	*Partner*
♡ Q 8 7 6 4 2	1 ♡	1 ♠
◊ 5 3	2 ♡	
♣ A 9		

You have 14 points. You should also bid 2 ♡ if partner responded 1 NT, 2 ♣, or 2 ◊.

To jump-rebid your own suit at the three-level, you need 17 to 19 points and a good six-card or longer suit. For example:

♠ 7	*You*	*Partner*
♡ A 6 2	1 ♣	1 ♡
◊ A 8 3	3 ♣	
♣ A K J 9 7 5		

You have 18 points. You should also bid 3 ♣ if partner responded 1 ◊ , 1 ♠ , or 1 NT.

You may rebid your own *major suit* at the game level with 20 to 22 points and a solid six-card suit, or a good seven-card or longer suit. You may also jump to game in your major suit with fewer than 20 points with exciting distribution; the point-count system does not do justice to highly distributional hands. For example:

♠ 7	*You*	*Partner*
♡ A K J 9 4 3 2	1 ♡	1 ♠
◊ A Q J 6	4 ♡	
♣ 6		

Although your hand counts only 18 points, you surely want to try your luck in game. If you bid only 3 ♡ your partner might pass, not realizing he has the meager values you need to make game. If partner's response were 1 NT, 4 ♡ would still be the best bid.

REBIDDING NOTRUMP

You may rebid 1 NT with 13 to 15 points and a balanced hand; stoppers in the unbid suits are *not* required. For example:

♠ K Q 10	*You*	*Partner*
♡ Q J 8	1 ◊	1 ♡
◊ A J 9 5	1 NT	
♣ 7 3 2		

You have 13 points and 1 NT describes your hand best.

♠ K 4	*You*	*Partner*
♡ 7 3 2	1 ♣	1 ♠
◊ K 10 8	1 NT	
♣ A K J 9 3		

You have 15 points (1 for the five-card suit). The 1 NT bid describes this hand accurately. A rebid of 2 ♣ to show your five-card suit would be inferior; remember, do not rebid a five-card suit if any other reasonable bid is available.

You may jump to 2 NT with 19 or 20 points, a balanced hand, and stoppers in the unbid suits. For example:

♠ A Q	*You*	*Partner*
♡ K 10 9 7 5	1 ♡	1 ♠
◊ A J 4	2 NT	
♣ K Q 2		

You have 20 points (1 for the five-card suit). This is the way to bid when your hand is too strong to open 1 NT. The 2 NT bid is not forcing, but your partner will bid again if he has the values to reach game; he knows you have 19 or 20 points.

After partner's suit response at the *one-level*, a leap to 3 NT shows a solid (or nearly solid) six- or seven-card suit, and stoppers in the unbid suits. For example:

	You	Partner
♠ 3	*You*	*Partner*
♡ K 8	1 ♣	1 ♠
◇ A 10 4	3 NT	
♣ A K Q 9 7 5 2		

You can run nine tricks with a heart lead, even if your partner has nothing. Do not use this bid unless you discuss it with your partner first; he may assume you have a balanced hand and make some bid you do not wish to hear (such as 4 ♠).

When your partner has responded 1 NT, you should pass with 13 to 16 points and a balanced hand (or rarely with a semibalanced hand), bid 2 NT with 17 to 19 points and a balanced or semibalanced hand, and bid 3 NT with 20 to 22 points and a balanced or semibalanced hand. Stoppers are not required to pass or raise a notrump response. Here are two examples:

	You	Partner
♠ A Q 3	*You*	*Partner*
♡ A Q 8 6 5	1 ♡	1 NT
◇ 6 2	P	
♣ J 9 2		

You have 14 points and partner has 6 to 10, so bidding game is out of the question. Rebidding 2 ♡ with only a five-card suit is inferior to a pass.

	You	Partner
♠ A Q 10 9 7	*You*	*Partner*
♡ J 2	1 ♠	1 NT
◇ A Q	2 NT	
♣ A 10 9 4		

You have 18 points and semibalanced distribution and 2 NT is a better bid than 2 ♣, the only alternative. If you had 20 points and the same distribution, the right bid would be 3 NT.

BIDDING A NEW SUIT

You may bid a new four-card suit at the one-level with from 13 to 19 points; your bid is not forcing. For example:

	You	Partner
♠ K 10 9 2	*You*	*Partner*
♡ Q 7 4	1 ♣	1 ♡
◇ A 8 3	1 ♠	
♣ K Q 5		

You have 14 points. You should resist the temptation to rebid 1 NT, as that would deny possession of a four-card major suit.

♠ 10 9 7 4	*You*	*Partner*
♡ K 3	1 ♣	1 ◊
◊ A 2	1 ♠	
♣ K Q 8 6 5		

You have 13 points. With 5-4 distribution, bid the five-card suit first and the four-card suit next; do not rebid the five-card suit and ignore the four-card suit. Your partner's 1 ◊ response does *not* deny a four-card major suit.

♠ K 9 7 3	*You*	*Partner*
♡ 7	1 ♣	1 ♡
◊ A K Q	1 ♠	
♣ A Q 10 6 4		

You have 19 points. Observe that a new-suit bid by the opening bidder does not describe his strength very accurately (he may have from 13 to 19 points) and his bid is not forcing.

You may bid a new four-card suit at the two-level with from 13 to 19 points, *provided the second suit ranks lower than the first.* For example:

♠ 7	*You*	*Partner*
♡ A Q 8 4 3	1 ♡	1 ♠
◊ A 9 7 6	2 ◊	
♣ K 10 2		

You have 14 points. It may seem tempting to bid 1 NT, but 2 ◊ is better; it is usually wrong to bid 1 NT with a singleton in your partner's suit. The 2 ◊ bid is not forcing.

♠ A K J 9 3	*You*	*Partner*
♡ 10 8 7 2	1 ♠	1 NT
◊ A 6 3	2 ♡	
♣ 5		

You have 13 points. Even with such a weak four-card suit it is better to bid it than to rebid your five-card suit. If your partner has an equal number of cards in your two suits, he will take you back to your first-bid suit; he knows you have five spades and may have only four hearts. If he has greater length in hearts you are likely to be better off in a heart contract; partner could even have ♠ 7 ♡ A-Q-J-9-4 ◊ 7-2 ♣ 9-8-6-4-3, in which case you are likely to make a game in hearts and may go down in a 2 ♠ contract.

♠ Q 10 4	*You*	*Partner*
♡ 9	1 ◊	1 NT
◊ A K J 8 7	2 ♣	
♣ A 6 5 2		

A club contract figures to be right here. Partner has denied a four-card or longer major suit, so he has *at most* six cards in the majors and *at least* seven cards in the minors. Unless he has four diamonds, in which case he will give you a preference for diamonds, he must have at least four clubs, and he may have five or six.

♠ A Q 8	*You*	*Partner*
♡ A J 7 4 2	1 ♡	1 ♠
◇ 8	2 ♣	
♣ K J 10 5		

This hand is too good to bid 2 ♠ and you need at least four trumps to jump to 3 ♠, so 2 ♣ is the best bid. You will more than likely support spades if you get another chance to bid.

If you have opened the bidding with 6-4 distribution, should you rebid the six-card suit or bid the four-card suit? There is no set answer. Sometimes it is right to rebid the six-card suit and sometimes it is right to bid the four-card suit, but giving priority to major suits is usually best. For example:

♠ 2	*You*	*Partner*
♡ A Q 10 7 4 3	1 ♡	1 ♠
◇ A J 9 5	2 ♡	
♣ 4 2		

With a six-card major and a four-card minor, it usually pays to rebid the major. You may never bid diamonds, depending on the subsequent bidding, but if partner's next bid is 2 NT or 3 ♣ you should bid 3 ◇; this bidding would describe your 6-4 distribution accurately.

♠ A Q 10 7 4 3	*You*	*Partner*
♡ A J 9 5	1 ♠	1 NT
◇ 2	2 ♡	
♣ 4 2		

In most cases you should bid a reasonably good four-card major suit rather than rebid a six-card suit. Your partner could have the magic hand, such as ♠ 5 ♡ Q-10-8-6-4-3 ◇ 9-3-2 ♣ A-8-7, in which case he should pass if you bid 2 ♠, but bid 4 ♡ if you bid 2 ♡.

THE JUMP SHIFT

A jump bid in a new suit is called a "jump shift" and shows 20 to 22 points (or maybe a good 19). The jump shift is forcing to game. For example:

♠ A J 10 7	*You*	*Partner*
♡ A Q	1 ◇	1 ♡
◇ A K J 10 3	2 ♠	
♣ 5 4		

You have 20 points and your partner has advertised at least 6, so you certainly want to bid at least a game, but where? You and your partner will have to exchange more information to decide.

```
♠ 74              You      Partner
♡ A J             1 ◊      1 ♡
◊ A Q J 10 6 2    3 ♣
♣ A K 8
```

Again you have enough points to reach at least a game, but need more bidding to decide where. A jump shift in a three-card suit is unusual, but necessary to force your partner to bid again.

THE REVERSE BID

Provided your partner has responded at the one-level, the requirement to bid a new suit at the two-level that ranks higher than your first suit is at least 17 points. This is called a "reverse bid" and implies greater length in your first suit than your second (usually 5-4, but maybe 6-4 or 6-5). For example:

```
♠ A 4 3           You      Partner
♡ A K J 9         1 ◊      1 ♠
◊ K Q 10 9 2      2 ♡
♣ 4
```

With 18 points, you are strong enough to reverse the bidding.

```
♠ 8 2             You      Partner
♡ A Q 10 8        1 ◊      1 ♠
◊ A Q J 10 7      2 ◊
♣ 4 3
```

You have only 14 points, not enough to reverse the bidding, so a bid of 2 ♡ is out. Rebidding a five-card suit should be avoided whenever possible, but no other bid is attractive, and you do have an excellent five-card suit.

In some nonexpert circles a reverse bid shows 17 to 19 points and invites the responder to bid again, but he is allowed to pass with a very weak hand and a tolerance for the second suit. To the contrary, *nearly every expert plays that a reverse bid is absolutely forcing for one round* so the bidder can explore for the best contract at a lower level of bidding without fear that his partner will pass. This method is obviously better, and I recommend that you make an agreement with your regular partners to play the reverse bid as forcing. Now you may reverse the bidding with 20 points or more, as well as with 17 to 19. For example:

```
♠ 2               You      Partner
♡ A K J 3         1 ♣      1 ♠
◊ A 8 5           2 ♡
♣ A K J 8 2
```

There is no need to jump the bidding with 21 points. Your reverse bid of 2 ♡ is forcing.

Although a reverse bid implies at least five cards in the first-bid suit, there are exceptional strong hands where it would be desirable to reverse with 4-4. For example:

	You	Partner
♠ A Q 7		
♡ A K J 4	1 ♣	1 ♠
◇ 6 2	2 ♡	
♣ A Q 10 9		

Although your hand has 20 points and is strong enough to insist on game, you need more bidding from your partner to decide which game to bid. The forcing 2 ♡ bid solves the problem neatly. (NOTE: The reverse bid with 4-4 is very rare and your partner should assume that you have at least five cards in your first-bid suit.)

The normal way to bid with two five-card suits is to bid the higher-ranking first, then bid and rebid the lower-ranking suit. *Never reverse the bidding with 5-5 distribution.* Here is one example:

	You	Partner
♠ K 2		
♡ A J 6 4 2	1 ♡	1 ♠
◇ 7	2 ♣	
♣ A K J 8 3		

You have 18 points. Your 2 ♣ bid shows 13 to 19 points but does not promise more than four clubs; to show your 5-5 shape you must rebid clubs at your next turn. If you had 20 points or more—for example, change the ♡ J to the ♡ K—your hand would qualify for a game-forcing bid of 3 ♣.

The normal way to bid with 6-5 distribution is to bid the six-card suit first and then bid and rebid the five-card suit, but this is complicated by the reverse-bid procedure, so there must be an exception. When the five-card suit is the higher-ranking and you have below 17 points, bid the five-card suit first; bid the hand as you would if you held two five-card suits. An exception to the exception is: With specifically six clubs and five spades, always bid clubs first. For example:

	You	Partner
♠ K Q 10 7 3		
♡ A Q 8 6 5 2	1 ♠	1 NT
◇ 3	2 ♡	
♣ 9		

With only 14 points you are not strong enough to reverse the bidding, so you must start with 1 ♠. If your six-card suit were clubs instead of hearts, a 1 ♣ opening would be correct.

	You	Partner
♠ 7		
♡ A K J 3 2	1 ◇	1 NT
◇ A Q J 7 5 3	2 ♡	
♣ 10		

You have 18 points, enough to reverse the bidding. Your plan should be to rebid hearts at your next turn to fully describe your 6-5 distribution.

You may also reverse with 6-4, but not unless you have at least 17 points. For example:

```
♠ A K J 9          You      Partner
♡ 8 5              1 ◇      1 NT
◇ K J 10 7 5 3     2 ◇
♣ 2
```

A bid of 2 ♠ is out, since you do not have the 17 points needed to reverse the bidding. Also, your partner would not have bid 1 NT if he held a four-card major, so the 2 ◇ bid is clearly right. If you change your diamonds to A-K-J-10-7-5, so you have 18 points, then 2 ♠ would be the right bid. ·

AFTER A TWO-OVER-ONE RESPONSE

If your partner has made a two-over-one response, any rebid you make below game is forcing; a two-over-one response promises another bid. (NOTE: If the responder bids a new suit at the two-level, a new suit bid by the opening bidder is forcing; to this everyone agrees. If instead the opener rebids 2 NT, rebids his original suit at the two-level, or raises his partner's suit to the three-level, his rebid is considered nonforcing in some bridge circles. So here is another subject to be ironed out with your partners. The modern trend is to play that any rebid the opener makes below game is forcing, and this is the way a vast majority of the experts play; this method is described in this book.)

Game is by no means certain after partner responds at the two-level (13 and 11 is 24, not enough points for game), so you must plan your bidding wisely to avoid getting to game when you should not. With a strong hand you usually jump the bidding to show extra values, but since any nonjump bid is forcing, you may use your judgment to make a nonjump bid with a strong hand. The four categories of rebids (bidding notrump, raising partner's suit, bidding a new suit, and rebidding your original suit) are explained as follows.

After a two-over-one response, a rebid of 2 NT shows a minimum opening bid (13 to 15 or 16 points), a balanced hand, and stoppers in the unbid suits. However, a 2 NT rebid should be avoided with fewer than 13 *high-card* points, or even with 13 high-card points if the hand is too barren, because the responder is required to bid again and he may bid 3 NT with just 11 points. Note the following two examples:

```
♠ K 10 9 6 3       You      Partner
♡ K 2              1 ♠      2 ♡
◇ A 10 4           2 NT
♣ K 10 9
```

You have 14 points, 13 in high cards. The 2 NT rebid is okay because you have good body cards, three tens and two nines. You may make a game even if partner bids 3 NT with only 11 points.

```
♠ K Q 4 3 2        You      Partner
♡ 8 6              1 ♠      2 ♡
◇ A 5 2            2 ♠
♣ A 7 6
```

Again you have 14 points, 13 in high cards, but notice how empty this hand is— four honor cards and nine deuces. If your partner has only 11 or 12 points, you must discourage him from bidding game, and there is a better chance of stopping below game if you rebid 2 ♠ instead of 2 NT. Although rebidding a five-card suit should be avoided, it is much more likely to be the best bid (or least of evils) after a two-over-one response than when your partner has responded at the one-level.

After a two-over-one response, you may jump to 3 NT with 17 to 19 points, a balanced or semibalanced hand, and the unbid suits stopped. For example:

♠ A Q	*You*	*Partner*
♡ A J 10	1 ◇	2 ♣
◇ A J 10 9 7 3	3 NT	
♣ 5 2		

With 18 points and the unbid suits securely stopped, 3 NT is the most attractive bid.·

After a two-over-one response, it is okay to raise your partner's minor suit with three good trumps, or to raise his 2 ♡ bid with any three trumps. For example:

♠ A K J 5 3	*You*	*Partner*
♡ 9 8 4	1 ♠	2 ♣
◇ 7 4	3 ♣	
♣ A Q 2		

Although your partner may have only a four-card club suit, he is prepared for you to raise him with three good trumps. He will obviously pursue a contract other than clubs if he has only a four-card club suit.

If partner's response were 2 ♡ (instead of 2 ♣), you should assume that he has a five-card or longer heart suit and raise him to 3 ♡ with your three small trumps.

If partner's response were 2 ◇, you should rebid 2 ♠.

Since a two-over-one response shows at least 11 points, you do not need as strong a hand to reverse the bidding as you do when your partner has responded at the one-level, promising only 6 points. The modern trend is to allow a reverse bid after a two-over-one response with a minimum opening, but a reverse bid sounds strong; so, although a reverse bid after a two-over-one response does not promise extra values, avoid it if you can with fewer than 15 points. Here are two examples:

♠ A K 8 2	*You*	*Partner*
♡ 7 4	1 ◇	2 ♣
◇ K Q 10 6 3	2 ◇	
♣ 5 2		

You have only 13 points, and 2 ◇ is a convenient rebid to show your minimum opening. If your hand were a little stronger—for example, change the spade holding to A-K-Q-2—a 2 ♠ bid would be recommended.

♠ A Q 7 5	*You*	*Partner*
♡ 9 5 3	1 ◇	2 ♣
◇ A Q J 2	2 ♠	
♣ 8 2		

This particular sequence (you 1 ◇, partner 2 ♣) sometimes presents a difficult rebidding problem. In this case, it seems silly to rebid the four-card diamond suit, or to bid 2 NT without a heart stopper, so the least of evils is to reverse the bidding with only 13 points; note that after a 2 ♣ response to 1 ◇, a reverse bid is common with two four-card suits.

If you answer your partner's two-over-one response by bidding a new suit at the three-level, you should have at least 15 points. As a result, with only 13 or 14 points, it is sometimes necessary to rebid a weak five-card suit. For example:

♠ Q 10 6 4 2	*You*	*Partner*
♡ 7	1 ♠	2 ♡
◇ A J 9 3 2	2 ♠	
♣ A 5		

With only 13 points you are too weak to bid 3 ◇. Rebidding a weak five-card suit is a deplorable act and is certainly not recommended for a steady diet, but it may be the only thing you can do with a weak hand if your partner's response deprives you of bidding your second suit at the two-level; if partner responded 2 ♣, 2 ◇ would be a routine bid. If you had 15 points—for example, change your spades to A-10-6-4-2—your hand would be strong enough to venture a bid of 3 ◇; there would be no need to rebid the ragged five-card spade suit.

You read on page 29 that with specifically five clubs and five spades, only 13 or 14 points, and a weak spade suit, you should open the bidding with 1 ♣. The reason for this should now be obvious—you wish to avoid rebidding a weak five-card spade suit. For example:

♠ J 9 7 4 3	*You*	*Partner*
♡ A 7	1 ♣	1 ◇
◇ 6	1 ♠	
♣ A Q 10 8 2		

Although it contains only 13 points, this attractive hand certainly qualifies for an opening bid. The exception to the rule "With two five-card suits, bid the higher-ranking suit first" is made here, to avoid an awkward rebidding problem. If you open the bidding with 1 ♠ and partner responds 2 ◇ or 2 ♡, you must either rebid the shabby spade suit or bid 3 ♣, which would imply that you have at least 15 points; hence the 1 ♣ opening. Bidding 1 ♣ here is the recommended bid, but it is not without fault; your partner will never know that you have a five-card spade suit, unless you get a chance to rebid the suit.

If you exchange the club suit and the spade suit (so you have ♠ A-Q-10-8-2 ♡ A-7 ◇ 7 ♣ J-9-7-4-3), you should open 1 ♠; if partner responds 2 ◇ or 2 ♡, rebid 2 ♠. If you had a couple of points more (change the heart suit to A-Q) it would be okay to open 1 ♠; if partner responds 2 ◇ or 2 ♡, you are strong enough to venture a 3 ♣ bid.

AFTER PARTNER HAS RAISED YOUR SUIT

When your partner raises your suit to the two-level (showing 6 to 10 points), always pass with a minimum-range opening bid (13 to 16 points), regardless of the quality of your suit. For example:

```
♠ A K 10 8 2        You      Partner
♡ K Q 9 3           1 ♠      2 ♠
◊ 7 4               P
♣ 6 5
```

After adding 2 points for the two doubletons, you have 15 points. The combined point count is between 21 and 25, not enough for game.

```
♠ A 9 6 3           You      Partner
♡ A K J 2           1 ♣      2 ♣
◊ 7 4               P
♣ J 5 2
```

You have 13 points. Although you may be concerned about the quality of your club suit, you must pass. You need at least 17 points to bid again.

When your partner raises your suit to the two-level and you have 17 to 19 points, *invite* game by (1) bidding three of the raised suit with good trumps; (2) bidding a new suit; or (3) bidding 2 NT with a balanced or semibalanced hand and stoppers in the unbid suits.

If your partner raises your suit to the two-level and you have 20 to 22 (or a good 19) points, bid game directly if you know where to play it, or bid a new suit if you do not. After your suit has been raised, any new suit bid is forcing for one round. Here are several examples:

```
♠ A K 9 8 3 2       You      Partner
♡ 7 6               1 ♠      2 ♠
◊ A 10              3 ♠
♣ K 4 2
```

After partner's raise, you have 18 points. Your partner should pass 3 ♠ with a minimum (6 or 7 points), or bid 4 ♠ with a maximum (9 or 10 points); with 8 points he must use his judgment, or guess. If you have 20 points or more—for example, replace the ◊ 10 with the ◊ K—you should bid 4 ♠ instead of 3 ♠.

```
♠ A K Q             You      Partner
♡ J 10 8 7 5        1 ♡      2 ♡
◊ 4                 3 ♣
♣ A J 4 3
```

You have 18 points. There is no question that you intend to play this hand in hearts, so the purpose of the 3 ♣ bid is to invite your partner to bid game; he may not pass 3 ♣. To reject your invitation he *must* bid 3 ♡ and you will pass. To accept your invitation he may make any other bid; usually he will bid 4 ♡, but he may bid a new suit or 3 NT. The advantage of inviting game by bidding 3 ♣ instead of 3 ♡ is that your partner can take his club holding into consideration in deciding whether or not to bid game; he will judge the ♣ K and ♣ Q to be of good value, while secondary honors in another suit (such as the ◊ K and ◊ Q) might be worthless.

If you had 20 points or more (for example, replace the ♡ J with the ♡ K), you should bid 4 ♡, not 3 ♣. You have all the information you need to bid a game in hearts, so a 3 ♣ bid would serve no purpose except to help your opponents to defend the hand.

	You	Partner
♠ J 10 9 7 4 2		
♡ A 3	1 ♠	2 ♠
◇ A Q 7 6 5	4 ♠	
♣ —		

You have only 11 high-card points, but your good distribution builds your point count to 18. Although the point-count requirement to bid 4 ♠ is 20 to 22, you should bid game with fewer points with this kind of distribution. A bid of 3 ◇ to invite game should be ruled out, because you can make game if your partner has the right 6 points and may not if he has the wrong 10 points, and there is no way to find out. When your partner raises your suit and you have freakish distribution, bid game first and count your points later.

	You	Partner
♠ K 10 8 2		
♡ K 5	1 ◇	2 ◇
◇ A Q J 7 4	2 NT	
♣ A 10		

You have 18 points (points for short suits should not be counted unless you intend to play a suit contract). Your 2 NT bid shows 17 to 19 points and stoppers in the unbid suits. With a minimum 2 ◇ bid, your partner should pass 2 NT or bid 3 ◇; with a maximum he should bid 3 NT or make some bid other than 3 ◇. Note that the 2 NT bid is better than 2 ♠ because your partner would not bid 2 ◇ with a four-card major.

If you held 20 to 22 points (for example, replace the ♣ 10 with the ♣ Q), you should bid 3 NT instead of 2 NT.

	You	Partner
♠ 7 6		
♡ A Q 10	1 ◇	2 ◇
◇ A Q J 5 2	2 ♡	
♣ A K 8		

Your 2 ♡ bid shows a heart stopper (not necessarily a four-card suit) and it is forcing. If your partner bids notrump, or bids 2 ♠ to show a spade stopper, you will play 3 NT; otherwise you will probably wind up in a 5 ◇ contract.

AFTER PARTNER HAS JUMPED THE BIDDING

When your partner jump-raises your suit to the three-level, jumps to 2 NT, or jump-shifts, all subsequent bids below game are forcing and often slam tries. If you know which game or slam to play, bid it. If the best contract is not obvious, make another bid below game to further describe your hand. For example:

	You	Partner
♠ J 8 7 4 2		
♡ 7	1 ♠	3 ♠
◇ A Q 10 6 3	4 ♠	
♣ K J		

You have a minimum opening and slam is out of reach, so bid 4 ♠ to end the auction. It would be clearly wrong to bid 4 ◇, as that would be a slam try. See "The Control-Showing Bid," page 190.

♠ 7 3 2	*You*	*Partner*
♡ A K 8	1 ◊	3 ◊
◊ A K 10 9 3	3 ♡	
♣ 6 5		

Your 3 ♡ bid shows a stopper. If partner has stoppers in spades and clubs, he should bid 3 NT. If he makes any other bid, you will probably wind up in a contract of 5 ◊.

♠ A Q 7	*You*	*Partner*
♡ A K 9 3 2	1 ♡	2 NT
◊ A Q J 5	3 ◊	
♣ 4		

You have 21 points and partner has shown 13 to 15, so it is clear that you should bid at least a small slam. The decision whether to play the hand in diamonds, hearts, or notrump will depend on the subsequent bidding; you may even wind up bidding a grand slam.

♠ A 5 3	*You*	*Partner*
♡ J 8	1 ◊	2 ♡
◊ A Q 10 7 4 2	3 ◊	
♣ K 9		

Your partner's jump-shift response shows 17 to 19 points, so with 16 points your hand is sufficiently strong to bid a slam. You must wait for partner's next bid to find out whether he has support for your suit, an independent heart suit, or a notrump-type hand; you will eventually bid a slam in diamonds, hearts, or notrump.

If your partner raises your major suit to the four-level (you 1 ♡, partner 4 ♡), or raises your minor suit to the four- or five-level (you 1 ◊, partner 4 ◊ or 5 ◊), he is showing a very weak hand with excellent trump support and distribution. For example:

♠ K Q J 5	*You*	*Partner*
♡ A K Q 2	1 ♣	5 ♣
◊ 7	P	
♣ K Q 10 8		

You most likely will need two aces from partner to make a slam, and preemptive bids are out of order with two aces. You had best hope he has one ace so you can make 5 ♣.

♠ K 10 7 6 4 2	*You*	*Partner*
♡ 3	1 ♠	4 ♠
◊ A K Q 8 4	4 NT	
♣ A		

If partner responds 5 ◊ to show one ace, you will bid 6 ♠. If he bids 5 ♣ to show no aces, you will sign off in 5 ♠; which should be a safe contract. It is rarely right to bid over your partner's preemptive raise, but your partner can have one ace and that is all you need to make a slam.

If your partner bids a new suit skipping two or three levels of bidding (you 1 ♡; partner 3 ♠, 4 ♠, 4 ♣, 5 ◊, etc.), he shows a very weak hand with a long and strong suit. For example:

♠ A 8 2	*You*	*Partner*
♡ 7	1 ◊	3 ♡
◊ K J 10 9 4 2	P	
♣ A Q 3		

Partner has advertised a hand that will win about five or six tricks if you allow him to play the hand in his suit; his hand may prove to be valueless unless the trump suit is hearts. It should be obvious that you have the wrong hand to bid again, so you must pass 3 ♡ and hope he can make that contract.

If partner's response were 3 ♠ instead of 3 ♡, it would be right to bid 4 ♠ with your good trump support and distribution.

AFTER YOU HAVE OPENED THE BIDDING IN THIRD OR FOURTH SEAT

When you open the bidding in third or fourth seat with subminimum values, your intention is not to bid again. But there are three cases in which you should change your mind: (1) when your partner forces you to bid again by jumping in a new suit; (2) when a pass would leave your partner to play a dreadful contract; and (3) when you discover an excellent trump fit and by adding points for short suits your hand builds up to full opening-bid strength. For example:

Partner	*You*	♠ K J 7 5 4
P	1 ♠	♡ 9 8 3
3 ♣	3 ♠	◊ A Q 2
		♣ 9 6

Your partner's 3 ♣ bid is forcing and guarantees a spade fit. He will perhaps bid 4 ♠ over your 3 ♠ bid if he believes his hand is good enough to make a game opposite a subminimum opening bid.

If partner's response were 2 ♣, you should pass; he shows a substantial five-card or longer club suit and 11 or 12 points.

If partner's response were 3 ♠, you should also pass; his bid shows good trump support and 11 to 13 points.

Partner	*You*	♠ J 10 6 2
P	1 ◊	♡ 5
1 ♡	1 ♠	◊ A J 9 8 2
		♣ A 10 4

Although you have a subminimum opening bid, you must not pass with a singleton heart; partner may have a weak four-card heart suit. Your partner will expect you to have a normal opening bid (at least 13 points) when you bid a second time, but the bidding is still very low and you will pass his next bid; you are unlikely to get into any trouble.

If partner's response were 1 ♠ (instead of 1 ♡), your hand improves so drastically that you should bid 2 ♠; if partner has a maximum passed hand he may bid 4 ♠ and make it.

When you open the bidding in third or fourth seat with a full opening bid, you should bid again if partner bids a new suit or jumps the bidding; exceptionally you may pass with 13 poor-quality points. For example:

Partner	You	
		♠ Q 6 4
P	1 ◇	♡ K 10 2
1 ♡	1 NT	◇ A Q 9 3
		♣ K 5 3

You have 14 points and your 1 NT rebid shows 13 to 15. If you pass and partner has a maximum passed hand, you could easily miss a game. If you pass and he has a poor hand, you make it easier for the opponents to enter the bidding and outbid you.

7

Rebids by the Responder

♣　　♦　　♥　　♠　　♣　　♦　　♥　　♠

The key word for the responder's first bid is *discipline*. The responder should, to the best of his ability, choose the bid that his bidding system dictates. He should not improvise to underbid, overbid, or gamble in any way.

The key word for the responder's second bid is *judgment*. An easy-to-figure-out second bid is often not available. The bidding abounds with close decisions, which sometimes force the responder to overbid or underbid slightly, or to make some ambiguous temporizing bid.

The first step before the responder chooses his second bid is to interpret the opener's bidding and consider the possibilities of the combined hands. If he has enough information to determine the best contract, he should bid it, or pass if that leaves him in the best contract. If he cannot determine the best contract, he should make the rebid that he judges best describes his hand. The rebid chart for the responder is:

> 6 to 10 points = the minimum range
> 11 or 12 points = the invitational range
> 13 or more points = the game range

These three ranges will be referred to throughout this chapter, which is divided into nine parts. In the first six parts the responder's first bid is at the one-level, but the titles are according to the opener's rebids. The last three are appropriately titled "After Responder Has Raised the Opener's Suit," "After Responder's First Bid Was a New Suit at the Two-Level," and "After Responder Has Jumped the Bidding."

AFTER RESPONDER'S SUIT HAS BEEN RAISED

When your partner raises your suit to the two-level, he shows a minimum-range opening bid (13 to 16 points) and usually four-card trump support; in rare cases he may raise with three good trumps. If your point range is from 6 to 10, always pass. For example:

Partner	You	
		♠ A Q 6 3
1 ♣	1 ♡	♡ Q 10 8 2
2 ♡	P	◊ 8 5
		♣ 9 8 4

You have 9 points after you add 1 point for the doubleton diamond. Since partner has 13 to 16, you know the combined total is between 22 and 25, not enough to hope for game. If you had 10 points it would be conceivable to bid again and hope partner had 16 points, but that would be highly speculative and would probably get you overboard.

When your partner raises your suit to the two-level and you have 11 or 12 points, you should bid again to *invite* game. There are many ways to invite game: You may bid three of the agreed suit, bid 2 NT, bid a new suit (a forcing bid), or bid three of partner's original suit. Here is an example of each:

Partner	You	
		♠ A 9 6
1 ◊	1 ♡	♡ K 10 9 8 4 2
2 ♡	3 ♡	◊ 7 4
		♣ 5 3

After your partner raises your suit and you add 2 points for your two doubletons, your hand becomes worth 11 points. When your chief asset is a long trump suit, invite game by bidding three of the agreed suit. Your partner should pass 3 ♡ with a minimum (13 or 14 points), or bid game with a maximum (15 or 16 points, or possibly with 14 if he likes his hand).

Partner	You	
		♠ J 7 4 2
1 ◊	1 ♠	♡ A Q 10
2 ♠	2 NT	◊ J 10 3
		♣ K 8 6

This is the way to invite game with only four cards in your suit and stoppers in the unbid suits. To reject your invitation to game, your partner should pass 2 NT with only three-card spade support, or bid 3 ♠ with four-card support; to accept, he should drive to game in some other way, choosing a 4 ♠ bid if he has four trumps for you.

Partner	You	
		♠ Q 10 8 5
1 ◊	1 ♡	♡ A Q 7 5
2 ♡	2 ♠	◊ K 4
		♣ 9 7 2

Your hand is worth 12 points after your partner raises your suit. Your 2 ♠ bid is meant to invite game, but you may have bid it with a much stronger hand; so 2 ♠ is forcing. Your partner may bid 2 NT or 3 ♡ to reject your invitation, or make any other bid to accept; *he may not pass.*

Partner	You	
		♠ K 7 4 2
1 ♣	1 ♠	♡ 8 2
2 ♣	3 ♣	◊ J 9 5
		♣ A K 4 3

You have 12 points. Your 3 ♣ bid shows 11 or 12 points and is invitational (although many experts play such a bid as forcing). It indicates that you have only four cards in your suit and good support for partner's suit. Partner should pass or bid 3 ♠ with a minimum, or make any other bid with a maximum.

AFTER THE OPENER REBIDS 1 NT

When your partner rebids 1 NT, he shows a balanced hand and from 13 to 15 points (with 16 he presumably would have opened the bidding with 1 NT). If you have 6 to 10 points you should rule out game. You may pass if 1 NT is an agreeable contract, or bid again to seek a better part-score contract. The bids you may make with 6 to 10 points are: bid your partner's suit at the two-level, rebid your own suit at the two-level, or bid a new suit at the two-level that ranks lower than your first suit. None of these bids is forcing and the opener may pass, or bid again in search of the best part-score contract. (NOTE: There is a modern trend among experts to play a new *minor* suit forcing after a 1 NT rebid, but this is far from standard and, therefore, not the way described in this book.) For example:

Partner	You	
1 ◊	1 ♡	♠ 10 7 6
1 NT	P	♡ K 10 8 5 3
		◊ A 5
		♣ 4 3 2

Your balanced hand suggests that 1 NT will make the best contract.

Partner	You	
1 ◊	1 ♡	♠ 7
1 NT	2 ◊	♡ A Q 6 3
		◊ Q 9 8 5
		♣ 10 4 3 2

With four diamonds and a singleton spade, 2 ◊ is the appealing contract.

Partner	You	
1 ♣	1 ♠	♠ J 10 8 7 5 2
1 NT	2 ♠	♡ 8 4
		◊ 9 3
		♣ A 6 2

Partner presumably has two or three spades (his 1 NT rebid suggests a balanced hand), so 2 ♠ is almost surely the best contract.

Partner	You	
1 ♣	1 ♡	♠ 7
1 NT	2 ◊	♡ Q 9 8 4 2
		◊ K J 6 3 2
		♣ 10 7

Your 2 ◊ bid is *not* forcing. (A new suit bid by the responder is forcing except when the opening bidder rebids 1 NT.) Partner should pass 2 ◊ with more diamonds, or bid 2 ♡ with equal or greater length in hearts; but he might conceivably bid 3 ◊ or 3 ♡ with 15 points and a very good fit in your suits.

If your partner rebids 1 NT and you have 11 or 12 points, you may invite game by bidding **2 NT** if you are satisfied to play the hand in notrump. For example:

Partner	You	
1 ◊	1 ♡	♠ 7 3
1 NT	2 NT	♡ K Q 10 8
		◊ 7 6 2
		♣ A Q 9 5

Your 2 NT bid shows 11 or 12 points, and your partner should pass 2 NT with 13 points and bid 3 NT with 14 or 15 points. If you build the point count of this hand up to 13, you should raise 1 NT to 3 NT.

After a 1 NT rebid by the opening bidder, any suit bid at the two-level (except a "reverse bid") is not forcing, but a jump in a suit to the three-level is forcing to game; there is no way to invite game. So, with 11 or 12 points and an unbalanced hand, you must use your judgment to bid at the two-level (an underbid), or bid at the three-level (an overbid). Here is one example:

Partner	You	♠ 7
1 ♣	1 ♡	♡ K 8 6 4 3
1 NT	2 ◊ or 3 ◊?	◊ A K 8 6 2
		♣ 9 5

Bid just 2 ◊ with this 12-point hand. Unless partner bids again, it is unlikely that you can make a game. The only game contract that looks promising is 4 ♡, but only if partner has three-card heart support. If he does have three hearts, he should certainly bid 2 ♡ over 2 ◊, in which case you might follow with a bid of 3 ◊ to show your 5-5 shape, or bid 4 ♡ directly if you feel lucky.

If your partner has rebid 1 NT and your hand is strong enough to insist on game, you must make a reverse bid or jump the bidding to force him to bid again. For example:

Partner	You	♠ A K 8 5
1 ◊	1 ♡	♡ K J 7 5 2
1 NT	2 ♠	◊ K 10 2
		♣ 3

Your 2 ♠ bid is a reverse bid. It is forcing and shows greater length in hearts than spades—probably 5-4, but maybe 6-4 or 6-5.

Partner	You	♠ A Q J 6 2
1 ◊	1 ♠	♡ A Q J 7
1 NT	3 ♡	◊ 9 4 3
		♣ 5

Your jump to 3 ♡ is necessary, since a nonjump bid of 2 ♡ would not be forcing.

AFTER THE OPENER REBIDS HIS SUIT

When your partner rebids his suit at the two-level, he shows a minimum-range opening bid (13 to 16 points) and a six-card or longer suit; rarely, a good five-card suit. When you have 6 to 10 points you should usually pass, but in rare cases you might bid again with a good six-card or longer suit. For example:

Partner	You	♠ A Q J 9 8 5
1 ♣	1 ♠	♡ 10 9 7
2 ♣	2 ♠	◇ 7 5 4
		♣ 3

With this wholesome six-card spade suit, it seems that 2 ♠ will make as good a contract as 2 ♣, or a better one.

Partner	You	♠ A Q 9 7 5
1 ◇	1 ♠	♡ J 4 3
2 ◇	P	◇ 2
		♣ 10 8 7 2

Partner may not be able to make his 2 ◇ contract, but if you bid again you will most likely make matters worse. Trouble is brewing, so pass before the opponents start doubling.

If, after your partner rebids his suit at the two-level, you bid a new suit, your bid is forcing; so bidding a new suit is a doubtful action with fewer than 11 points. Here is one example:

Partner	You	♠ A 10 8 4 3
1 ♣	1 ♠	♡ A K 9 2
2 ♣	2 ♡	◇ 7 4
		♣ 6 2

You have 12 points, so there is still hope for game. Your 2 ♡ bid is forcing for one round.

If your partner rebids his suit at the two-level and you have 11 or 12 points, you may bid 2 NT with the unbid suits stopped, or raise partner's suit to the three-level with adequate trump support. These bids are invitational, not forcing. For example:

Partner	You	♠ Q 10 6 4
1 ◇	1 ♡	♡ K 9 5 3
2 ◇	2 NT	◇ 6 3
		♣ A Q 2

Your 2 NT rebid shows 11 or 12 points and stoppers in clubs and spades. Your partner should pass, or bid 3 ◇, to reject your game invitation, or make any other bid to accept. If you add 2 more points to this hand (to make 13 points), your correct bid would be 3 NT.

   If your partner had opened the bidding with 1 ♣ and rebid 2 ♣, the proper bid with this hand would be 3 ♣.

The responder does not always have to rebid below game. If he has the required strength and knows which game he wants to play, he should by all means bid it. For example:

Partner	You	♠ A Q 6 3 2
1 ♡	1 ♠	♡ K 5
2 ♡	4 ♡	◇ A 8 6 5
		♣ 7 4

On this auction, partner must have at least a six-card heart suit. If he has 5-3-3-2 distribution his proper rebid is 1 NT. If he has a four-card minor suit, he should bid it rather than rebidding a five-card suit. So raising him to game with a doubleton is okay.

AFTER THE OPENER BIDS A NEW SUIT

With from 6 to 10 Points

If your partner's rebid is in a new suit at the one-level, or in a new suit at the two-level that ranks lower than his first suit, he may have anywhere from 13 to 19 points. Although his bid is not forcing, you should bid again with many hands in the 6-to-10-point range not only to find a better part-score contract, but also because there is still hope for game. Here are twelve illustrations showing when to pass, and when and what to bid:

Partner	You	
		♠ Q 10 6 4
1 ♢	1 ♡	♡ A Q 5 3
1 ♠	2 ♠	♢ 9 8 7
		♣ 9 2

Your raise of partner's suit to the two-level shows at least four trumps and about 7 to 10 points. If partner has a minimum-range opening bid (13 to 16), he should pass 2 ♠. If he has an invitational-range opening (17 to 19), he should bid again.

Partner	You	
		♠ J 7 3
1 ♢	1 ♡	♡ A J 9 5
1 ♠	P	♢ 6 4 2
		♣ 10 8 2

Although partner may have as many as 19 points, his 1 ♠ bid is not forcing. Since game seems out of reach and 1 ♠ looks like a reasonable contract, you should pass.

Partner	You	
		♠ 7 4
1 ♢	1 ♡	♡ J 10 9 8
1 ♠	1 NT	♢ 5 4 2
		♣ A J 6 3

The 1 NT rebid shows 7 to 10 points and a balanced hand. Rebidding 1 NT with only 6 points is not recommended as a steady diet, but it is the least of evils here. If you pass 1 ♠, you are almost certainly leaving partner in a 4-2 fit; the opponents have him outnumbered in trumps.

Partner	You	
		♠ 6 3
1 ♣	1 ♡	♡ A K 5 4 2
1 ♠	2 ♣	♢ 10 2
		♣ 9 8 7 3

Rebidding your five-card suit would be a poor choice; partner may have a singleton or void in hearts. If partner happens to have a three-card club suit, he will automatically have three hearts; he will bid 2 ♡ over your 2 ♣ bid.

Partner	You	♠ A 10 6 4 2
1 ♡	1 ♠	♡ 3
2 ◇	P	◇ Q 9 5
		♣ 8 7 6 4

Once again, you should not rebid your five-card suit. You have a very weak hand and a clear preference for diamonds over hearts; passing is the only reasonable choice.

Partner	You	♠ Q 2
1 ♠	1 NT	♡ A Q 9 5
2 ♡	3 ♡	◇ 8 6 4
		♣ J 9 7 3

Your 1 NT response showed 6 to 10 points. Your 3 ♡ bid says you have *at least four trumps* and your high cards are in the right places; do not raise your partner's second suit directly with fewer than four trumps. Your partner should pass 3 ♡ with a minimum opening bid, or bid 4 ♡ with something extra.

Partner	You	♠ 7
1 ♠	1 NT	♡ K 10 8 6 2
2 ♡	4 ♡	◇ A 10 9 5 4
		♣ 6 3

Sometimes your hand improves dramatically. Even if partner has a dead-minimum opening bid, he should be able to make a game with this marvelous dummy.

Partner	You	♠ K J 7 4 2
1 ♡	1 ♠	♡ J 3
2 ◇	2 ♡	◇ J 5
		♣ K 10 8 2

It is common practice to "take a preference" with a doubleton, and 2 ♡ is clearly the best bid here. Passing is wrong because partner must have at least five hearts and he may have only four diamonds. Bidding 2 ♠ is inferior to 2 ♡ because you know the combined hands have at least seven hearts; partner has at most four black cards and should bid 2 ♠ over your 2 ♡ bid if he has three spades and one club. Finally, bidding 2 NT is out of the question because that would show extra values—11 or 12 points.

Note that partner will most likely pass your 2 ♡ bid if he has a minimum-range opening bid, but will bid again with 17 to 19 points to invite you to bid game. For example, if he bids 3 ♡ you should bid 3 NT with your 9 high-card points; with a weaker hand you should pass 3 ♡.

Partner	You	♠ Q 2
1 ♠	1 NT	♡ 7 6 4 3
2 ♣	2 ♠	◇ 8 7 5 3
		♣ A Q 9

You have three key cards in partner's two suits and should most emphatically *not* pass 2 ♣; remember, partner may have as many as 19 points. Also, you must *not* raise clubs with only three-card support. The 2 ♠ preference is the only sensible way to "keep the bidding open." If partner bids again over 2 ♠, showing 17 to 19 points, you should bid game eagerly. If he passes, 2 ♠ should be a cozy contract.

Partner	You	
		♠ 6 2
1 ♠	1 NT	♡ K Q J 9 6
2 ◇	2 ♡	◇ 7 4
		♣ 10 9 8 7

You could not bid 2 ♡ directly over 1 ♠ because you do not have the required 11 points or more. Bidding 1 NT first and following with 2 ♡ shows 6 to 10 points and a very strong five-card suit, or any six-card or longer suit. In effect, your 2 ♡ bid says: "Partner, I have no support for your two suits, but I have a *very substantial* suit of my own; I am prepared to play my suit even if you pass with a singleton heart."

Partner	You	
		♠ 6 2
1 ♠	1 NT	♡ K 7 5 3 2
2 ◇	2 ♠	◇ K 4
		♣ 10 9 8 7

Your heart suit is too weak to bid 2 ♡ and you must not pass 2 ◇ with equal length in partner's two suits. Although the spade preference with a worthless doubleton is an ugly choice, it is not as bad as any other bid.

Partner	You	
		♠ 4 2
1 ♠	1 NT	♡ 6 5 3
2 ◇	3 ♣	◇ 5 2
		♣ A Q J 10 8 7

Your bidding, 1 NT followed by 3 ♣, shows 6 to 10 points and a very good six-card or any seven-card suit.

With 11 or 12 Points

Hands with 11 or 12 points are the toughest to rebid. The recommended procedure is to make a second forward-going bid that allows your partner to stop bidding below game if he has a weak opening bid. However, as you have already seen in this chapter, in many auctions no second forward-going bid is available; the responder must choose between a weak nonforcing bid (showing at most 10 points) and a strong forcing bid (showing at least 13 points).

To help overcome these problems, some players use certain jump bids to describe 11- and 12-point hands that invite the opener to bid game, rather than to describe a stronger hand that is forcing to game. The problem with playing any of responder's jump bids as invitational is that it adds uncertainty to the average player's game; even the experts do not agree on which jump rebids should be forcing and which should be invitational.

My recommendation is that you play that *all jump rebids by the responder are forcing to game* (unless he is a passed hand, of course). If you decide that you prefer to play any of these jump bids as invitational, you must make an agreement with your partner to that effect; without such an agreement, it should be assumed that you are playing the forcing style.

Here are four typical auctions that pose rebidding problems for the responder:

Opener	Responder	Opener	Responder
1 ♣	1 ♡	1 ♣	1 ♡
1 ♠	1 NT or 2 NT?	1 ♠	2 ♠ or 3 ♠?

Opener	Responder	Opener	Responder
1 ◇	1 ♡	1 ◇	1 ♡
1 ♠	2 ♡ or 3 ♡?	1 ♠	2 ◇ or 3 ◇?

In each case the nonjump rebid indicates a maximum of 10 points and is not forcing, while the jump bid indicates 13 points or more and is forcing. It may appear that I have presented a good case for playing jump rebids as invitational, showing 11 or 12 points. It is true that on these four auctions you would be much better off playing jump rebids as invitational if you held 11 or 12 points, but you would be much better off playing these jump rebids as forcing if you held 13 points or more. As stated earlier, I recommend that you play all jump rebids by the responder as forcing, and that is assumed in the following pages. My purpose in showing you these four auctions is so that you will be aware when you are in a tough spot, and then to explain how you should handle the bidding with 11 or 12 points. Here is how to do it:

Partner	You		1. ♠ 7 4 2		2. ♠ 7 4 2
1 ♣	1 ♡		♡ A Q 10 9		♡ A Q 6 4
1 ♠	?		◇ K Q 10		◇ K Q 8
			♣ 10 9 8		♣ 7 5 3

You have 11 points and the choice is strictly between bidding 1 NT (showing about 7 to 10 points) and a game-forcing 2 NT (showing at least 13 points). The slight overbid of 2 NT is recommended with #1 because of the good spot cards, and the slight underbid of 1 NT is recommended with #2 because of the lack of good spot cards.

Partner	You		1. ♠ Q J 8 2		2. ♠ A K 7 2
1 ♣	1 ♡		♡ A K 7 2		♡ Q J 8 2
1 ♠	?		◇ 9 6 5		◇ 9 6 5
			♣ 4 3		♣ 4 3

After adding 1 point for the doubleton you have 11 points and must decide whether to bid 2 ♠ or 3 ♠; no other bid is reasonable. A game-forcing bid of 3 ♠ is best with #1 because of the good location of your high cards—the Q-J in your partner's suit and the A-K in a side suit. Bid only 2 ♠ with #2 (showing about 7 to 10 points), because the ♡ Q-J may be useless; when your partner bids two suits, queens and jacks in the other suits are of doubtful value.

Partner	You		1. ♠ A 6 3		2. ♠ A 6 3
1 ◇	1 ♡		♡ K J 10 7 5 2		♡ K J 7 5 3 2
1 ♠	?		◇ Q 8 4		◇ 9
			♣ 9		♣ Q 8 4

This time it is desirable to rebid your six-card suit and, although you have 12 points, you must choose between 2 ♡ (showing 6 to 10 points) and 3 ♡ (showing at least 13 points). Bid 3 ♡ with #1 because you have the ♡ 10 and your honor cards seem to be in the right places. Bid only 2 ♡ with #2; your heart suit is a bit shabby and you have the stray ♣ Q.

Partner	*You*	1.	♠ 2	2.	♠ 2
1 ◇	1 ♡		♡ A 10 6 4 2		♡ Q J 6 4 2
1 ♠	?		◇ A K 8 5		◇ A K 8 5
			♣ 10 7 3		♣ 10 7 3

If you count 2 points for the singleton spade, hand #1 counts 14 points and #2 counts 13; since we are talking about 11- and 12-point hands, they seem out of place here! But two things must be taken into account: Short-suit points should not be counted unless you intend to play the hand in the agreed trump suit, and you need about 29 points to bid game in a minor suit. So game is by no means certain.

The choice is whether to make a forcing 3 ◇ bid, or a discouraging 2 ◇ bid. The good quality of your points in #1 suggests you should bid 3 ◇. With #2 a bid of 2 ◇ is recommended, but you may still get to game if partner takes another bid; for example, he may bid 2 ♡ over 2 ◇ to show three-card heart support and then you will bid again to make up for your previous underbid. If he passes 2 ◇, it is very unlikely that you will miss a game.

There is no problem rebidding with 11 or 12 points if the responder intends to bid the unbid suit, to raise opener's second suit from two to three, or to rebid 2 NT over two of a suit. For example:

Partner	*You*	♠ 7 2
1 ♣	1 ♡	♡ A Q 10 9 8
1 ♠	2 ◇	◇ A J 7 4
		♣ 6 3

You have 12 points, so it is still unclear whether or not you should bid a game. Your 2 ◇ bid is forcing for one round.

Partner	*You*	♠ A Q 7 2
1 ◇	1 ♠	♡ 7 5
2 ♣	3 ♣	◇ Q 10 8
		♣ K 10 7 4

You have 12 points. Your 3 ♣ bid shows about 11 or 12 points and at least four-card club support. Your partner may pass with a minimum opening bid, or bid again with something extra.

Partner	*You*	♠ K 10 9 3
1 ♡	1 ♠	♡ J 4
2 ♣	2 NT	◇ A J 10
		♣ Q 9 5 2

You have 11 points. With the diamond suit securely stopped, 2 NT is a better bid than 3 ♣.

AFTER THE OPENER REVERSES THE BIDDING

If your partner makes a "reverse bid" (for example, partner 1 ♣, you 1 ♠, partner 2 ◇), he promises at least 17 points and you should assume that he has greater length in his first-bid suit. The reverse bid is forcing for one round, but remember in yesteryear it showed 17 to 19 points and was not a forcing bid (see page 48).

If your partner makes a reverse bid after you have responded at the one-level with a weak hand, you must choose between bidding 2 NT, bidding three of partner's first suit, or rebidding your own suit. Although the practice of many experts is to play that the opening bidder promises to bid again if he has reversed the bidding, none of these rebids by the responder is defined as a forcing bid in nonexpert circles. So if your partner makes a reverse bid and you want to reach game (you have 9 points or more), do not make any of these nonforcing rebids. To make sure that your partner does not pass you below game, you must bid a new suit, raise your partner's second suit, or jump the bidding in various ways. For example:

Partner	You	
		♠ Q 7 4 2
1 ◊	1 ♠	♡ Q 8 3
2 ♡	2 NT	◊ 9 7 2
		♣ K 6 5

This is the way to bid when you have a weak hand with a stopper in the unbid suit. Your 2 NT bid is not forcing, so with a couple more high-card points you should jump to 3 NT to be sure you get to game.

Partner	You	
		♠ 7 4 3
1 ◊	1 NT	♡ K 7 6
2 ♡	3 ◊	◊ 9 5 3
		♣ K 10 8 2

Since partner has advertised at least a five-card diamond suit, 3 ◊ is the most attractive bid and should lead to the best contract. You should not raise your partner's second suit without four trumps, you should not bid 2 NT without a spade stopper, and you *may not pass* your partner's reverse bid.

Partner	You	
		♠ A 10 6 2
1 ♣	1 ♠	♡ 7
2 ♡	4 ♣	◊ 8 7 4 2
		♣ K 10 9 2

Your hand has improved in value tremendously because of partner's bidding. With four strong clubs, a singleton in partner's side suit, and an ace, you certainly want to reach game and you may even have a slam. If you bid just 3 ♣, your partner might pass.

AFTER THE OPENER HAS JUMPED THE BIDDING

When you have from 6 to 10 points and your partner jumps the bidding to show an invitational-range opening bid (17 to 19 points), he expects you to reject his game invitation with a minimum, or accept with a maximum. It may seem that 6 or 7 points should be considered a minimum, while 8, 9, or 10 points is a maximum, but it is not always right to reject partner's game invitation with 7 points and accept with 8 points. You may be able to make game if you have the right 7 points and you may not be able to make game if you have the wrong 8 points, or more. There is a lot of guesswork in bidding, but good judgment in valuing your hand will help you guess right most of the time. The following illustrations demonstrate how to use your judgment.

When your partner jump-raises your suit to the three-level, showing 17 to 19 points and at least four-card trump support, he is leaving it up to you whether to pass, or bid on to game. For example:

Partner	You	♠ Q J 6 4
1 ◇	1 ♠	♡ 9 7
3 ♠	4 ♠	◇ 6 3 2
		♣ A 8 5 4

You have 8 points (1 for the doubleton) and partner's 3 ♠ bid shows 17, 18, or 19 points. The total is 25, 26, or 27 points, so accepting partner's game invitation is a good gamble with this hand because all of your points are "working" (they are of good quality). If you reverse the club and spade holdings (so you have ♠ A-8-5-4, ♡ 9-7, ◇ 6-3-2, ♣ Q-J-6-4), you should pass 3 ♠ because the club honors are doubtful values; although the queen and jack of clubs will be useful if partner holds something like ♣ A-X-X, they may be worthless if he has another holding such as ♣ X-X

When your partner jump-rebids his original suit at the three-level, showing 17 to 19 points and a good six-card or longer suit, his bid is invitational. For example:

Partner	You	♠ J 4 3
1 ♡	1 NT	♡ 5 2
3 ♡	P	◇ K J 8 4
		♣ Q 9 5 2

In most cases, you should reject partner's invitation to game with only 7 points.

Partner	You	♠ 7 5 2
1 ♡	1 NT	♡ K 10
3 ♡	4 ♡	◇ A 7 4 2
		♣ 9 8 6 3

The ♡ K is a key card and any ace figures to be of great value, so you must upgrade this marvelous 7-point hand and bid game. Since partner's bid promises at least a good six-card suit, it is correct to raise him with a doubleton trump, even a worthless doubleton.

Partner	You	♠ Q 10 9 2
1 ♡	1 ♠	♡ Q 3
3 ♡	3 NT	◇ K J 8
		♣ J 10 9 4

Not only must you decide whether or not to accept partner's invitation to game, you must bid the *right* game. This balanced 9-point hand with scattered honors figures to play better in 3 NT than in 4 ♡; it has notrump written all over it. This is a rare case, however; normally choose the major suit when an eight-card fit is available.

When your partner raises your 1 NT response to 2 NT, he shows from 17 to 19 points and a balanced or semibalanced hand. For example:

Partner	You	♠ A Q 7
1 ◊	1 NT	♡ 9 3 2
2 NT	3 NT	◊ 9 8 5
		♣ K 10 8 2

On this auction you must rely heavily on point count. With a balanced hand and 6 or 7 points, pass 2 NT, and with 8, 9, or 10 points, bid 3 NT. With an unbalanced hand you must use your judgment to pass, bid 3 NT, or bid a suit.

When your partner *jumps the bidding* to 2 NT, he shows 19 or 20 points, a balanced hand, and stoppers in the unbid suits. Although his bid is invitational (it is *not* forcing), you should always bid again with 7 points and usually with 6 high-card points. For example:

Partner	You	♠ K 10 9 8
1 ◊	1 ♠	♡ 7 2
2 NT	3 NT	◊ 6 4 3
		♣ K 10 5 2

Although it is a close decision whether to pass or bid 3 NT with 6 points, the good spot cards should influence you to be aggressive. With an unbalanced hand you may elect to bid a suit; any bid you make below the game level is forcing.

If the opening bidder's rebid is a jump bid and you have a very strong hand, there is no need to jump the bidding; any bid you make below game is forcing. For example:

Partner	You	♠ A Q J 6 5 2
1 ♡	1 ♠	♡ 7
3 ♡	3 ♠	◊ A J 8
		♣ 10 7 3

Your partner has shown 17 to 19 points and you have 14, so you know you have a game and you may have a slam. It is true that the 3 ♠ bid does not reveal your strength, but it is forcing and is the proper step in the auction to get your side to the best contract. If partner's rebid was 2 NT, 3 ♣, or 3 ◊ (instead of 3 ♡), 3 ♠ would still be the right bid.

When your partner jumps the bidding in a new suit—jump-shifts—his bid shows 20 points or more (or maybe a good-quality 19 points) and is forcing to game. For example:

Partner	You	♠ Q 7 4 2
1 ♡	1 ♠	♡ 8 3
3 ◊	3 NT	◊ J 10 3
		♣ K 6 5 4

If your hand were any weaker than this you probably would not have bid in the first place, but even if your hand were weaker, *you are not allowed to pass 3 ◊ or any subsequent bid below game.* With a stopper in the unbid suit, 3 NT appears to be the best chance for game; without a club stopper you would have to find some other bid.

AFTER RESPONDER HAS RAISED THE OPENER'S SUIT

When your partner bids again after you raise his suit to the two-level, he shows at least 17 points; he should most emphatically pass with 13 to 16 points. When he "reraises" the agreed suit (partner 1 ♠, you 2 ♠, partner 3 ♠), he describes a hand with a good trump suit and from 17 to 19 points; you should pass with a minimum (6 or 7 points), bid again with a maximum (9 or 10 points), and use your judgment with 8 points. If, after you have raised your partner's suit to the two-level, he follows by bidding a new suit, his bid is absolutely forcing for one round; with a minimum raise, you should bid three of the agreed suit, and with a maximum you should make any other bid. For example:

Partner	You		
		♠	K 10 8
1 ♠	2 ♠	♡	7 6 3 2
3 ♣	4 ♠	◇	9 5 3
		♣	K J 5

Partner's 3 ♣ bid is a *game try,* showing length in clubs and at least 17 points. The reason he chose the 3 ♣ bid for his game try is so that you could take into account your holding in his side suit when deciding whether or not to accept his game invitation. Note that the aggressive 4 ♠ bid with only 7 points is indicated because of your strong club holding. If partner had bid 3 ◇ (instead of 3 ♣) your club honors might be useless; you should reject the invitation to game by bidding 3 ♠.

Partner	You		
		♠	K Q 10
1 ◇	2 ◇	♡	7 3
2 ♡	3 NT	◇	Q 6 5 4
		♣	Q 10 9 8

Partner's 2 ♡ bid shows a stopper (it is not necessarily a four-card or longer suit) and is an attempt to reach 3 NT. Your 3 NT bid shows a maximum 2 ◇ response with stoppers in clubs and spades.

Partner	You		
		♠	6 4
1 ◇	2 ◇	♡	6 3 2
2 ♡	3 ♣	◇	K 10 8 7 4
		♣	A J 5

Your 3 ♣ bid tells your partner that you have a maximum 2 ◇ bid with a stopper in clubs. If your partner has a spade stopper he should bid 3 NT; otherwise the hand will be played in diamonds.

Partner	You		
		♠	7 4
1 ♣	2 ♣	♡	8 5 3
2 ♠	3 ♣	◇	9 7 4 2
		♣	A Q 10 8

By returning to three of the agreed suit, you show a minimum raise and discourage your partner from bidding further. If you have a maximum 2 ♣ bid with particularly good distribution and trump support, you may jump to 4 ♣, or even 5 ♣.

When your partner bids 2 NT after you have raised his suit to the two-level, he shows 17 to 19 points, a balanced or semibalanced hand, and stoppers in the unbid suits. With a minimum raise, you should pass 2 NT or bid three of the agreed suit. With a maximum you should bid 3 NT, bid a new suit, or jump the bidding in the agreed suit. Here is one example:

Partner	You	
		♠ A Q 10 6
1 ♠	2 ♠	♡ 7
2 NT	4 ♠	◊ 9 8 4 3
		♣ 8 7 5 2

Partner should have 5-3-3-2 distribution with stoppers in all three unbid suits; otherwise, why would he suggest a notrump contract after you have raised his major suit? With 8 quality points you should accept partner's invitation to game, and your especially good trump support and distribution make it clear that 4 ♠ is the best game.

AFTER RESPONDER'S FIRST BID WAS A NEW SUIT AT THE TWO-LEVEL

When you respond in a new suit at the two-level, you show 11 points or more and promise to bid again if partner's rebid is below game. (NOTE: As was mentioned on page 50, the old style was to play that a two-over-one response does not promise another bid; the opener must bid a new suit or jump the bidding to force the responder to bid again. Most authorities would agree that the modern style—a two-over-one response promises another bid—is much better, and that is the way it is explained in the following pages.)

When you bid again and have just 11 or 12 points, be sure not to make any further encouraging bids. Your partner already knows you have at least 11 points, and he will not stop bidding below game unless he has a dead-minimum opening bid. The nonforcing rebids available with 11 or 12 points are to raise your partner's suit, to bid 2 NT (or 3 NT if partner's last bid was at the three-level), to rebid your own suit, or to take a preference for your partner's first suit. For example:

Partner	You	
		♠ K 7
1 ♠	2 ♣	♡ 6 4 3
2 ♠	3 ♠	◊ 9 3
		♣ A K 8 7 5 2

When your partner rebids his suit and you raise him to the three-level, you show 11 or 12 points and your bid is not forcing; with a stronger hand you must bid 4 ♠. It is okay to raise your partner with a doubleton honor after he has rebid his suit, and 3 ♠ is a far better bid than 3 ♣. Your partner knows you may have raised him with a doubleton honor; he will take his suit quality into account when deciding whether to pass 3 ♠ or bid game.

Partner	You	
		♠ 7
1 ♠	2 ♣	♡ 6 4 3
2 ◊	3 ◊	◊ K 9 8 7
		♣ A K J 5 2

Your hand becomes worth 14 points after your partner's 2 ◊ bid. Since game in a minor suit requires 29 points in the combined hands, you may raise your partner's minor suit with a slightly stronger hand (13 or 14 points), but you must have four-card trump support to raise his second suit directly. Your 3 ◇ bid is not forcing and partner should pass with a minimum opening bid, or bid again with something extra. If you held a hand strong enough to insist on game and chose to raise diamonds, you must jump to 4 ◇ to force him to bid again.

Partner	You	♠ K 10 6
1 ♡	2 ♣	♡ 7 4
2 ♡	2 NT	◇ A Q 7 4
		♣ K 9 5 2

Your 2 NT bid shows 11 or 12 points and stoppers in the unbid suits. Note that the first response of 2 ♣ is correct; with 11 or 12 points always bid a new suit, and with two four-card suits bid up the line. Your partner may pass 2 NT or bid 3 ♡ to reject your game invitation. If you held 1 more high-card point, your proper rebid would be 3 NT, not 2 NT.

Partner	You	♠ 7
1 ♠	2 ♡	♡ K Q 8 6 4 2
2 ♠	3 ♡	◇ A J 9
		♣ 5 3 2

Your 3 ♡ bid shows 11 or 12 points and a reasonably good six-card suit. Your partner may pass 3 ♡ if he has a minimum opening bid and judges that there is no game.

Partner	You	♠ K 10
1 ♠	2 ♣	♡ 8 7 5
2 ◇	2 ♠	◇ Q 4 2
		♣ A Q 10 6 3

Your 2 ♠ bid shows 11 or 12 points. It may seem strange to tell your partner that you prefer spades to diamonds when you have more diamonds, but you may not pass partner's new-suit bid, and no other reasonable bid exists: You should not raise your partner's second suit unless you have at least four trumps (his second suit is usually a four-carder); you should not rebid clubs with only a five-card suit; you should not bid 2 NT without a heart stopper; but it is okay to give your partner a preference for his first suit with a doubleton honor. If your partner has 5-5 distribution he should rebid his diamond suit, unless he has a minimum opening and decides to pass 2 ♠.

If you make a two-over-one response and follow by bidding a new suit, your bid shows 11 points or more—no upper limit—and is forcing for one round. For example:

Partner	You	♠ A Q 9 2
1 ♡	2 ♣	♡ 7 3
2 ♡	2 ♠	◇ 8 4
		♣ A J 10 7 6

With a two-suited hand, you should bid the longer suit first; it would be an error to respond 1 ♠ with this hand. This bidding guarantees that you have more clubs than spades (5-4, 6-4, or 6-5), and you must of course have at least 11 points. Since your new-suit bid is forcing, you may bid this way with much stronger hands.

Partner	You	
Partner	*You*	♠ 7 6
1 ♡	2 ♣	♡ 8 2
3 ♣	3 ♢	♢ A 10 8
		♣ A Q 9 5 4 2

After a minor suit has been raised, a new-suit bid below 3 NT shows a stopper; it is not necessarily a four-card or longer suit. In this case your partner should bid 3 NT if he has a spade stopper, or make any other bid to describe his hand without a spade stopper; he may not pass your new-suit bid. If partner does not bid 3 NT, it is very possible that you will stop bidding below game, in 4 ♣.

If, after your two-over-one response, your partner bids 2 NT, he shows a balanced hand that was too weak to open the bidding with 1 NT. Even if you have only 11 points you must bid again, choosing the bid that best describes your hand. For example:

Partner	*You*	
1 ♠	2 ♢	♠ K 5
2 NT	3 NT	♡ 8 7 2
		♢ A Q J 9 3
		♣ 9 4 2

Your wholesome diamond suit should be very productive in 3 NT, so partner should be a favorite to make his contract.

Partner	*You*	
1 ♠	2 ♡	♠ 8
2 NT	3 ♡	♡ K J 8 6 5 2
		♢ A Q 4
		♣ 9 7 2

Your 3 ♡ bid shows a six-card heart suit with 11 or 12 points. Your partner must decide whether to pass or bid on to game; the 3 ♡ bid is not forcing.

There is an extraordinary difference in the meaning of the responder's rebid when his first bid was at the two-level, in contrast to when his first bid was at the one-level. *The meaning of any rebid is always within the framework of the meaning of any earlier bid, or bids.* For example:

Partner	*You*	
1 ♡	2 ♣	♠ 9 5 4
2 ♢	2 ♡	♡ K 10 5
		♢ 7 2
		♣ A K 10 6 3

Your 2 ♡ bid limits your hand to 11 or 12 points and is not forcing. If you held a stronger hand and wanted to insist on game, you would have to jump to 3 ♡. Note the difference in the following hand, where the clubs and spades have been reversed and your first response was at the one-level.

Partner	*You*	
1 ♡	1 ♠	♠ A K 10 6 3
2 ♢	3 ♡	♡ K 10 5
		♢ 7 2
		♣ 9 5 4

The choice of rebids is between 2 ♡, which is not a forward-going bid and shows from 6 to 10 points, and a jump to 3 ♡, which is forcing to game; no other bid makes any sense. Since there is no way to invite game, the aggressive action is clearly right, as partner would pass a 2 ♡ bid with many hands that would make game.

AFTER RESPONDER HAS JUMPED THE BIDDING

Any jump response to an opening suit bid of one is forcing to game. For example:

Partner	*You*	♠ 8 4 2
1 ♠	2 NT	♡ A 10 9 8
3 ♢	3 ♠	♢ A Q 5
		♣ K J 3

The 2 NT response showed 13 to 15 points, a balanced hand, and stoppers in the unbid suits. Since you have committed the partnership to game, your partner may make any bid below game with a minimum opening in search of the best game contract, or with a powerful slam-going hand. He obviously has a two-suited hand and wants you to describe your hand further. With three-card spade support you should bid 3 ♠ as shown; with only two spades you would choose some other bid, such as 4 ♢ with four-card support, or 3 NT with the clubs and hearts securely stopped. Your partner will reveal his extra strength, if any, in the subsequent bidding.

8

Opening Preemptive Bids

♣   ♦   ♥   ♠   ♣   ♦   ♥   ♠

Any opening suit bid at the three-level, or the four-level, or a minor suit at the five-level, is a *preemptive bid*. These bids describe a hand with a long suit and very limited high-card strength. For example:

♠ K Q J 10 7 4 2	This hand is ideal for an opening bid of 3 ♠. If allowed
♡ 7 3	to play a spade contract the hand can win six tricks,
◊ 9 4	while in defense against a different trump contract it is
♣ 8 5	unlikely to win any tricks.

The main purpose of a preemptive bid is to deprive your opponents of bidding space. They may walk into a trap and take a big set, be shut out of the bidding entirely, or be steered into reaching the wrong contract. For example:

Opp.	You	
3 ♠	?	♠ 7 4 2
		♡ A 5
		◊ K 9 8 6 2
		♣ A K J

If you pass and your partner has a reasonable hand and passes as well, you may miss a game. If you bid and your left-hand opponent has a strong hand, you may get doubled and suffer a big penalty. And, finally, if you bid and your partner does have a good hand, it is less likely that you will reach the best contract than if you were able to start bidding at the one-level. The recommended call with this hand is pass (see Chapter 14, Bidding over Preemptive Bids).

While the main purpose is to deprive the opponents of bidding space, an opening preemptive bid describes a hand accurately and the responder can judge wisely whether to pass, bid a game or slam, or take a good sacrifice.

If an opponent doubles your preemptive bid and the double is left in, you can expect to be set a few tricks if your partner has a worthless hand. But the doubled penalty will not be a serious loss, because the opponents, in most cases, could have made a big score by bidding and making a game or slam.

Daring tactics are in order when you open the bidding with a preemptive bid, but just how daring depends very heavily on the vulnerability. The safety factor is in the quality of your long suit. For example, if you are vulnerable and your opponents are not, you need a good seven-card suit to bid at the three-level, at least A-Q-10-X-X-X-X or Q-J-10-X-X-X-X. If the opponents are vulnerable and you are not, you may bid at the three-level with any seven-card suit, or a strong six-card suit, as J-X-X-X-X-X-X or K-Q-J-X-X-X. At the higher levels of bidding the suit must be more substantial.

When you open the bidding with a preemptive bid you must not have too many high cards. You may mislead your partner into missing a game or slam, or into taking a "phantom sacrifice." An opening preemptive bid should usually contain in the neighborhood of 6 to 9 high-card points, but you may have slightly more or less depending on the vulnerability. The high cards should be concentrated in your long suit, but it is acceptable to have one high card—an ace or king—in a side suit. In general, an opening preemptive bid describes a hand too weak to open with a one-bid, but at the game level—such as an opening 4 ♠ bid—it may be in the category of a minimum opening one-bid.

As was indicated in Chapter 1, the point-count system is entirely inaccurate when it comes to highly distributional hands. So do not count points to value your hand for an opening preemptive bid, except to make sure you do not have too many high-card points. Instead, count your tricks; estimate how many tricks you think your hand can win. This procedure is explained in the following examples, but first let us see how the vulnerability affects our decision whether or not to open the bidding with a preemptive bid or how high to bid— whether to preempt at the three-level, the four-level, or in a minor suit at the five-level.

1. With unfavorable vulnerability—your side is vulnerable and the opponents are not—overbid by two tricks. For example, when you bid 3 ♠ you have estimated that your hand can win seven tricks.
2. With equal vulnerability—both sides are vulnerable or both sides are not— overbid by three tricks. For example, when you bid 3 ♠ you have estimated that your hand can win six tricks.
3. With favorable vulnerability—the opponents are vulnerable and your side is not—overbid by three, four, or even five tricks. It is with favorable vulnerability that bidding at a high level with a trashy suit is desirable; the amount you lose if your contract is doubled and set, as compared to the amount you lose if your opponents bid and make a game or slam, is usually a bargain.

Here are several examples:

♠ 4

♡ Q J 10 9 7 5 4

♢ 8 5 3

♣ A 3

You should count five tricks in hearts and one for the ♣ A. With six tricks you should open the bidding 3 ♡ with equal or favorable vulnerability. With unfavorable vulnerability you should pass or bid 2 ♡ if you play "weak two-bids" (see Chapter 9).

♠ J 4
♡ 3
◇ A Q 10 9 8 5 2
♣ 8 7 5

Counting the number of winning tricks is not always as clear-cut as in the first example. You should estimate six tricks for this diamond suit. You may lose two diamond tricks to the king and jack—leaving only five winners—but with so few diamonds outstanding it is unlikely. So this hand qualifies for an opening 3 ◇ bid with equal or favorable vulnerability. If you play weak two-bids, you should bid 2 ◇ with unfavorable vulnerability.

♠ 7
♡ Q 9
◇ 3 2
♣ A K Q 9 8 7 5 3

Here you have eight club tricks. Open the bidding 4 ♣ with unfavorable vulnerability, or 5 ♣ with equal or favorable vulnerability. If this hand were any stronger—say the heart holding was ♡ A-9 (or even K-9) instead of ♡ Q-9—the recommended bid would be 1 ♣.

♠ K Q J 10 9 8 2
♡ 4
◇ 10 8 3 2
♣ Q

If in addition to your long trump suit you have a four-card suit on the side, it will usually win a trick. Estimate any side four-card suit to be worth a trick, so this hand is worth seven tricks—six spades and one diamond. Open the bidding 3 ♠ with unfavorable vulnerability, or 4 ♠ with equal or favorable vulnerability. (NOTE: Many authorities say you should not open the bidding with a preemptive bid if you have a side four-card *major suit*, but I have been known to break that rule if my four-card major is weak.)

♠ 10 8 7 5 4 3 2
♡ K 2
◇ 3
♣ 9 8 6

This ragged seven-card suit should produce about four tricks, and the ♡ K is worth one-half of a trick. With favorable vulnerability, open the bidding with 3 ♠, but with any other vulnerability, *pass*.

When you are in third or fourth seat, you may open the bidding with a preemptive bid at the game level with a stronger hand than in first or second seat. For example:

♠ 5
♡ A K Q J 10 4 3
◇ 8 2
♣ K J 4

In first or second seat the correct opening bid with this hand is 1 ♡; if you open 4 ♡ your partner will expect a weaker hand and may pass with the values that would make a slam.

In third or fourth seat the best bid is 4 ♡. Since your partner is a passed hand, it is unlikely that his hand is strong enough to make a slam; and, even if he did have the magic hand to make a slam, it would be very difficult to bid. A much more important consideration is that the opponents may have a game in spades or a good sacrifice against your makable 4 ♡ contract; the 4 ♡ opening bid may keep them out of the bidding.

The requirements to open the bidding with a preemptive bid below the game level in third seat are about the same as in first or second seat. But in fourth seat you should never make a preemptive opening bid of any kind unless you expect a profit; if you pass, the bidding is over. So, to open the bidding with a preemptive bid in fourth seat, you need the equivalent of a minimum opening one-bid; but if you are considering an opening bid of 3 ♠, your hand may be slightly weaker (see the discussion of the "spade-suit theory" for opening one-bids in fourth seat, page 30). For example:

♠ 7
♡ A J
◇ 8 5 2
♣ A Q J 10 9 7 2

In first or second seat, open 1 ♣. In third seat, open 1 ♣; but since partner is a passed hand, 3 ♣ is within reason. In fourth seat, open 3 ♣; your partner will expect you to have a good hand and will bid something if there is a chance for game.

♠ K Q J 10 7 4 3
♡ 9
◇ Q J 10
♣ 8 2

This hand is worth seven tricks (six spades and one diamond). So in first, second, or third seat, you should open 3 ♠ with unfavorable vulnerability and 4 ♠ with equal or favorable vulnerability.

In fourth seat you should open 3 ♠ regardless of the vulnerability. This is rather a weak hand in high cards for a fourth-seat opening, but you are a favorite to find partner with two of the high cards you need to make 3 ♠ (it is even possible that you have a game), and both opponents are passed hands and so it is unlikely they will dare to compete at the four-level. If your spade holding were in any other suit, the recommended call would be to pass; the opponents are more likely to compete at the three-level, and since your hand has so little defensive strength, they are likely to make anything they bid.

RESPONSES TO OPENING PREEMPTIVE BIDS

When responding to an opening preemptive bid, value your hand by counting tricks, not points. Here is a typical hand for an opening preemptive bid; you can see the values in the responder's hand needed to produce tricks:

♠ A J 10 9 8 7 3
♡ 7 5
◇ 6 5
♣ 8 2

In the nontrump suits this hand has six losing tricks, and the only high cards that the responder can have to help are quick tricks (A-K, A-Q, A, K-Q, K-X). Note that stray queens and jacks would be worthless.

In the trump suit any honor figures to be useful; notice how useful the ♠ K or ♠ Q would be here. The responder should count a full trick for a king or queen in the opener's suit.

Provided the responder has trump support, he should count tricks for singletons and voids in the side suits. For example, if the responder had only one club, a trick could be won by trumping the second club.

An opening preemptive bid describes a hand that will win numerous tricks if played in the long suit, but may not win any tricks if the hand is played in a different trump suit or notrump. This suggests that the responder should be reluctant to make any bid other than raising the opener's suit. Since an opening preemptive bid shows a very substantial suit, the responder should be glad to raise with a doubleton and willing to raise with a singleton. In rare cases, when your side is vulnerable and the opponents are not, it may even be right to raise with a void suit; the opener's suit must be very good when he preempts with unfavorable vulnerability.

An opening preemptive bid describes the trick-taking power of a hand accurately. For example, an opening suit bid of three shows a hand that can win seven tricks with unfavorable vulnerabiity, six tricks with equal vulnerability, and four, five, or six tricks with favorable vulnerability. The responder should estimate how many tricks he thinks his hand can win and add the total to the number of tricks the opener has indicated; this will give him a good idea of how many tricks can be won if the hand is played in the opener's long suit. For example:

Partner	You	
3 ♠	?	♠ 7 4
		♡ K Q J 3
		◊ Q J 9
		♣ K Q J 2

You should pass regardless of the vulnerability. Your hand has only two tricks, ♡ K-Q and ♣ K-Q; the ♡ J, ◊ Q-J, and ♣ J are apt to be useless. So with unfavorable vulnerability you figure to make just 3 ♠, with equal vulnerability you figure to be set one trick, and with favorable vulnerability you may be down even more than one trick.

If you are thinking 3 NT may be a good contract, forget it; you will almost surely lack the entries to dummy to run your partner's long suit, and even if you could run the suit a diamond lead could still beat you.

Partner	You	
3 ♠	?	♠ 7
		♡ A K 8 4
		◊ A 10 8 2
		♣ J 9 7 3

This time you have three tricks for your partner, so it's right to bid 4 ♠ with unfavorable vulnerability. With equal or favorable vulnerability you should pass.

Partner	You	
3 ♡	?	♠ A K 9 7 2
		♡ K 9 4
		◊ 3
		♣ 10 8 7 5

You have what looks like four winning tricks: two for the ♠ A-K, one for the ♡ K, and one for the singleton diamond. So bid 4 ♡ regardless of the vulnerability.

Partner	You	
3 ◊	?	♠ 2
		♡ A K Q 5 3
		◊ K 7 4
		♣ A K 9 7

If partner has an ace, you can almost surely make a slam. So bid 4 NT to find out; if he has an ace you will bid 6 ◊ and if he has no aces you will bid 5 ◊.

(NOTE: With three or more trumps it usually pays to raise your partner's opening preemptive bid with a poor hand, to further the cause of blocking the opponent's bidding or as a sacrifice. This subject is covered in Chapter 16.)

Bidding 3 NT in response to an opening preemptive bid is rare, but if your partner opens the bidding with three of a *minor suit*, bid 3 NT provided you have a fit in partner's suit—at least X-X-X or K-X—and the equivalent of an opening bid with stoppers in the three unbid suits. For example:

Partner	You	
3 ♣	3 NT	♠ J 10 7 6
		♡ A Q 2
		◇ A 10 9 4
		♣ K 9

If partner has a poor club suit (as Q-10-X-X-X-X-X), 3 NT may fail, but the odds are in your favor and it is the only game contract that has a good chance to make.

Partner	You	
3 ◇	?	♠ A K 9 2
		♡ A K 5
		◇ 7 3
		♣ A 6 5 4

Without a fit in diamonds it would be a mistake to bid 3 NT; unless partner has a running diamond suit, or a one-loser diamond suit and a side entry, you will not be able to run his suit. The right bid with five quick tricks is 5 ◇, or if the vulnerability is unfavorable you should bid 6 ◇.

If your partner opens the bidding with three of a *major suit*, it is almost never right to bid 3 NT; if you have a strong hand, raise his suit instead. The one time responding 3 NT to a major suit may be right is when you can win nine tricks without running your partner's suit. For example:

Partner	You	
3 ♠	3 NT	♠ 7
		♡ K 2
		◇ A J 4
		♣ A K Q J 9 6 3

If the opening lead is a heart, you have your own nine tricks. Note that 3 NT figures to be a much better game contract than 4 ♠ or 5 ♣.

When your partner opens the bidding with a preemptive bid, especially in a major suit, it seldom pays to bid your own suit, because partner's hand may be trickless unless his suit is the trump suit. However, it is occasionally right to bid your own suit, and if your bid is below game, it is forcing—that is, unless you passed originally. A new-suit bid shows a hand strong enough to hope for game and a long and strong suit (usually six cards long, but it may be a strong five-card suit); your partner should raise your suit with a doubleton honor, or three small trumps. For example:

Partner	You	
3 ◇	3 ♠	♠ A K J 7 5 2
		♡ 6 2
		◇ A
		♣ A 9 8 3

If partner bids 4 ♠ you will pass. If he bids 4 ◇ you should bid 5 ◇ with unfavorable vulnerability and pass with favorable vulnerability (he may have a trashy suit); with equal vulnerability the decision is very close.

Partner	You	♠ A K J 10 9 8
3 ◊	P	♡ K 7 3
		◊ 2
		♣ 7 6 4

If you bid 3 ♠ with this hand you are asking for trouble. In the first place, 3 ◊ is probably the only contract that has a chance to succeed, although the odds are against it. Secondly, a 3 ♠ bid would be forcing; when your partner bids at the four-level it is not unlikely that the opponents will double and set your senseless contract two or three tricks.

When your partner opens the bidding with a preemptive bid and you bid a new suit at the game level, your suit must be independently strong and your partner must pass, even if he is void in your suit. For example:

Partner	You	♠ —
3 ♠	4 ♡	♡ A K Q J 10 9 5
		◊ A Q 10 6
		♣ J 2

You clearly want to play 4 ♡ with this hand, and let's hope your partner will know enough to pass.

REBIDS AFTER OPENING WITH A PREEMPTIVE BID

Many years ago I visited New York City and stayed in the apartment of my friend Charlie Goren while he was out of town. Perusing his library, I noticed a book with a rather strange title: *Rebids by the Opening Preemptive Bidder.* When I opened the book, I found 300 blank pages.

Goren was trying to tell his "readers" something important. When you open the bidding with a preemptive bid, bid as high as you dare the first time and then pass throughout. Do not bid again unless your partner makes a bid that invites or commands you to do so. After you have made a preemptive bid, your partner is the captain; he is responsible for all of the subsequent bidding. If you wish to see what happened to me in a rubber-bridge game when my partner broke this rule, turn to page 184.

9

Opening Suit Bids of Two

♣   ♦   ♥   ♠   ♣   ♦   ♥   ♠

There are two popular methods for opening suit bids of two. You have a choice:

1. Opening bids of 2 ♣, 2 ◊, 2 ♡, and 2 ♠ are all very strong and forcing bids. This method is called "strong two-bids."
2. Opening bids of 2 ◊, 2 ♡, and 2 ♠ are weak, and only 2 ♣ is used as a strong opening bid. This method is called "weak two-bids" and the "strong artificial two-club opening."

Except for the experts and in duplicate bridge circles, a vast majority of players in America use strong two-bids. Since strong two-bids are so popular, you must know how to play them, and that is what the first part of this chapter is all about. Weak two-bids and the strong artificial two-club opening are far superior to strong two-bids, and perhaps, one day they will be standard with all players. Therefore they are covered later in this chapter, and you should learn them and use them in preference to strong two-bids anytime you have a competent partner willing to use the more modern method.

STRONG TWO-BIDS

You generally need about 23 points (including distribution) to open a strong two-bid, but you may shade it down 1 or 2 points with a long and strong suit, or a good two-suited hand. For example:

♠ A K Q J 9 8 2   Open 2 ♠ with 21 points (3 points for the length in
♡ 5   spades).
◊ A K J
♣ 10 4

♠ A 10 8
♡ A K Q J 10 7 4 3
◊ 6 2
♣ —

Open 1 ♡ with 18 points. Although you have nine sure tricks, your hand does not qualify for a strong two-bid. Never open a strong two-bid with fewer than 17 high-card points.

♠ A K Q 8 2
♡ K Q J 9 7
◊ A 4
♣ 3

Open 2 ♠ with 21 points and two strong five-card major suits.

♠ K Q
♡ K 9 7 4 2
◊ A K J 7 3
♣ A

Open 1 ♡ with 22 points and a poor-quality heart suit.

RESPONSES TO STRONG TWO-BIDS

The opening suit bid of two is absolutely forcing; the responder may not pass. The "negative response" is 2 NT, showing 0 to 6 high-card points, or 7 high-card points of poor quality; the bid says nothing about the responder's distribution. (NOTE: If your right-hand opponent bids or doubles over your partner's strong two-bid, pass becomes the negative response; your partner will get another chance to bid.) Here are three examples:

Partner	You	
2 ♡	2 NT	♠ 9 5 4
		♡ 7 5
		◊ 10 8 3 2
		♣ 8 6 4 3

Even with 0 points you must bid 2 NT. Only if your right-hand opponent bid or doubled should you pass.

Partner	You	
2 ♡	2 NT	♠ K 10 9 8 6 4
		♡ 8
		◊ 9 8 7 5 2
		♣ 3

Your 2 NT bid does not indicate anything about your distribution. You must wait until the next round of bidding to bid your spade suit.

Partner	You	
2 ♡	4 ♡, or	♠ 8 3
	2 NT	♡ K 10 7 4
		◊ 9 8 7 5
		♣ 6 3 2

A jump-raise of a major suit is a highly specialized bid showing four or more trumps headed by the ace, king, or queen, and no first- or second-round controls in the side suits—no aces, kings, singletons, or void suits. It is very possible that your partner will misunderstand your 4 ♡ response, so it would be wiser to respond 2 NT unless you are confident that he knows a jump raise of a major suit shows a weak hand with good trump support.

Any response to a strong two-bid other than 2 NT (or the jump raise of a major suit) is a "positive response," showing 8 or more high-card points, or 7 points of good quality, such as an ace and a king, or A-Q-J in the same suit. The possible bids are to raise your partner's suit to the three-level with three trumps or more; to bid your own five-card or longer suit (on occasion, it may be necessary to bid a strong four-card suit); or to jump to 3 NT with a balanced hand and 8 to 10 high-card points. For example:

Partner	*You*	♠ 8 6 4
2 ♡	3 ♡	♡ 10 7 5
		◊ A Q 10 2
		♣ A Q 3

With this strong hand you should be wondering whether you have a small slam or a grand slam, but the first step is to raise partner's suit.

Partner	*You*	♠ 10 5
2 ♠	3 ♣	♡ 7 3 2
		◊ 9 8 2
		♣ A Q J 6 4

This is the least you might have to give a positive response. Your subsequent bidding should be conservative.

Partner	*You*	♠ A K J 2
2 ♡	2 ♠	♡ 3
		◊ 9 8 5 3
		♣ 9 7 6 4

No bid except 2 ♠ makes any sense, so here is a rare case where you must make a positive response in a strong four-card suit.

Partner	*You*	♠ K 10 8
2 ♡	3 NT	♡ K 2
		◊ Q J 9 7
		♣ 8 6 5 3

Your 3 NT bid is not forcing, but your partner knows you have 8 to 10 high-card points, and he should bid a slam if that is enough. If you had 11 high-card points or more you should insist on reaching a slam and would have to find some response other than 3 NT.

REBIDS AFTER AN OPENING STRONG TWO-BID

An opening strong two-bid is forcing to game unless the responder gives a negative response of 2 NT and the opener rebids three of his original suit. For example:

♠ A	*You*	*Partner*
♡ A Q J 10 8 7 2	2 ♡	2 NT
◊ A J 9	3 ♡	
♣ K 3		

You need some help from your partner to make a game, and your 3 ♡ bid says just that. Your partner should pass if he judges his hand to be worthless, or bid game if he can provide a trick.

	You	Partner
♠ A Q J 10 2	2 ♠	2 NT
♡ 9	3 ◇	
◇ A K J 10 5		
♣ A Q		

Your 3 ◇ bid is absolutely forcing to game.

If the responder makes a positive response, the opening bidder should be looking for a slam, but he should not bid beyond the game level unless he has something extra. For example:

	You	Partner
♠ A K 8	2 ♡	3 ◇
♡ A K Q 4 2	3 NT	
◇ 6 4		
♣ A Q 9		

Your 3 NT bid is not forcing, but your partner heard your strong two-bid and will not pass if he thinks you can make a slam.

	You	Partner
♠ A K Q J 6 3	2 ♠	3 ♣
♡ 7 5	4 ◇	
◇ A Q 2		
♣ K Q		

Your 4 ◇ bid is a "control-showing" bid (see Chapter 17, Slam Bidding), and the decision whether or not to bid a slam depends on whether or not your partner's subsequent bidding is encouraging.

After giving a negative response of 2 NT, the responder must be aware of two very important factors at his next turn to bid: (1) Unless the opener rebids his original suit at the three-level, he may not pass below game. (2) If he thinks his hand may contribute a trick or two to his partner's contract, he should bid aggressively (maybe even jump the bidding). For example:

Partner	You	
2 ♠	2 NT	♠ 7
3 ♡	3 NT	♡ 9 5
		◇ J 10 6 3 2
		♣ 8 6 5 4 2

You may not pass 3 ♡, so you have no choice but to bid 3 NT and hope for the best.

Partner	You	
2 ♡	2 NT	♠ 7 6 2
3 ♡	4 ♡	♡ K 9
		◇ 10 8 5 4 2
		♣ 6 4 3

Partner's 3 ♡ bid is not forcing, but he fully expects you to bid on to game if you can produce a trick.

Partner	You	♠ K 9 4
2 ♠	2 NT	♡ 10 8 5 2
3 ◇	4 ♠	◇ Q 3
		♣ 9 8 6 4

Your 4 ♠ bid tells your partner that you have about 5 or 6 useful high-card points; this may be all he needs to bid a makable slam. If you take away the ♠ K and/or the ◇ Q, 3 ♠ would be the right bid.

WEAK TWO-BIDS

Opening bids of 2 ◇, 2 ♡, and 2 ♠ are "weak two-bids" and show a hand with 5 to 11 *high-card points* and a reasonably good six-card suit, but the requirements are governed to a large extent by the vulnerability. A weak two-bid should not include a side four-card major suit, except perhaps in third or fourth seat. For example:

♠ 6 ♡ A J 10 9 8 3 ◇ K 4 ♣ 9 5 4 2	Open 2 ♡ regardless of the vulnerability. If you exchange the clubs and spades, so you have a side four-card major suit, you should pass in first or second seat but open 2 ♡ in third or fourth seat.
♠ Q 10 7 5 3 2 ♡ J ◇ 9 8 ♣ K 10 7 3	Open 2 ♠ with favorable vulnerability only, but in fourth seat pass; you should be happy to throw the hand in with only 6 high-card points.
♠ 7 6 3 ♡ 5 ◇ A Q J 10 9 2 ♣ K J 4	Open 2 ◇ regardless of the vulnerability. This is a maximum weak two-bid.
♠ A K 10 7 6 2 ♡ A 9 5 ◇ 4 3 ♣ 7 5	Open 1 ♠. With three quick tricks, this hand is simply too good for a weak two-bid. However, you might open 2 ♠ in fourth seat; a weak two-bid opening in fourth seat shows a slightly stronger hand than in first, second, or third seat.

Although very rare, you may open a weak two-bid with a seven-card suit. For example:

♠ 5 2 ♡ A Q 8 7 6 4 2 ◇ J 7 ♣ 9 3	Open 3 ♡ with equal or favorable vulnerability, and open 2 ♡ with unfavorable. When you are vulnerable and the opponents are not, it is too risky to bid at the three-level with this broken seven-card suit.

You may open a weak two-bid with a *very strong* five-card suit in third or fourth seat only. For example:

♠ A K J 10 9 ♡ Q 4 2 ◇ 9 8 7 5 ♣ 4	Pass this hand in first or second seat, but open 2 ♠ in third or fourth seat.

RESPONSES TO WEAK TWO-BIDS

When your partner opens the bidding with a weak two-bid, you must use your judgment to pass, raise his suit, bid a new suit, bid games directly, or bid 2 NT (an artificial and forcing response). These five categories are treated separately as follows:

Pass your partner's weak two-bid if you have nothing constructive to say and let your partner's bid take its effect on the opponents. For example:

Partner	You	
2 ♡	P	♠ A Q 7 3
		♡ 2
		♢ A 10 5 4
		♣ K J 7 6

> With this obvious misfit you should pass, even though you have 14 high-card points.

Raise your partner's suit when you have good trump support and not much defensive strength; the purpose is to further impede the opponents' bidding. Your raise of partner's suit is not only nonforcing, your partner is *barred* from bidding again. For example:

Partner	You	
2 ♡	3 ♡	♠ 7 4
		♡ Q 10 2
		♢ 9 6 5 2
		♣ A Q 8 3

> It is not unlikely that the opponents can make a game in spades, and your 3 ♡ bid may keep them out of the bidding. You can expect the 3 ♡ contract to be set a trick or two, but your minus score figures to be a good one; the opponents could probably win more by bidding and making a spade contract. It may appear risky to bid 3 ♡ if the vulnerability is unfavorable, but then partner can be relied upon to have a good weak two-bid with a strong suit; there is very little chance that you will get doubled, and even then the penalty will not be severe.

Partner	You	
2 ♠	4 ♠	♠ K 8 6 3
		♡ J 4
		♢ 7
		♣ K 10 9 7 6 2

> The opponents can make a game in hearts or diamonds and they may even have a slam. Your 4 ♠ bid may keep them out of the bidding. If they double the 4 ♠ contract you will most likely be set a trick or two, but if partner has the magic hand you may even make it.

Answer your partner's weak two-bid by bidding a new suit with from 7 to 13 high-card points and a strong suit, usually at least six cards long. A new-suit bid is *not* forcing, but the opening bidder should bid again if he has a maximum weak two-bid and support for the responder's suit. (NOTE: Many players play a new-suit response is forcing for one round. So come to an agreement with your partner whether or not a new-suit response is forcing and avoid a mishap.) For example:

Partner	You	
2 ♡	2 ♠	♠ A K 10 9 3 2
		♡ 5 3
		♢ 10 9 6
		♣ 8 4

A 2 ♠ contract may or may not be better than 2 ♡, but this is not the main reason for bidding. If you pass, your left-hand opponent may bid notrump; a spade lead may be needed to beat 3 NT, and you cannot expect your partner to lead the suit unless you bid it.

Your partner will usually pass your 2 ♠ bid, but if he bids 3 ♠ you should pass with this weak hand; if you had a stronger hand (for example, change the diamonds to ♢ A-9-6), you should accept his game invitation and bid 4 ♠.

If you have a strong hand and know where you want to play it, bid game directly. Your partner must pass your bid. For example:

Partner	You	
2 ♠	4 ♠	♠ K 10
		♡ A K J 2
		♢ K Q J 5 4
		♣ 6 2

When you raise your partner to game you can have a weak hand or a strong hand. This sometimes poses problems for the opponents.

Partner	You	
2 ♠	3 NT	♠ 7
		♡ K Q 9
		♢ A K Q J 8 4
		♣ K J 10

This is the logical game contract, and your partner must pass 3 NT.

The only forcing response to a weak two-bid is 2 NT. The 2 NT bid shows a hand strong enough to at least have hope for game, but it does not indicate that you have a balanced hand; you may bid 2 NT with any distribution. Your partner's next bid will help you decide whether or not to bid a game (or slam), and which game (or slam) to bid. For example:

Partner	You	
2 ♡	2 NT	♠ K Q 4 2
		♡ A 10 8
		♢ 8 6
		♣ K Q 7 3

Your 2 NT bid is artificial and forcing. Its purpose is to find out if partner has a "minimum" or a "maximum" weak two-bid. If partner's next bid indicates he has a minimum (such as ♡ K-Q-J-X-X-X and nothing else), you will play 3 ♡. If his next bid indicates he has a maximum (such as ♡ K-Q-X-X-X-X and a side ace), you will play 4 ♡.

Partner	You	
2 ♢	2 NT	♠ A K J 8 5
		♡ 6 3
		♢ A 4
		♣ A Q 9 2

This time your hand is strong enough to bid game even if partner has a minimum weak two-bid, but where? You would like to play 4 ♠ if partner has three trumps for you, or 3 NT if he has a stopper in hearts, or as a last resort you will probably bid 5 ♢. Note that you cannot bid 2 ♠ right away as that bid would not be forcing. So you bid 2 NT with the intention of bidding 3 ♠ over partner's next bid (a new-suit bid following 2 NT is forcing); your partner should raise 3 ♠ to 4 ♠ with three trumps, or else choose some other bid to further describe his hand.

If the opponents enter the bidding after your partner has opened the bidding with a weak two-bid, the meanings of the various responses are the same as in noncompetitive auctions insofar as possible. When the opponent's intervention does deprive you of making your normal bid, you must use your judgment to pass, bid something, or double. Since an opening weak two-bid describes the offensive strength and defensive strength of a hand within narrow limits, you should be able to figure the trick-taking potential of both sides fairly accurately and therefore make the winning decision most of the time. Good luck.

REBIDS AFTER AN OPENING WEAK TWO-BID

The requirements for rebids after an opening weak two-bid depend on your partner's response:

1. If partner raises your suit, you must pass.
2. If partner bids a new suit, you should generally pass, but you may raise his suit with three or more trumps.
3. If partner bids any game contract or any slam contract, you must pass.
4. If partner responds 2 NT, you must bid again to give a more detailed description of your hand as follows: (1) With a minimum hand (5, 6, 7, or maybe 8 high-card points), rebid your suit at the three-level. (2) With a maximum hand (9, 10, 11, or maybe 8 high-card points), show a "feature" by bidding a side suit headed by an ace, king, or queen. (3) With a solid suit headed by A-K-Q, bid 3 NT.

For example:

	You	Partner
♠ K 9 3	*You*	*Partner*
♡ A Q J 10 6 3	2 ♡	3 ♡
◊ 8 7 6	P	
♣ 2		

Even though you have a maximum weak two-bid you *must* not bid again when your partner raises your suit. His bid is to harass the opposition, not to invite you to bid game.

	You	Partner
♠ Q 4 2	*You*	*Partner*
♡ 7 2	2 ◊	2 ♠
◊ A K 10 6 5 3	3 ♠	
♣ 8 7		

With good trump support, you should bid 3 ♠ and invite your partner to bid game. Without support for his suit, you should pass; for example, if partner's response were 2 ♡ instead of 2 ♠, you should pass.

	You	Partner
♠ 8 6	*You*	*Partner*
♡ Q J 9 5 4 2	2 ♡	2 NT
◊ K 10 4	3 ♡	
♣ 7 3		

Your 3 ♡ simply tells your partner that you have a minimum weak two-bid; it says nothing about the quality of your suit. Your partner may pass 3 ♡, or bid again if he judges a game can be made in spite of your minimum.

```
♠ 8 5              You       Partner
♡ A Q 9 7 6 4     2 ♡       2 NT
◇ K J 2           3 ◇
♣ 9 4
```

Your 3 ◇ bid indicates that you have a maximum weak two-bid and some high-card strength in the diamond suit; it does not say that you have length in diamonds. Your partner will undoubtedly bid again and you will most likely reach some game contract, depending on his hand.

```
♠ A K Q 10 6 2    You       Partner
♡ 7 4             2 ♠       2 NT
◇ 8 3             3 NT
♣ 9 5 2
```

The 3 NT bid is reserved to show that your suit is headed by the ace, king, and queen. Your partner should take you back to spades, unless he has the unbid suits stopped and thinks 3 NT is the best game.

THE STRONG ARTIFICIAL TWO-CLUB OPENING BID

The sister convention of the weak two-bid is the strong artificial two-club opening bid. Since opening bids of 2 ◇, 2 ♡, and 2 ♠ are weak, all very strong hands are opened with 2 ♣. An opening 2 ♣ bid is forcing and shows one of two kinds of hands:

1. A balanced hand with a minimum of 23 high-card points.
2. A powerful unbalanced hand. These requirements are the same as for strong two-bid openings; see page 83.

RESPONSES AND REBIDS AFTER A STRONG ARTIFICIAL TWO-CLUB OPENING BID

The only "negative response" to a 2 ♣ opening is 2 ◇. The 2 ◇ bid is artificial and shows 0 to 7 high-card points. On the rare occasions that an opponent bids over a 2 ♣ opening, responder passes to show a negative response. Any response other than 2 ◇ is a natural bid and a "positive response," showing 8 or more high-card points (or 7 points with one and a half quick tricks). The normal positive responses are 2 ♡, 2 ♠, 3 ♣, 3 ◇, and 2 NT to show a balanced hand.

It is the opening 2 ♣ bidder's rebid that reveals the nature of his hand. With a balanced hand, he rebids 2 NT with 23 or 24 high-card points (a nonforcing bid), 3 NT with 25 to 27, and 4 NT with 28 to 30. With an unbalanced hand, he rebids in a suit; a suit bid is absolutely forcing. For example:

```
♠ A Q 2           You       Partner
♡ A K 9 7         2 ♣       2 ◇
◇ K Q 10          2 NT
♣ A J 5
```

You have 23 points. If partner's response were 2 ♡ or 2 ♠, you should still rebid 2 NT. If his response were 2 NT, or 3 ♣ or 3 ◇, you should rebid 3 NT.

♠ A K J 5	*You*	*Partner*
♡ A Q 3 2	2 ♣	2 ◇
◇ A K	3 NT	
♣ K J 10		

With 25 points, your rebid is a jump to 3 NT.

♠ A Q	*You*	*Partner*
♡ A K 8	2 ♣	2 ◇
◇ A Q J 4	4 NT	
♣ A K Q 10		

With 29 points you must bid beyond game. If your partner's hand is worthless the 4 NT contract might be set, but there is a much greater chance that he will have the 4 or 5 points needed to bid a makable slam. Note that your 4 NT is *not* Blackwood.

♠ A K J 7 2	*You*	*Partner*
♡ A K Q J 5	2 ♣	2 ◇
◇ —	2 ♠	
♣ K 8 6		

You have 23 points and with two five-card suits must bid the higher-ranking first.

♠ A Q	*You*	*Partner*
♡ A K J 2	2 ♣	2 ◇
◇ 3	3 ♣	
♣ A Q J 10 9 4		

With one suit longer than any other, bid it first and await developments.

♠ 5	*You*	*Partner*
♡ A Q J	2 ♣	2 ◇
◇ A K 10 8 7	3 ◇	
♣ A K J 3		

Here you are bidding a new suit, as you did in the previous examples. Partner's 2 ◇ bid is artificial. Note that if the final contract should be played in diamonds, your partner will be the declarer.

If the opening bidder rebids 2 NT after a 2 ◇ response, the responder should treat it just like a 2 NT opening bid, except that a 2 NT opening shows 21 or 22 points while 2 ♣ followed by 2 NT shows 23 or 24. For example:

Partner	*You*	♠ 7 2
2 ♣	2 ◇	♡ K 10 8 6
2 NT	3 ♣	◇ 8 6 5 3
		♣ 9 7 2

Your 3 ♣ bid is Stayman, asking for a four-card major. If partner bids 3 ♡ you will bid 4 ♡; if he bids 3 ◇ or 3 ♠, you will bid 3 NT. Note that although 2 NT is not forcing you should not pass this hand; with one king you have enough to bid a game.

When the opener rebids 3 NT or 4 NT you must be alert to slam possibilities with very meager holdings. For example:

Partner	You	
2 ♣	2 ◇	♠ K 10 8
4 NT	6 NT	♡ 7 3 2
		◇ Q 9 5 4
		♣ 9 8 6

Partner's 4 NT bid shows 28 to 30 high-card points, so the combined total is 33, 34, or 35, enough to bid a slam.

The Second Negative Response

If the opening 2 ♣ bidder follows a 2 ◇ response by bidding a new suit, the responder must bid again. It then becomes desirable for responder to describe his point count more accurately. With 0 to 4 high-card points (but never an ace), the responder makes a "second negative" bid. This is done by bidding 3 ♣ over 2 ♡ or 2 ♠, 3 ◇ over 3 ♣, and 3 NT over 3 ◇. This variation of the second negative is sometimes called the "cheaper minor" and is probably the most popular, although there are other methods.

The main advantage of the second negative is obtained when responder makes any other bid, which shows 5 to 7 high-card points. This is, of course, forcing to game and sometimes enables the opening bidder to bid a makable slam.

You can play the strong artificial two-club opening bid without using the second negative; you and your partner must decide. If you decide it is too complicated for you at this stage of your game, simply play that all rebids by responder are natural: Raise the opener's suit with trump support, bid a long suit of your own, or bid notrump with a balanced hand; unless you jump the bidding, all of these responses show from 0 to 7 points.

The following six illustrations show how the second negative works:

Partner	You	
2 ♣	2 ◇	♠ 7 6
2 ♠	3 ♣	♡ 9 5 4 2
		◇ J 8 6 3
		♣ 10 9 5

Your 3 ♣ bid is completely artificial; it simply says you have from 0 to 4 high-card points. You would make the same bid if partner's rebid were 2 ♡ instead of 2 ♠.

Partner	You	
2 ♣	2 ◇	♠ 5 3 2
3 ♣	3 ◇	♡ J 9 7 6
		◇ 8 3
		♣ 10 6 4 2

When partner rebids 3 ♣, 3 ◇ becomes the second negative.

Partner	You	
2 ♣	2 ◇	♠ 10 9 7 6 2
3 ◇	3 NT	♡ J 6 3
		◇ 8
		♣ Q 4 3 2

When partner rebids 3 ◇, 3 NT is the second negative.

Partner	You	
		♠ 7 3
2 ♣	2 ◇	♡ 10 9 6 4
3 ♣	4 ♣	◇ K 10 8
		♣ K 5 3 2

When partner rebids 3 ♣, any bid other than 3 ◇ shows 5 to 7 points. This information may enable your partner to bid and make a slam.

Partner	You	
		♠ K 10 8 6 3
2 ♣	2 ◇	♡ Q J 9
3 ◇	3 ♠	◇ 7
		♣ 10 7 5 2

The 3 ♠ bid shows 5 to 7 points and a five-card or longer spade suit.

Partner	You	
		♠ Q 9 5 4
2 ♣	2 ◇	♡ 7 3
2 ♡	2 NT	◇ J 7 6 2
		♣ K 10 8

With 6 points and a balanced hand, 2 NT describes your hand accurately.

After the responder has made a positive response—showing 8 or more high-card points—it is not unlikely that a slam can be made, and it may be up to the responder to bid it. For example:

Partner	You	
		♠ A Q 10 2
2 ♣	2 NT	♡ 9 8 7
3 NT	6 NT	◇ Q 10 7
		♣ Q 5 3

Your partner has 23 or 24 high-card points and you have 10. The 6 NT bid should be automatic.

Partner	You	
		♠ A J 4 2
2 ♣	2 NT	♡ 9 6 2
3 ♣	3 ♠	◇ K 10
		♣ 10 8 7 5

The 3 ♣ bid is Stayman, asking for a four-card major suit. If your partner has a real club suit, he will have to bid the suit a third time to show it.

Partner	You	
		♠ K 10 9 5 3
2 ♣	2 ♠	♡ A 6 2
3 ♡	4 ♡	◇ 4 2
		♣ 8 7 4

Your 4 ♡ bid tells your partner that you have minimum values for your positive response and you are satisfied to stop bidding in game. Your partner should pass 4 ♡ with a minimum 2 ♣ opening, or bid on to slam with something extra.

Partner	You	♠ K 7 2
2 ♣	3 ◊	♡ 8 4
3 ♠	6 ♣	◊ A K 9 8 5
		♣ 10 7 6

Your hand is strong enough to insist on a slam after partner bids 3 ♠. It is not necessary to bid 6 ♠ right away—any forcing bid would be okay as long as you intend to bid a slam eventually—but a bid of 4 ♠ would be dead wrong; partner may pass.

   An opening 2 ♣ bid is forcing to game, with two exceptions: (1) The responder may pass with a worthless hand when the opener rebids 2 NT (this was explained earlier in this chapter). (2) The responder may pass with a worthless hand if the opener rebids his suit. For example:

♠ A Q 2	You	Partner
♡ A K Q J 7 3	2 ♣	2 ◊
◊ 9 5	2 ♡	3 ♣
♣ K Q	3 ♡	

Your 3 ♡ bid is not forcing. The responder's 3 ♣ bid was the second negative, but he should still bid game if he thinks his hand can take a trick.

♠ A K Q J 10 4	You	Partner
♡ 2	2 ♣	2 ◊
◊ A K J 9	2 ♠	3 ♣
♣ A 4	3 ◊	

Your 3 ◊ bid is unconditionally forcing to game. You certainly want to reach game with this powerful hand and therefore must not make a nonforcing bid of 3 ♠. Since partner has revealed a hand with 0 to 4 points—3 ♣ is a second negative—it may seem right to bid 4 ♠ and end the auction, but 3 ◊ is a better bid, as it may lead to a good slam.

10

Overcalls

♣　　♦　　♥　　♠　　♣　　♦　　♥　　♠

The first bid by your side after your opponents have opened the bidding is an *overcall*. There are many kinds described in this chapter: overcalls at the one-level, overcalls at the two-level, notrump overcalls including the "unusual notrump," strong jump overcalls, weak jump overcalls, and preemptive overcalls. However, overcalls of your opponents' opening preemptive bids are treated separately in Chapter 14.

Getting your side into the bidding is important for several reasons: You may bid and make a contract your way, you may have a good sacrifice, you may push your opponents too high, or you may indicate a good opening lead to your partner; and an overcall has a general nuisance value as it uses up your opponents' bidding space and makes it harder for them to bid accurately.

Although there is much to be gained by overcalling, you should do so only when your hand qualifies. If you bid without the recommended values, you may get doubled and suffer a big penalty, or you may mislead your partner into bidding too much. The requirements to overcall are quite liberal, depending on *level of bidding* and *vulnerability*, so you will have plenty of opportunities to bid.

OVERCALLS AT THE ONE-LEVEL

The point-count requirements to overcall at the one-level range from about 9 to 17 points. You may overcall with as few as 9 points provided you have a *good* five-card or longer suit to bid. With such a weak hand you are a favorite to be outbid and you must be prepared for your partner to lead your suit. For example:

Opp.	You	
1 ♣	1 ♦	♠ 4 2
		♥ 8 6 5
		♦ A K J 10 3
		♣ 10 6 5

Although you have only 9 points, you should bid 1 ♦ regardless of the vulnerability.

Opp.	You	♠ 7 2
1 ♣	P	♡ K Q 10 9 4
		◊ 8 3 2
		♣ 6 5 3

You have only 6 points and are too weak to overcall. It is tempting to bid 1 ♡ (especially with favorable vulnerability) to direct a heart lead, and it is unlikely that you will get doubled because you have a strong suit; but you must not bid because you may mislead your partner into bidding too much.

Opp.	You	♠ K 10 9 8 7
1 ♡	1 ♠	♡ 9 6 3
		◊ 8 2
		♣ A Q 10

You have 10 points and a reasonably good suit (thanks to the body cards), so the 1 ♠ overcall is recommended regardless of the vulnerability. Lacking the body cards (for example, change your suit to ♠ K-8-5-3-2), you should still overcall 1 ♠ if you are not vulnerable, but it would be more discreet to pass if you are vulnerable.

Opp.	You	♠ 8 7 6 4 2
1 ♡	P	♡ 9 6 3
		◊ K 2
		♣ A Q 10

Your 10 points is enough to overcall, but your suit is too weak, so you should pass regardless of vulnerability. You are a favorite to be outbid by your opponents and do not want to direct a spade lead.

It may be right to overcall with a worthless five-card suit if you have a strong hand; the odds favor that you will outbid the opponents and you are less concerned with directing the lead. For example:

Opp.	You	♠ 8 7 6 4 2
1 ♡	1 ♠	♡ A Q 3
		◊ 5
		♣ A K 5 2

With this good-quality 14 points you should overcall 1 ♠. Obviously you do not wish to encourage a spade lead, but with this good hand you are less likely to be defending.

In general, you should not overcall with a four-card suit, but you may be a little adventurous *at the one-level* with a very strong suit. For example:

Opp.	You	♠ 5 3
1 ◊	1 ♡	♡ A K J 10
		◊ 7 6 4
		♣ A J 6 5

Note that it would be wrong to double for takeout with this hand, because you are not prepared for your partner to bid spades.

The maximum strength to overcall is about 17 points. If you overcall with a stronger hand, your partner might pass holding sufficient values to make a game. If you have an overcall-type hand with more than 17 points, the best procedure is to double first and bid your suit later; see Chapter 11, Takeout Doubles. For example:

Opp.	You	
1 ♣	1 ♡	♠ 7 2
		♡ A Q 10 6 4
		◊ K 8 3
		♣ A K 8

Even though you have 17 points, the correct bid is a simple overcall at the one-level.

When holding two five-card or longer suits, a nonjump overcall is the best bid with as many as 18 or 19 points. Although you run the risk that your partner will pass and you may miss a game, there is no better way to handle the strong two-suited hands using standard bidding methods. For example:

Opp.	You	
1 ♣	1 ♡	♠ 7 2
		♡ K J 9 6 4
		◊ A K Q 10 3
		♣ A

You have 19 points and your plan is to jump the bidding in diamonds if you get another chance to bid. Note that with two five-card suits you bid the higher-ranking first, whether it is stronger or not.

OVERCALLS AT THE TWO-LEVEL

You need a better trick-producing hand to bid at the two-level than at the one-level, because your opponents are more anxious to double you and your partner will expect more. However, it is not necessary to have a strong hand in high cards. You may overcall at the two-level with as few as 9 or 10 high-card points, provided you have a substantial suit, especially when you are not vulnerable. For example:

Opp.	You	
1 ♡	2 ◊	♠ 4 2
		♡ 7 6
		◊ K Q J 9 7 5
		♣ A 10 8

By virtue of the excellent diamond suit, this hand qualifies for an overcall at the two-level whether you are vulnerable or not.

Opp.	You	
1 ♡	2 ◊	♠ K 2
		♡ A 3
		◊ Q 10 8 5 4 2
		♣ 9 6 5

With this mediocre diamond suit, you should pass if you are vulnerable, but bid 2 ◊ if you are not.

```
Opp.    You     ♠ 6 4
1 ♠     P       ♡ A Q 10 5 3
                ◇ K Q 9
                ♣ 7 5 2
```

This hand qualifies for an overcall at the one-level, but it would be dangerous to overcall at the two-level. If you bid 2 ♡ and unluckily find your partner with a singleton heart and a poor hand, you may get doubled and suffer a huge penalty. If you bid 2 ♡ and luckily find your partner with good trump support and a good hand, he will more than likely bid too much and you will go down. You can't win.

You may overcall at the two-level with a weaker suit than is normally recommended if you have excellent distribution (such as two five-card suits), because the chances of bidding and making a game are much greater, while the chances of being doubled and taking a big set are much smaller. For example:

```
Opp.    You     ♠ 6
1 ♠     2 ♡     ♡ A Q 10 5 3
                ◇ K Q 9 4 2
                ♣ 7 5
```

The only difference between this hand and the preceding one is the distribution (5-5-2-1 as compared to 5-3-3-2), but this time you should bid 2 ♡ whether you are vulnerable or not. This bid is not without risk, but the odds are good. If partner has a fit with one of your suits and a couple of key cards, you will probably bid and make a game (note that this would not be true with the preceding hand). If your 2 ♡ bid gets doubled, you can run to 3 ◇; it would be very unlucky if partner did not have a tolerance for one of your suits.

Be wary of overcalling with all doubtful hands when you have length in the enemy suit, because the opponent behind you is likely to be short in that suit and, therefore, more apt to double you. For example:

```
Opp.    You     ♠ Q J 10 2
1 ♠     P       ♡ A Q 9 5 3
                ◇ 7 6
                ♣ K 8
```

If you bid 2 ♡ there is a good chance that you will get doubled, because you have four cards in the spade suit, so you should pass vulnerable or not. If you exchange the clubs and spades (so you have ♠ K-8 and ♣ Q-J-10-2), you should venture a 2 ♡ bid if you are not vulnerable, but a pass is still recommended if you are vulnerable.

It is usually right to pass with a very strong hand if an opponent opens the bidding in your longest suit. For example:

```
Opp.    You     ♠ A J 10 8 2
1 ♠     P       ♡ 7
                ◇ A Q 9 4
                ♣ K Q 3
```

You have the wrong kind of hand for any bid. It is wrong to double because you have a singleton heart. It is wrong to bid 1 NT because you do not have a balanced hand. It is wrong to bid 2 ♠ because that is a cue bid; it does not mean that you have spades. Your best chance for a profit here is by beating the opponents in their eventual contract.

If it is necessary to overcall at the three-level, you logically need a better hand than at the two-level. For example:

Opp.	Partner	Opp.	You	♠ 7 2
1 ♠	P	2 ♠	3 ♣	♡ A 8
				◇ 9 8 7
				♣ A Q J 10 6 3

This is about the least you should have to overcall at the three-level, but with such a good suit the 3 ♣ bid is recommended whether you are vulnerable or not.

You need a better hand to overcall an opening bid of 1 NT than an opening bid of one of a suit. There is a greater chance of being doubled and suffering a big penalty, and a lesser chance of bidding and making a game. For example:

Opp.	You	♠ 7 2
1 NT	P	♡ K J 9 8 4
		◇ A Q 4
		♣ K 5 3

You should pass regardless of vulnerability. The right time to overcall a 1 NT opening bid is when you have a very good suit, or exciting distribution; this hand lacks both. If you change the ♠ 2 to the ♡ 2, which improves the quality of your suit and your distribution, a 2 ♡ overcall is recommended regardless of the vulnerability.

RESPONSES TO OVERCALLS

When your partner overcalls and you have the values to bid, the common responses are to raise your partner's suit, to bid your own suit, or to bid notrump. *None of these responses is forcing, not even if you jump the bidding.* If your hand is strong enough to insist on game, you must bid game directly, or cue-bid the opponent's suit to force your partner to bid again.

Since the requirements for a vulnerable overcall suggest the need for a stronger hand and a better suit than a nonvulnerable overcall, the requirements to respond are just the opposite; you need a stronger hand to respond to a nonvulnerable overcall than you need to respond to a vulnerable overcall. Although this is an important consideration when responding to an overcall, the recommended bids in the following illustrations should be made regardless of vulnerability unless otherwise stated.

Raising Partner's Suit

A reasonable guide for raising your partner's overcall at the one-level when you have three or more trumps for him is to raise to the two-level with 7 to 11 points, jump-raise to the three-level with 12 to 14 points, and raise him to game (or cue-bid the opponent's suit; see page 104) with 15 points or more. You may also raise partner to game as a preemptive bid. For example:

Opp.	Partner	Opp.	You	♠ K 6 3
1 ♣	1 ♠	P	2 ♠	♡ 8 3 2
				◊ A 10 7 4
				♣ 9 8 6

You have 7 points and adequate trump support, so the 2 ♠ bid is a must.

Opp.	Partner	Opp.	You	♠ J 9 5
1 ♣	1 ♠	P	3 ♠	♡ A K 4 2
				◊ A 8 7
				♣ 10 5 3

You have 12 points. Note that your jump bid is not forcing; your partner should pass 3 ♠ if he has a minimum overcall.

Opp.	Partner	Opp.	You	♠ Q J 6
1 ♣	1 ♠	P	4 ♠	♡ K J 9 2
				◊ A K Q 3
				♣ 8 5

With 16 high-card points and adequate trump support, you should insist on game.

Opp.	Partner	Opp.	You	♠ K 9 6 4 3
1 ♣	1 ♠	P	4 ♠	♡ 2
				◊ Q J 10 8 5
				♣ 5 2

Even though you have a weak hand in high cards, the raise to game is correct with excellent trump support and distribution. You have poor defensive values, so the opponents are likely to have a game their way and your bid makes it difficult for them to bid accurately. If your partner has the right hand he may make his contract; it is possible that both sides can make a game.

When your partner overcalls at the two-level, you can expect him to have a better hand than when he overcalls at the one-level. Consequently, you do not need as strong a hand to raise his suit (or bid your own suit or notrump).

A reasonable guide for raising your partner's overcall at the two-level when you have three or more trumps (or on rare occasions with a doubleton honor) is: to raise him to the three-level with 7 to 11 points, and to jump-raise him to the four-level or cue-bid the opponent's suit with 12 points or more. For example:

Opp.	Partner	Opp.	You	♠ A K 8 4
1 ♡	2 ◊	P	3 ◊	♡ 6 3 2
				◊ K 9
				♣ 10 7 6 5

You have 10 high-card points of top quality and must bid something; if partner has a good overcall he can make a game. Since you cannot bid a four-card suit and you cannot bid notrump without a stopper in the opponent's suit, you have no choice but to raise diamonds with a doubleton. The raise to 3 ◊ is correct regardless of vulnerability.

Opp.	Partner	Opp.	You	♠ 6 5 3
1 ♠	2 ♡	P	4 ♡	♡ J 7 4 2
				◊ A Q 10 9
				♣ A 4

You have 12 points and four-card trump support, so partner should be able to make game even if he has a minimum nonvulnerable overcall.

Responding in Your Own Suit

If you answer your partner's overcall by bidding your own suit, you should have between 8 and 13 points; your new-suit bid is constructive, *not* forcing. At the one-level you may bid a five-card suit; at the two-level you should have at least a strong five-card or a six-card suit; at the three-level you need at least a strong six-card suit. For example:

Opp.	Partner	Opp.	You	♠ 7 5 2
1 ♣	1 ◊	P	1 ♡	♡ A J 10 6 4
				◊ K 8 6
				♣ 5 3

You have 9 points and should bid this good five-card major suit, rather than raise diamonds. However, do not bid your own suit if you have three-card support for your partner's *major* suit. For example, if partner had overcalled 1 ♠, your proper response would be 2 ♠, not 2 ♡.

Opp.	Partner	Opp.	You	♠ 8 5 2
1 ♠	2 ♣	P	2 ♡	♡ A Q 10 6 4
				◊ A Q 9
				♣ 5 3

You have 13 points, and since your bid is not forcing, this is the most you should have to bid your own suit. Although you can expect a better hand from your partner if your side is vulnerable, the 2 ♡ bid is recommended regardless of the vulnerability.

You may jump the bidding in your own suit with a strong six-card or longer suit and about 12 to 14 points. The jump shift is a strong invitation for your partner to bid again, but it is *not* forcing. (NOTE: Some authorities recommend that the jump shift is forcing, so this is another point to clear up with your favorite partners.) For example:

Opp.	Partner	Opp.	You	♠ 8
1 ♣	1 ♠	P	3 ♡	♡ A K J 10 7 5
				◊ A 9 2
				♣ 7 6 4

With 14 points and a strong six-card suit, 3 ♡ is the right bid here. If your partner is ashamed of his overcall, he may pass.

When you respond in your own suit and skip two or more levels of bidding, your bid is preemptive (similar to an opening preemptive bid; see Chapter 8). However, you may bid your own suit at the game level with a weak or strong hand. For example:

Opp.	Partner	Opp.	You	♠ K Q 10 9 8 6 4
1 ♣	1 ◊	P	3 ♠	♡ 7
				◊ 8 5
				♣ J 6 2

If you exchange the ♣ J for the ♠ J (so your spade suit becomes ♠ K-Q-J-10-9-8-6-4), you should bid 4 ♠.

Opp.	Partner	Opp.	You	♠ —
1 ◊	1 ♠	P	4 ♡	♡ A Q J 10 9 7 5
				◊ 7 2
				♣ A J 10 3

The only other conceivable bid with this hand is a cue-bid of 2 ◊. But slam chances appear remote and you surely want to reach game, so you might as well bid 4 ♡ right away.

Responding in Notrump

Any notrump response to an overcall suggests a balanced or semibalanced hand and stoppers in the unbid suits (although these are not firm requirements) and guarantees at least one stopper in the opponent's suit. The approximate point-count requirements to respond to a one-level overcall are: 1 NT shows about 8 to 11, 2 NT shows 12 to 14, and 3 NT shows 15 or more. The high-card-point requirements to respond to a two-level overcall are: 2 NT shows about 9 to 11, and 3 NT shows 12 or more. Do not forget that a vulnerable overcall promises a better hand than a nonvulnerable overcall, so you might be a bit more aggressive when your side is vulnerable.

Opp.	Partner	Opp.	You	♠ 8 7 3
1 ♣	1 ♡	P	1 NT	♡ 6 2
				◊ A Q 9 5
				♣ K 10 4 3

With as many as 9 high-card points it is wrong to pass your partner's overcall, and the bid that best describes your hand is 1 NT. Note that the bid is recommended without a spade stopper.

Opp.	Partner	Opp.	You	♠ A 5 3 2
1 ♣	1 ♡	P	2 NT	♡ J 4
				◊ Q 10 9 7
				♣ A Q 10

You have 13 high-card points. Your partner may pass with a minimum. If your partner rebids 3 ♡, you should pass; if he bids a new suit below game, you must bid again. If you had a couple more high-card points (for example, change the hearts to ♡ K-4), your proper response would be 3 NT instead of 2 NT. Also, if your side is vulnerable, it is a fair gamble to bid 3 NT with the actual hand.

Opp.	Partner	Opp.	You	♠ K 8
1 ♠	2 ◇	P	2 NT	♡ 10 6 5 2
				◇ Q 9 3
				♣ A J 10 4

You have 10 high-card points and your 2 NT bid is not forcing. Your partner should pass or bid 3 ◇ with a minimum; he should bid a new suit, jump to 4 ◇ , or bid game directly with a maximum. If you had 12 or more high-card points, your proper response would be 3 NT.

Cue-Bidding the Opponent's Suit

If you respond to your partner's overcall by bidding the opponent's suit, it *does not* say that you have length in that suit, first-round control of that suit, or trump support for your partner's suit. The cue-bid does say you have a strong hand and need partner's help to decide which game to bid, whether or not to bid a game, or whether or not to bid a slam. The cue-bid is the only forcing response, and it gives you time to explore for the best contract by making bids below game without fear that your partner will pass.

Cue-bids in response to overcalls are *not* forcing to game. If, after cue-bidding, you are not willing to stop below game, you must bid a new suit, jump the bidding, or bid game yourself. If you follow your cue-bid by raising partner's suit below game, or bidding 2 NT, your bid is not forcing; your partner may pass, but only with a minimum overcall.

Here are two examples:

Opp.	Partner	Opp.	You	♠ Q 6 3 2
1 ♣	1 ♠	P	2 ♣	♡ A 7 4
				◇ A Q 9 8 5
				♣ 8

You have 15 points and excellent trump support, so you should be able to make a game in spades even if partner has a minimum overcall. The 2 ♣ cue-bid is better than a direct raise to 4 ♠ because it saves bidding room to explore for a possible slam.

Opp.	Partner	Opp.	You	♠ A Q 10 3 2
1 ◇	1 ♡	P	2 ◇	♡ K 6
				◇ 8 5
				♣ A J 10 9

With 15 points you should be anxious to reach game, but where? Your 2 ◇ cue-bid is the first step toward finding out.

THE DIRECT CUE-BID

A direct cue-bid of an opponent's opening suit bid of one shows a powerful hand, usually 22 points or more. Similar to the takeout double, it asks your partner to bid one of the unbid suits, but the cue-bid is forcing to game; your partner may be required to bid two or three times with nothing. These cue-bids do not promise control of the opponent's suit—such as an ace or a void—and they are not meant as a natural overcall with length in the opponent's suit. For example:

Opp.	You	♠ A K 10 3
1 ◇	2 ◇	♡ A K Q 10
		◇ —
		♣ A J 9 7 2

You want to reach game even if partner has absolutely nothing, but you need his help to pick the trump suit. If partner gives you any encouragement, you may even bid a slam.

Opp.	You	♠ A K J 6 3
1 ♣	2 ♣	♡ A K J 9 8
		◇ A
		♣ J 2

If partner bids 2 ◇, you will bid 2 ♠. Over his next bid you will bid hearts and will reach game in one of the major suits when your partner makes his choice. If he happens to bid spades or hearts, you will of course raise him to game. In any event, your partner may not pass until you reach game.

Opp.	You	♠ 7
1 ♣	P	♡ 8 4 2
		◇ A J 3
		♣ A Q J 10 6 2

Since an opening bid of 1 ♣ or 1 ◇ may be a short suit, some players like to play the cue-bid of a minor suit as a natural overcall and would bid 2 ♣ with this hand. You may make an agreement with your partner to play this way if you wish, but it is not considered standard. If you do pass this hand, you may get a chance to bid your excellent club suit later if the bidding does not get too high.

Here is just one hand to show you the responsibility of the responder when his partner cue-bids the opening bidder's suit:

Opp.	Partner	Opp.	You	♠ 3
1 ♣	2 ♣	P	2 ◇	♡ 10 7 5
P	2 ♠	P	3 ◇	◇ J 9 7 6 2
P	3 ♡	P	4 ♡	♣ 8 6 4 3

Once your partner made his 2 ♣ cue-bid, you were not allowed to pass below game. Although you bid three times, none of your bids was constructive; with a singleton spade and three trumps to the ten, this hand is better than it might have been.

WEAK JUMP OVERCALLS AND PREEMPTIVE OVERCALLS

Leaping bids in a suit (skipping two or more levels of bidding) are, and always have been, used to describe a weak hand with a very long suit. For example, if your right-hand opponent opens the bidding with 1 ♡, a bid of 3 ♠, 4 ♣, 4 ◇, or any higher suit bid is a *preemptive overcall*.

Single-jump bids in a suit (skipping exactly one level of bidding) are also used to describe a weak hand with a long suit. For example, if your right-hand opponent opens the bidding with 1 ♡, a bid of 2 ♠, 3 ♣, or 3 ◇ is a *weak jump overcall*. The weak jump overcall is today a normal part of standard bidding, having replaced the strong jump overcall over thirty years ago. However, many players stubbornly refuse to change, or possibly have never been exposed to weak jump overcalls. So to avoid a bidding disaster, make an arrangement in advance with your partners as to whether your single-jump overcalls are weak or strong. Just in case you encounter a partner who insists on playing the strong jump overcall, here is how it works:

Opp.	You	
1 ♡	2 ♠	♠ A K Q J 9 2
		♡ 7 2
		◇ 8 4
		♣ A Q J

Your 2 ♠ bid shows a hand with a strong six-card (or longer) suit and 18, 19, or 20 points. Your partner should pass, unless he has at least 6 or 7 useful points. (Note that if you were playing weak jump overcalls you would double with this hand, intending to bid spades later. Since you do not need two ways to bid a strong-overcall-type hand, the single-jump overcall is more useful as a weak bid.)

The requirements for weak jump overcalls and preemptive overcalls are very similar to the requirements for opening preemptive bids (see page 76); you must have a hand with a long and strong suit and at most about 10 high-card points. To decide how high to bid, estimate how many tricks you think your hand can win and then overbid according to the vulnerability:. If you are vulnerable and the opponents are not, overbid by two tricks; if the vulnerability is equal, overbid by three tricks; if the opponents are vulnerable and you are not, overbid by three, four, or even five tricks.

Here are several examples:

Opp.	You	
1 ◇	?	♠ Q J 10 8 5 2
		♡ 7 2
		◇ 6 4
		♣ 9 8 5

With four probable tricks, bid 2 ♠ with favorable vulnerability, but pass with equal or unfavorable.

Opp.	You	
1 ♣	?	♠ 6 3
		♡ Q J 10 9 5 2
		◇ 9 4 3
		♣ K 8

If the ♣ K comes home, your hand should win five tricks. So bid 2 ♡ with equal or favorable vulnerability, but pass with unfavorable.

Opp.	You	
1 ♡	?	♠ A K Q J 10 3
		♡ 6 4
		◇ 6 3
		♣ 8 5 2

With six tricks, bid 3 ♠ with equal or favorable vulnerability, but bid only 2 ♠ with unfavorable.

Opp.	You	♠ A Q J 9 8 5
1 ♡	?	♡ A 10 6
		◊ 7
		♣ J 4 2

Bid 1 ♠ regardless of the vulnerability. This hand is too good for a jump overcall.

Opp.	You	♠ 5
1 ♠	?	♡ 8 2
		◊ Q 10 8 7 6 4 2
		♣ 9 5 3

Bid 3 ◊ with favorable vulnerability, but pass with equal or unfavorable.

Opp.	You	♠ 4 2
1 ♡	?	♡ J 10
		◊ 5
		♣ A Q 10 8 7 6 3 2

You have seven winners, so bid 4 ♣ with equal or favorable vulnerability, and bid 3 ♣ with unfavorable.

Opp.	You	♠ A K Q J 10 9 2
1 ♣	?	♡ 3
		◊ K J 10
		♣ 8 4

Bid 4 ♠ regardless of vulnerability. When you jump to game in a suit, you may have much more than 10 high-card points provided you are willing to give up on slam.

RESPONSES TO WEAK JUMP OVERCALLS

The weak jump overcall is a devastating weapon against your opponents, as it often causes them to bid too much, to bid too little, or to play the hand in the wrong trump suit. The player who makes the weak jump overcall seldom gets into trouble, *unless his partner gets into the act*. So responding to jump overcalls is an important topic, and the most prudent call in a vast majority of cases is *to pass*. For example:

Opp.	Partner	Opp.	You	♠ K J 9 2
1 ◊	2 ♡	P	P	♡ 7
				◊ K 8 6
				♣ A Q J 5 4

You may already be overboard in 2 ♡. If you bid with this hand you can look forward to getting doubled in your eventual contract and being set several tricks.

When you do have the right hand to bid in response to a weak jump overcall, you may raise your partner's suit, bid your own suit, bid notrump, or cue-bid the opponent's suit.

If you raise your partner's jump overcall, you show a mediocre hand with trump support. The purpose of the raise is to further impede the opponent's bidding, or to set the stage for a possible sacrifice. For example:

Opp.	Partner	Opp.	You	
1 ♣	2 ♠	P	3 ♠	♠ Q 9 5
				♡ A 2
				◊ A 10 8 5 3
				♣ 9 7 2

The opponents can probably make a game in hearts, and your 3 ♠ bid may keep them out of it. If you change the ♡ 2 to the ♠ 2, a bid of 4 ♠ would be appropriate. You may also raise your partner to game with a strong hand, so your opponents usually have a difficult decision deciding the best action. Your partner should pass anytime you raise his suit.

You may bid your own long and strong suit if you judge it will make a better trump suit than your partner's. Your partner should then pass, unless he has support for your suit and decides to raise you. For example:

Opp.	Partner	Opp.	You	
1 ♣	2 ◊	P	2 ♡	♠ 9 8 4
				♡ A K J 10 6 2
				◊ 6 4
				♣ K 3

This contract should be better than 2 ◊. Another advantage of your 2 ♡ bid is that the opponents may outbid you and a heart lead from partner should give you the best chance to beat their contract.

You may respond by bidding 2 NT or 3 NT with a very strong hand, stoppers in the other three suits, and a good fit in your partner's suit. For example:

Opp.	Partner	Opp.	You	
1 ♠	3 ◊	P	3 NT	♠ K 8
				♡ K 9 7 4 2
				◊ A Q 9
				♣ A J 10

Partner should have a seven-card diamond suit headed by the king, so with the expected spade lead you have nine tricks. The 3 NT bid is right regardless of vulnerability; any other bid will most likely lead to an unmakable suit contract.

When you have a powerful hand but are uncertain whether or not to bid a game, or which game to bid, your first step should be a cue-bid of the opponent's suit. In the following example, assume that the vulnerability is favorable:

Opp.	Partner	Opp.	You	
1 ◊	2 ♠	P	3 ◊	♠ K 2
				♡ A K Q
				◊ 7 5 4 2
				♣ A 9 8 3

Since the vulnerability is favorable, your partner may have a very poor hand (such as ♠ Q-J-10-X-X-X ♡ X-X ◊ X-X ♣ X-X-X), in which case his next bid should be 3 ♠ and then you should pass. With something extra, partner should find some bid other than 3 ♠ and you will reach a 4 ♠ contract. With any other vulnerability you could depend on partner having a better hand, so you should bid 4 ♠ directly; there would be no point in cue-bidding 3 ◊.

If your right-hand opponent bids over your partner's weak jump overcall and you have support for partner's suit, it may be right to bid competitively in a part-score battle, or to take a sacrifice. In the following two examples, assume that neither side is vulnerable:

Opp.	Partner	Opp.	You	
1 ♣	2 ♠	3 ♣	3 ♠	♠ K 5
				♡ 9 8 7 4 2
				◇ A K 10 3
				♣ 5 2

With equal vulnerability, you should assume that your partner's hand will win five tricks. So it looks like the 3 ♠ contract can be set one trick, while the opponents are likely to succeed in their 3 ♣ contract if you pass and let them play it. But maybe your partner will make 3 ♠, or maybe the opponents will bid 4 ♣ and you will set them.

Opp.	Partner	Opp.	You	
1 ♡	2 ♠	4 ♡	4 ♠	♠ J 10 5
				♡ 9 2
				◇ A K Q 10 9 4
				♣ 8 4

Since the opponents have bid strongly and your partner's weak jump overcall promises a poor defensive hand, it is reasonable to assume that the 4 ♡ contract would succeed. If you get doubled in 4 ♠, you are unlikely to be set more than one or two tricks, while if the opponents bid 5 ♡ you may set them. (For more detailed information about "sacrifice bidding," see Chapter 16.)

RARE SITUATIONS WHERE WEAK JUMP OVERCALLS DO NOT APPLY

The weak jump overcall should not be used over an opening 1 NT bid, in the balancing seat, or over an opposing preemptive bid. In these three cases, a jump overcall is strong. For example:

Opp.	You	
1 NT	3 ♠	♠ K J 10 8 6 4 2
		♡ 7
		◇ K 2
		♣ A Q J

Weak jump overcalls are not desirable over an opening 1 NT bid because there is a greater chance of taking a big penalty and lesser chance your bid will hinder the opponents from reaching a good contract, so this 3 ♠ bid is very strong, showing a hand that can win about eight tricks.

Opp.	Partner	Opp.	You	
1 ◇	P	P	2 ♡	♠ 3 2
				♡ A K Q 10 8 5
				◇ 7 4
				♣ A J 9

The weak jump overcall is useless after your right-hand opponent passes. Your 2 ♡ bid is strong and shows the ability to win about seven tricks. (See Chapter 13 for more details about "balancing bids.")

Opp.	You	♠ 7
3 ♣	4 ♡	♡ A K J 9 6 5 2
		◊ A Q J 10
		♣ 3

Over any opposing weak bids, all jump bids are strong.

1 NT OVERCALLS AND RESPONSES

If your right-hand opponent opens the bidding with a suit bid of one, a 1 NT overcall shows a balanced hand with 16 to 18 high-card points (as would a 1 NT opening bid) and at least one stopper in the opponent's suit. For example:

Opp.	You	♠ A Q 5
1 ♠	1 NT	♡ 6 3 2
		◊ A Q 10
		♣ A J 9 4

You have 17 points. If the opening bid were 1 ♡ instead of 1 ♠, you should not bid 1 NT; without a heart stopper, you should double for takeout instead.

If your partner makes a 1 NT overcall, you should respond in very much the same way you do when he opens the bidding with 1 NT. For example:

Opp.	Partner	Opp.	You	♠ 7 4
1 ♠	1 NT	P	2 NT	♡ J 3 2
				◊ 10 8 7 5
				♣ A Q J 10

Your 2 NT bid shows 8 or 9 points. With 1 point fewer, you should pass. With 2 points more, you should bid 3 NT.

Opp.	Partner	Opp.	You	♠ 4
1 ♠	1 NT	P	2 ♡	♡ Q J 10 4 2
				◊ 8 7 5 3
				♣ 9 7 5

Your 2 ♡ bid shows 0 to 7 (or 8) points and a five-card or longer suit; your partner is expected to pass. If your long suit were diamonds, you would bid two of that suit.

Opp.	Partner	Opp.	You	♠ K J 10 7 4
1 ♡	1 NT	P	3 ♠	♡ 6 3
				◊ 7 2
				♣ A J 10 8

Your jump to 3 ♠ shows 10 points or more (or maybe 9 points) and a five-card or longer suit. Your partner is forced to bid again; he should usually bid 4 ♠ with three or more spades, or 3 NT with only two spades.

Opp.	Partner	Opp.	You	♠ 7
1 ♠	1 NT	P	2 ♣	♡ K J 10 7
				◇ 8 6 3 2
				♣ A Q 10 8

Your 2 ♣ bid is the Stayman Convention, asking partner if he has four cards in an unbid major suit; in this case he must bid 2 ♡ with four hearts and 2 ◇ without four hearts—he may not make any other bid. Since you have 10 points you should insist on game; if partner bids 2 ♡ you will bid 4 ♡, and if he bids 2 ◇ you will bid 3 NT.

(NOTE: Using a 2 ♣ response to a 1 NT overcall as Stayman is debatable. Many prefer to use a cue-bid—in the hand above, a bid of 2 ♠—to inquire about partner's major suits, and use the 2 ♣ response to show a five-card or longer suit and a weak hand, the same as a two-level response in any other unbid suit. The modern trend is to play 2 ♣ as Stayman, so I suggest you roll with the tide and play this way too. Also note that if 2 ♣ is Stayman, a direct jump to 3 ♣ is used to show the weak hand with a long club suit; see page 21. Be sure to clarify these points with your regular partners.)

THE UNUSUAL 2 NT OVERCALL AND RESPONSES

When your right-hand opponent opens the bidding with a suit bid of one and you have a very strong notrump-type hand—19 high-card points or more—you should always double, with the intention of bidding notrump at your next turn to bid. Therefore, a direct 2 NT overcall of an opening suit bid of one does not show a strong balanced hand; it is the "unusual notrump." The unusual 2 NT overcall describes a hand with at least five cards in each of the *lower-ranking* unbid suits, and the responder is expected to bid one of them. The main purpose of the unusual notrump is to find a good sacrifice, so the 2 NT bidder usually has a relatively weak hand in high cards, at most about 12 high-card points.

If your right-hand opponent opens the bidding with 1 ♡ or 1 ♠, a 2 NT overcall shows a hand with at least five cards in each minor suit. For example:

Opp.	You	♠ 7
1 ♡	2 NT	♡ 2
		◇ K Q J 10 3
		♣ J 10 9 8 6 4

This is an ideal hand for the unusual notrump, as the opponents probably can make a game (or maybe a slam) in a major suit and prospects for a good sacrifice are excellent. With this 6-5 distribution, the 2 NT bid is recommended regardless of the vulnerability. With only 5-5 in the minors (say we change the ♣ 4 into the ♠ 4), the 2 NT bid would be too risky unless the vulnerability is favorable.

The fact that a 2 NT overcall over an opening bid of 1 ♡ or 1 ♠ is unusual, asking partner to bid a minor suit, is generally known. But a 2 NT overcall over an opening bid of 1 ♣ or 1 ◇ is also unusual, asking partner to bid one of the two lower-ranking unbid suits (over a 1 ♣ opening it shows diamonds and hearts, and over a 1 ◇ opening it shows clubs and hearts); this is not generally known. So do not use this convention over a 1 ♣ or 1 ◇ opening unless you are confident that your partner will understand. Here is one example:

Opp.	You	♠ 6
1 ◇	2 NT	♡ Q 10 8 5 3
		◇ 7
		♣ A K J 10 9 2

Your partner is expected to choose between clubs and hearts. This sound hand qualifies for a 2 NT overcall regardless of the vulnerability.

You may also use the unusual 2 NT overcall when the opponents have bid two suits, asking partner to choose between the two unbid suits. For example, if the bidding went opponent 1 ◇, partner P, opponent 1 ♠, a 2 NT bid would be unusual and appropriate with this hand.

The unusual 2 NT overcall may also be used over a strong two-bid, or a 1 NT bid, especially with favorable vulnerability when a good sacrifice is most likely. However, a 2 NT overcall is not unusual over an opening weak two-bid. For example:

Opp.	You	♠ 7
2 ♡	?	♡ 3
		◇ Q J 10 9 7 2
		♣ A Q J 10 8

If the 2 ♡ bid is strong, then a bid of 2 NT would be unusual and appropriate with this hand. If the 2 ♡ bid is weak, you should bid 3 ◇, as a 2 NT bid would show a balanced hand and about 16 to 19 high-card points.

Note that if the opponents are using the strong artificial 2 ♣ opening bid, you should bid 2 NT with this hand over a 2 ♣ opening and your bid would be unusual; the 2 ♣ bid is *artificial,* so the two lower-ranking unbid suits are clubs and diamonds.

Also, over an opening bid of 1 NT, an unusual 2 NT overcall would be correct with this hand.

Although it is very rare, you may also use the unusual 2 NT overcall with strong hands—about 17 high-card points or more. With the in-between hands (13 to 16 high-card points), a 2 NT overcall is not desirable because you may be faced with a difficult rebidding problem. For example:

Opp.	You	♠ K 2
1 ♠	2 NT	♡ 7
		◇ A Q 10 9 3
		♣ A K Q J 6

Your partner will assume that you have at most 12 high-card points, but you will reveal your extra strength by bidding again at your next turn.

Opp.	You	♠ 6
1 ♠	2 ◇	♡ K 2
		◇ A Q 9 8 5
		♣ A Q 10 7 4

The best approach here is simply to bid 2 ◇, with a plan to bid clubs at your next turn if the bidding does not get too high. It would be wrong to overcall 2 NT, because you would have no convenient rebid; if partner responds 3 ♣ or 3 ◇, you are too strong to pass and too weak to bid.

Responding to the Unusual 2 NT Overcall

When your partner makes an unusual 2 NT overcall, you should know by now that you are expected to bid one of his two suits. This often involves bidding a three-card suit, or in rare cases a two-card suit. For example:

Opp.	Partner	Opp.	You	
1 ♠	2 NT	P	?	♠ J 8 6 4
				♡ K Q 10 7 3
				◊ 8 2
				♣ 7 5

Partner has shown the two minor suits, so bid 3 ♣. With an equal number of cards in the two suits, bid the lower-ranking and hope for the best. If your right-hand opponent had doubled your partner's 2 NT bid, you should pass with an equal number of cards in the two suits; let partner pick the suit, as he may have six of one and five of the other.

If you bid 3 ♡ with this hand you are asking for trouble; partner is unlikely to have more than one heart and he could be void. You may bid the suit your partner does not have if you are prepared to play it opposite a singleton or a void; for example, if your heart suit were Q-J-10-X-X-X-X it would be right to bid 3 ♡.

It is unlikely that you will encounter an uncomfortable bidding situation like the one in the preceding illustration (you usually have at least three cards in one of his suits), but if you do, be an obedient partner and bid one of your partner's suits; leave passing from fright to the amateurs. If, in response to an unusual 2 NT bid, you have good support for one of your partner's suits, good distribution, and a high card or two, you should jump the bidding. For example:

Opp.	Partner	Opp.	You	
1 ◊	2 NT	P	4 ♣	♠ A 6 5
				♡ 7
				◊ 9 7 5 3 2
				♣ K 8 4 3

Partner has clubs and hearts. Your jump bid is meant to show a good supporting hand to play in clubs; it does not promise a lot of high cards, or defensive strength, and it is not forcing.

Except for aces, high cards in the two suits your partner does not have are probably useless. If you exchange the ♠ A and the ♣ K, so you have ♠ K-6-5 and ♣ A-8-4-3, you should consider the ♠ K to be of doubtful value and bid 3 ♣ instead of 4 ♣.

If your partner makes an unusual 2 NT overcall and you have a hand strong enough to insist on game, you may bid game directly, or cue-bid the opponent's suit if you need to exchange more information.

3 NT AND 4 NT OVERCALLS

A 3 NT overcall of an opening suit bid of one is not unusual and does not show a strong balanced hand. So the only sensible use of a 3 NT overcall is to show a hand with a long solid minor suit and a stopper in the opponent's suit. For example:

Opp.	You	♠ Q
1 ♡	3 NT	♡ K 5
		◊ A K Q J 9 7 3
		♣ A 8 2

With a heart lead you have nine tricks. Many players would gamble a 3 NT bid without the ♣ A, although they would probably run to 4 ◊ if they got doubled in 3 NT.

A 4 NT overcall of an opening major suit bid of one is unusual; it is intended to show a highly distributional hand and to jam the opponents' bidding as much as possible. For example, with favorable vulnerability:

Opp.	You	♠ 2
1 ♡	4 NT	♡ —
		◊ Q J 9 8 6 3
		♣ A Q J 7 6 4

Your partner is expected to bid his better minor suit. If your partner gets doubled and goes down in his contract, it is likely to be a good sacrifice. If the opponents bid over 5 ♣ or 5 ◊, they will have a more difficult time reaching their best contract, and they might be in serious trouble.

NOTE: Overcalls of 3 NT and 4 NT are rarely made except over opening preemptive bids. This topic is covered in Chapter 14; see "Notrump Overcalls of Preemptive Bids," page 154.

11

Takeout Doubles

♣   ♦   ♥   ♠   ♣   ♦   ♥   ♠

A takeout double asks your partner to bid one of the unbid suits, and this convention is indispensable to good bidding. Together with the overcall, it makes up the two common ways to get your side into the bidding when your opponents open the bidding ahead of you. There are many auctions where a double is meant for takeout, but by far the most frequent usage is a double of your right-hand opponent's opening suit bid of one. This is where we will begin, and the more ambiguous kinds of takeout doubles will be covered later.

The minimum requirements to double your right-hand opponent's opening suit bid of one vary, depending primarily on your distribution and, to a lesser degree, on the level of bidding at which partner must respond and the vulnerability. The ideal distribution is to have at least four cards in each of the three unbid suits (5-4-4-0, or 4-4-4-1); then you may double with as few as 10 or 11 points. For example:

Opp.	You	
1 ♣.	DBL	♠ K 9 7 2
		♡ A 8 5 2
		◊ K 9 8 4
		♣ 7

This 10-point hand is okay for a double because of your excellent distribution.

When you have 4-4-3 in the unbid suits, you need a slightly stronger hand to double; about 12 points is the least you should have. For example:

Opp.	You	
1 ♡	DBL	♠ A J 7 2
		♡ 7 3
		◊ K J 6 4
		♣ K 10 8

With 12 points you have just enough to venture a double with 4-4-3 in the unbid suits. Notice that as your distribution becomes less attractive, you need more high cards to compensate.

When you have 4-3-3 in the unbid suits, you need at least 13 points to double, and if some of your points are in the opponent's suit, you should have slightly more. For example:

Opp.	You	
1 ♣	DBL	♠ A Q J
		♡ Q J 8 5
		◇ Q J 9
		♣ 7 4 2

The double of 1 ♣ is all right because none of your 13 points is in the club suit and the bidding is very low; partner can bid his suit at the one-level. If the opening bid were 1 ◇, 1 ♡, or 1 ♠, you should pass.

When you double a 1 ♣ opening bid your partner must go to the two-level to bid his suit, so you need a slightly more substantial hand to double and the vulnerability may influence your decision. For example:

Opp.	You	
1 ♠	?	♠ J 8
		♡ A Q 7 2
		◇ J 4 2
		♣ K J 8 5

Aggressive bidding is a winning style, but if you double and find your partner with a worthless hand you may get doubled and suffer a big penalty. This is a close decision. So take the chance and double if you are not vulnerable, but pass if you are vulnerable.

When you have a doubleton, a singleton, or a void in one of the three unbid suits, it is risky to double unless you have a very strong hand. Mathematical common sense tells you that your short suit is the one your partner will most likely bid. If you double first and bid a new suit at your next turn, you show a hand too strong to overcall (18 points or more). If you double first and bid notrump at your next turn, you show a hand too strong to overcall 1 NT (19 points or more). On rare occasions it is advisable to shade these requirements down to 17 points, or maybe 16 points, but I warn you: *do not double with minimum values if you are short in any of the unbid suits, especially an unbid major suit.* Note the following three examples:

Opp.	You	
1 ♣	DBL	♠ A K J
		♡ 8 2
		◇ A K Q 10 9 7
		♣ 6 3

With 19 points, your hand is too strong to overcall 1 ◇. By doubling first and bidding diamonds at your next turn, you show your strong hand; this will encourage your partner to bid on to game with modest values.

Opp.	You	
1 ♠	DBL	♠ A Q 7
		♡ 8 4
		◇ A Q 10 9
		♣ A K J 2

It is rare to double when you are short in an unbid major, but if partner bids 2 ♡ you will rebid 2 NT to describe your strong hand accurately.

Opp.	You	
1 ♠	P	♠ A 6 2
		♡ Q 5
		◇ Q 9 7 6
		♣ A K 8 4

If you double with this hand you can expect your partner to bid 2 ♡ if he has a four-card heart suit. Then you are stuck. Your hand is not strong enough to bid again, and if you pass, 2 ♡ will be a frightful contract if partner has a poor suit, such as ♡ 10-X-X-X. Note that this hand is too weak for an immediate overcall of 1 NT, but 1 NT would be far better than a double.

RESPONSES TO TAKEOUT DOUBLES

A takeout double by your partner asks you to bid one of the unbid suits, with emphasis on unbid major suits; it may be necessary to bid with a worthless hand. The requirements for the various responses are explained below in five categories: with 0 to 5 points, with 6 to 9 points, with 10 to 12 points, with 13 points or more, and preemptive responses. These point ranges include distributional points.

Responses with 0 to 5 Points

Bid one of the three unbid suits. Bid over a redouble only when you have a clear preference for one of the unbid suits. (Do not bid 1 NT and do not bid over an intervening bid.)
   For example:

Opp.	Partner	Opp.	You	
1 ◇	DBL	P	1 ♠	♠ 8 5 4 2
				♡ 9 6 4
				◇ 8 7 3
				♣ J 10 5

You must not pass (from fright) because if you do, 1 ◇ doubled will be the final contract and the doubled overtricks the opponents will probably make will be very expensive.

Opp.	Partner	Opp.	You	
1 ◇	DBL	P	1 ♡	♠ 9 5 3
				♡ 8 6 3
				◇ Q 10 6 4
				♣ 7 5 2

With 0 to 5 points you must bid one of the three unbid suits. When your only four-card or longer suit is the one bid by the enemy, it is necessary to bid a three-card suit. The 1 ♡ bid is better than 1 ♠ or 2 ♣ because it keeps the bidding lower. It is tempting to bid 1 NT with this hand, but that is clearly wrong with only 2 points.

Opp.	Partner	Opp.	You	
1 ♡	DBL	P	1 ♠	♠ J 10 7 4
				♡ 8 2
				◇ 9 2
				♣ J 10 6 5 3

Although the normal action in a vast majority of cases is to bid your longest suit, it is usually better to bid a four-card major ahead of a five-card minor suit.

Opp.	Partner	Opp.	You	♠ Q 7 4 3
1 ♠	DBL	RDBL	2 ♣	♡ 9 2
				◇ 5 2
				♣ 8 7 6 4 3

When your right-hand opponent redoubles and you have a clear preference for one of the unbid suits, you should bid right away. If you pass, your partner may rescue himself by bidding 2 ◇ or 2 ♡ and get doubled; then you must bid 3 ♣, or pass and leave your partner in an inferior contract.

Responses with 6 to 9 Points

Bid the suit of your choice (which shows 0 to 9 points), or bid freely over an intervening bid by your right-hand opponent. Bid 1 NT with at least one stopper in the opponents' suit, a balanced hand, and no unbid four-card major suit. For example:

Opp.	Partner	Opp.	You	♠ K 2
1 ♣	DBL	1 ♠	2 ♡	♡ J 9 7 6
				◇ K J 10 5
				♣ 8 4 3

Your free bid of 2 ♡ shows 6 to 9 points and a four-card or longer heart suit. If your right-hand opponent had passed, your normal rebid would be 1 ♡ to show 0 to 9 points.

Opp.	Partner	Opp.	You	♠ K 10 7
1 ♠	DBL	P	1 NT	♡ 6 4 3
				◇ 9 7 5 2
				♣ A J 10

Your 1 NT bid shows 6 to 9 (or 10) points, at least one stopper in the spade suit, and no four-card heart suit.

Responses with 10 to 12 Points

Jump the bidding in an unbid suit. Jump to 2 NT with at least one stopper in the opponent's suit, a balanced hand, and no unbid four-card major suit. When your partner doubles an opening bid of 1 ♣ or 1 ◇, cue-bid the opponent's suit with four cards in both major suits and 10 or more points; your rebid will clarify whether you have 10 to 12 points or 13 or more points.

One of the most common mistakes of the average player is his failure to jump the bidding with 10, 11, or 12 points; it is sometimes right to jump with a good 9 points. The jump response is *not* forcing; the doubler should pass with minimum values.

Here are a few examples:

Opp.	Partner	Opp.	You	♠ 7 3
1 ◇	DBL	P	2 ♡	♡ K 10 9 4
				◇ 9 8 2
				♣ A K 6 4

Your jump bid shows 10 to 12 points and at least a four-card heart suit.

Opp.	*Partner*	*Opp.*	*You*	♠ 7 4
1 ◊	DBL	P	2 NT	♡ K 10 9
				◊ K 9 7 3
				♣ A J 10 2

With 11 points and a diamond stopper, 2 NT is a better bid than jumping to 3 ♣ with only a four-card suit. The doubler has implied he has the spades stopped, so there should be nothing to worry about there.

Opp.	*Partner*	*Opp.*	*You*	♠ Q 10 9 3
1 ♣	DBL	P	2 ♣	♡ A J 6 4
				◊ A 7
				♣ 8 5 3

Your cue-bid asks partner to bid a four-card major suit. When he bids 2 ♡ or 2 ♠, you will raise him to the three-level to show 10 to 12 points. If you had 13 points or more, you would raise him to game.

Responses with 13 Points or More

Bid game directly if you know where to play it. Cue-bid the opponent's suit if you do not know which game to play, or think you may have a slam. For example:

Opp.	*Partner*	*Opp.*	*You*	♠ 6 3
1 ◊	DBL	P	3 NT	♡ 8 5 2
				◊ A Q 9
				♣ A Q J 10 4

With two stoppers in the opponent's suit, the prospects of making 3 NT are much brighter than making a game in clubs. Partner's double implies that he has the major suits stopped.

Opp.	*Partner*	*Opp.*	*You*	♠ K 8
1 ♣	DBL	P	2 ♣	♡ Q 7 4 2
				◊ A K J 9 3
				♣ 7 3

Your 2 ♣ cue-bid is the first step toward deciding which game to bid. If partner bids 2 ♡, you will raise him to game. If he bids 2 ♠, you will follow with a forcing bid of 3 ◊.

Opp.	*Partner*	*Opp.*	*You*	♠ K Q J 7 3
1 ♡	DBL	P	2 ♡	♡ 9 8 6 3
				◊ 5
				♣ A Q 2

It is reasonably clear that this hand will play in spades. A direct response of 4 ♠ is not as good as the 2 ♡ cue-bid, because you could easily miss a slam; partner could have ♠ A-10-4-2 ♡ 7 ◊ A-9-8-3 ♣ K-J-10-2, or other good-fitting hands.

Preemptive Responses

Any leaping bid in a suit, skipping two or more levels of bidding, shows a weak hand with a long and strong suit. Since a takeout double implies support for the unbid suits, your suit need not be as long and strong as is recommended in other areas of preemptive bidding; a broken six-card suit is usually good enough. You may also leap to game with a weak hand, but the suit must be more substantial. For example:

Opp.	Partner	Opp.	You	
1 ◊	DBL	P	3 ♠	♠ K 10 8 6 5 2
				♡ 3
				◊ 7 6 3
				♣ 9 6 4

Note that the 3 ♠ bid skips two levels of bidding and is therefore a weak bid. Partner should be able to judge accurately whether to pass or bid 4 ♠, and, at the same time, your bid will make it difficult for the opponents in case it is their hand.

Opp.	Partner	Opp.	You	
1 ♡	DBL	2 ♡	4 ♠	♠ Q J 10 9 8 6
				♡ 6 4
				◊ 2
				♣ K J 10 7

With this exciting distribution you should have a good chance to make 4 ♠ and the opponents may be able to make 4 ♡, so bidding 4 ♠ directly is the most sensible bid.

WHEN TO PASS YOUR PARTNER'S TAKEOUT DOUBLE

There are three situations where it is right to pass your partner's takeout double: (1) Your right-hand opponent bids over your partner's double and you have 0 to 5 points. (2) Your right-hand opponent redoubles and you have a relatively equal number of cards in the three unbid suits. (3) You have a potent holding in the opponent's suit—a five-card or longer holding that you are confident will win a minimum of three tricks. For example:

Opp.	Partner	Opp.	You	
1 ♣	DBL	1 ♡	P	♠ K 9 6 3
				♡ 10 5 4
				◊ 9 5 2
				♣ 8 7 2

Any bid by your right-hand opponent relieves you of the obligation to bid. You should pass with fewer than 6 points.

Opp.	Partner	Opp.	You	
1 ♣	DBL	RDBL	P	♠ J 7 4
				♡ 9 6 3
				◊ J 7 2
				♣ 8 6 5 2

With no clear preference for any of the unbid suits, you must pass and let your partner select the suit. Your pass suggests that you have a tolerance for all three unbid suits; it does *not* suggest that you want to play a contract of 1 ♠ doubled and redoubled. *Your partner must bid.*

Opp.	Partner	Opp.	You	
1 ◊	DBL	P	P	♠ 7 3
				♡ A J 9
				◊ Q J 10 9 7
				♣ 10 4 2

This is about the minimum trump holding in the opponent's suit that you should have to pass; passing is then right regardless of your strength in the other suits. By passing, you convert your partner's takeout double into a penalty double. If 1 ◊ doubled becomes the final contract, your partner should lead a trump.

Let me emphasize that if your diamond holding were any weaker you should not pass; if you change the diamonds in this hand to Q-10-8-6-3, it would be better to bid 1 NT.

REBIDS BY THE DOUBLER

When a player responds to a takeout double by bidding one of the unbid suits, he may have zero points—0 to 9—and a weak four-card suit (rarely, a three-card suit). Therefore, the doubler should not bid again unless he has a strong hand, usually at least 16 points. If the responder bids 1 NT or makes a free bid, he indicates 6 to 9 points, and the doubler may logically bid again with a slightly weaker hand. If the responder jumps the bidding, he shows 10 to 12 points, but his bid is not forcing and the doubler should pass unless he has something extra.

When the doubler does have the values to bid again, he may raise the responder's suit, bid a new suit, bid notrump, or cue-bid the opponent's suit. The requirements for these rebids are described as follows.

Raising Your Partner's Suit

When your partner bids a suit in response to your takeout double, *you must have at least four trumps to raise him directly.* If he responds by bidding a major suit at the one-level, raise him to the two-level with 16 to 18 points, jump-raise him to the three-level with 19 to 21 points, or jump-raise him to game with 22 points or more. If partner responds by bidding a new suit at the two-level, you need about 18 to 20 to raise him to the three-level, or an even stronger hand to jump-raise him to the four-level. If partner jumps the bidding in a new suit, his bid is *not* forcing; you need at least 15 (or a good 14) points to raise him. Here are several examples:

Opp.	Partner	Opp.	You	
		1 ◊	DBL	♠ A Q 10 6
				♡ K Q J
P	1 ♠	P	2 ♠	◊ 4 3
				♣ A 9 7 2

Your 2 ♠ raise shows 16 to 18 points and at least four-card trump support. If partner's response were 1 ♡, you should pass; you should not raise him directly with fewer than four trumps, and you should not bid a new suit unless it is at least five cards long.

Opp.	Partner	Opp.	You	♠ A J 7 3
		1 ♣	DBL	♡ K Q 9 5
P	1 ♡	P	3 ♡	◇ A Q J 2
				♣ 6

You have 19 points and your jump raise shows 19 to 21 points and at least four trumps.

Opp.	Partner	Opp.	You	♠ A Q 10 6 2
		1 ◇	DBL	♡ A K
P	1 ♠	P	4 ♠	◇ 8 6
				♣ K Q J 3

You have 22 points. If partner has absolutely nothing, the 4 ♠ contract might fail, but he needs so little to make a game that you would be a pessimist if you did not bid it.

Opp.	Partner	Opp.	You	♠ 9
		1 ♠	DBL	♡ A Q J 8
P	2 ♡	P	3 ♡	◇ A K 10 2
				♣ K 9 5 3

You have 19 points. When your partner responds at the two-level, you need 18 to 20 points and at least four trumps to raise him.

Opp.	Partner	Opp.	You	♠ A K 8 3
		1 ♡	DBL	♡ 7 2
P	2 ♣	2 ♡	3 ♣	◇ A Q 6
				♣ Q 10 9 4

You have 16 points, not enough for a normal raise to 3 ♣. But in competitive situations it is desirable to lower the requirements to raise your partner's suit a point or two, provided you have excellent trump support. If your right-hand opponent had passed over your partner's 2 ♣ bid, you should pass also.

Opp.	Partner	Opp.	You	♠ A J 8 4
		1 ◇	DBL	♡ K 9 8 2
P	2 ♣	P	P	◇ 4 2
				♣ A 10 3

After adding 1 point for your doubleton diamond, you have 13 points—not enough to hope for game when partner has 10 to 12 points. If you had a couple more points (for example, change the hearts to ♡ K-Q-8-2), you should bid 4 ♣.

Bidding a New Five-Card or Longer Suit

A simple overcall may be as strong as 17 points. If your hand is too strong to overcall—18 points or more—the accepted procedure is to double first and bid your long suit later. For example:

Opp.	Partner	Opp.	You	
		1 ♣	DBL	♠ A 5 3
P	1 ♠	P	2 ♡	♡ A K 9 7 4
				◇ 8 2
				♣ A K 8

You have 19 points. Your 2 ♡ bid shows 18 to 20 points and at least a five-card heart suit.

When you have a two-suited hand that includes a side four-card major suit, it is considered good technique to double with a slightly weaker hand—16 or 17 points. For example:

Opp.	Partner	Opp.	You	
		1 ♠	DBL	♠ 6 2
P	2 ♣	P	2 ◇	♡ A Q 10 4
				◇ A K Q 9 6
				♣ 8 7

You have 16 points, but a double is better than a 2 ◇ overcall because of your four-card heart suit. You were hoping your partner could bid hearts, but when he bids 2 ♣ you have no choice but to bid 2 ◇. Never double first and follow by bidding a new suit with a weaker hand than this one; by doing so with only 16 points you are already taking liberties.

If you double first and then jump the bidding in a new suit, you show a hand with about 21 or 22 points and a self-sufficient suit. Your bid is *not* forcing. For example:

Opp.	Partner	Opp.	You	
		1 ◇	DBL	♠ K Q J 10 7 4
P	1 ♡	P	2 ♠	♡ A Q 8
				◇ 3
				♣ A K 2

You have 21 points. This is about the strongest nonforcing bid you can make. Your partner should bid again if he thinks he can take a trick.

If your partner answers your takeout double by bidding 1 NT, you do not need additional values to bid a new suit. For example:

Opp.	Partner	Opp.	You	
		1 ♡	DBL	♠ A 10 8 2
P	1 NT	P	2 ◇	♡ —
				◇ K Q 9 6 4
				♣ K 7 5 4

Partner's 1 NT response is disappointing, and 1 NT does not appear to be a good contract. Your 2 ◇ bid does not show a strong hand and is not forcing. If you do have a strong hand and want your partner to bid again, you must jump the bidding, or cue-bid the opponent's suit.

Bidding a New Four-Card Suit

If the takeout doubler rebids in a new suit, it must be at least five cards long. This is a good rule, but note the following two exceptions:

Opp.	Partner	Opp.	You	♠ K 10 9 2
		1 ♣	DBL	♡ A Q 5
P	2 ♣	P	2 ♠	◊ K J 6 3
				♣ 7 3

Your partner's 2 ♣ bid is a cue-bid, asking you to bid a four-card major suit if you have one. You must obey orders.

Opp.	Partner	Opp.	You	♠ A J 7 6
		1 ◊	DBL	♡ Q 10 8 2
RDBL	P	P	1 ♡	◊ 2
				♣ K J 10 4

If your partner had a clear preference for one of the unbid suits, he would have bid it over the redouble. His pass indicates he has an equal number of cards in each unbid suit (maybe 3-3-3, or 4-3-3) and he wants you to select the suit. You may be in serious trouble here and must try to escape playing a doubled contract, especially if you are vulnerable. The 1 ♡ bid is better than 1 ♠ or 2 ♣ because it keeps the bidding lower and increases your chances of escaping a doubled contract. If your left-hand opponent doubles 1 ♡ and your partner passes, you might run to 1 ♠; you must do your best to find the least expensive contract. If you are thinking you might do better by passing 1 ◊ redoubled, you are dead wrong; that figures to be a complete disaster.

Bidding Notrump

With any balanced hand containing 19 or more high-card points, the normal procedure is to double first with the intention of bidding notrump at your next turn. When you have a four-card major it may be desirable to double first and rebid 1 NT with a slightly weaker hand—17 or 18 high-card points. In all cases, the primary requirement to rebid 1 NT, 2 NT, or 3 NT is that you have at least one stopper in the opponent's bid suit. A 1 NT rebid shows 17 to 20 high-card points, a jump to 2 NT shows 21 or 22, a nonjump bid of 2 NT shows 19 to 21, and 3 NT shows a hand too strong to bid 2 NT.

If your partner has answered your takeout double by bidding 1 NT or 2 NT and your hand looks good to play notrump, raise 1 NT to 2 NT with 17 or 18 points and to 3 NT with 19 or more, and raise 2 NT to 3 NT with 15 points or more. Stoppers in the opponent's suit are not required to raise your partner's notrump bid.

Note the following examples:

Opp.	Partner	Opp.	You	♠ A J 10 2
		1 ◊	DBL	♡ Q 7
P	1 ♡	P	1 NT	◊ A K 4
				♣ A J 8 5

Your 1 NT rebid shows a balanced hand with at least one diamond stopper and 17 to 20 points.

Opp.	Partner	Opp.	You	♠ A Q 10 2
		1 ◊	DBL	♡ K Q 10
P	1 ♡	P	2 NT	◊ A Q 5
				♣ K J 9

If there were no bids ahead of you, you would open the bidding with 2 NT. When your right-hand opponent opens the bidding, you double first and follow with a jump to 2 NT to show a balanced hand with at least one diamond stopper and 21 or 22 points.

Opp.	Partner	Opp.	You	
		1 ♡	DBL	♠ A Q 10 2
				♡ A Q
P	2 ♣	P	2 NT	◇ K 10 9 7
				♣ A 8 4

Your nonjump rebid of 2 NT shows a balanced hand with at least one heart stopper and 19 to 21 points.

Opp.	Partner	Opp.	You	
		1 ◇	DBL	♠ A K 3
				♡ 7 5
P	1 ♡	P	3 NT	◇ A 5
				♣ A K Q J 10 8

Now that partner has bid hearts you can assume that the opponents cannot run the first five heart tricks. With nine sure tricks, 3 NT is the only sensible bid.

Opp.	Partner	Opp.	You	
		1 ♡	DBL	♠ A Q J 7
				♡ 6 3
P	1 NT	P	2 NT	◇ A Q 9 8
				♣ K Q 10

Partner has 6 to 9 high-card points and at least one heart stopper, so with 18 points you should bid 2 NT to invite him to game; with a point or two more, you should raise to 3 NT.

Cue-bidding the Opponent's Suit

When you have doubled with a very strong hand (21 points or more) and cannot raise your partner's suit, bid a new suit, or bid notrump, your only recourse is to cue-bid the opponent's suit. For example:

Opp.	Partner	Opp.	You	
		1 ♠	DBL	♠ 6 3
				♡ A Q 7 2
P	2 ◇	P	2 ♠	◇ A K J
				♣ A K J 8

Your cue-bid shows an extremely strong hand and is forcing for one round. Since your partner is forced to bid again with nothing, you should pass any minimum rebid he makes, such as 2 NT or 3 ◇. If your partner has any values (as few as 4 or 5 points), he should realize that a game is very likely and jump the bidding.

REBIDS BY THE RESPONDER

The average player tends to overbid his strong hands and underbid his weak hands; he does not recognize the value of one or two key cards when his partner has done some strong bidding. This is typically true of many players when their partners make a takeout double. Note the following five hands to see if you are a timid soul.

Opp.	Partner	Opp.	You	♠ K 10 9 3
1 ♡	DBL	P	1 ♠	♡ 8 6 5 2
P	2 ♠	P	4 ♠	◇ K J 9 8
				♣ 7

Your partner's 2 ♠ bid shows 16 to 18 points and at least four trumps. When you add 2 points for your singleton club you have 9 points, so you should have an excellent play for game. If partner's rebid were 3 ♠, you should bid 4 ♠ with as few as 5 or 6 points.

Opp.	Partner	Opp.	You	♠ K 10 8 2
1 ◇	DBL	P	1 ♠	♡ 9 7 3
P	2 ♡	P	3 ♡	◇ 9 7 6 4
				♣ K 5

Partner has 18 to 20 points and a five-card or longer heart suit, so you have the values to invite him to game. If partner jumped to 3 ♡, it would be a good gamble to bid 4 ♡ without the ♣ K.

Opp.	Partner	Opp.	You	♠ 9 2
1 ♡	DBL	P	2 ◇	♡ 8 7 3
P	2 NT	P	3 NT	◇ A Q 9 6
				♣ 10 6 4 2

The 2 NT rebid shows 19 to 21 points, so you have enough to bid game.

Opp.	Partner	Opp.	You	♠ Q J 9 4
1 ♠	DBL	P	2 ◇	♡ 8 5
P	2 ♠	P	3 NT	◇ Q 10 7 6 3
				♣ 3 2

The 2 ♠ cue-bid shows a powerful hand, at least 21 points. With the spade suit securely stopped and 5 high-card points, you should be optimistic about your chances to make 3 NT. You are forced to bid again over the 2 ♠ cue-bid, and if you bid only 2 NT, or some other nonjump bid, your partner will expect you to have nothing and may pass.

Opp.	Partner	Opp.	You	♠ 7 6
1 ♠	DBL	P	2 ♡	♡ Q 10 8 6 3
P	P	2 ♠	3 ♡	◇ K 2
				♣ 9 8 5 4

Your 2 ♡ bid showed nothing and this hand is worth about 8 points; since partner must have good heart support to double 1 ♠, you should count points for your short suits. Your 3 ♡ bid shows about 6 to 9 points; if you had fewer than 6 points you should pass, and if you had 10 points you would have jumped to 3 ♡ on your previous bid.

MORE TAKEOUT DOUBLES

So far in this chapter we have only taken up doubles of opening suit bids of one, and now we are getting into less common auctions where doubles are for takeout. Here is where confusion about the meaning of a double may develop—one player doubles for penalty and his partner thinks it is for takeout, or vice versa. So before we get involved with more takeout doubles, note the following situations where a double is for penalty:

1. If the doubler's partner has entered the auction (taken any action other than passing), the double is for penalty.
2. A double of any notrump bid is for penalty, with the one exception noted later in this chapter.
3. A double of any game bid is for penalty, with the exception of preemptive bids (see Chapter 14).
4. A double of any artificial bid (such as a Stayman 2 ♣ bid, a cue-bid, or a response to Blackwood) is for penalty, for lead-directing purposes.

A double of any natural suit bid below the game level (4 ◇ or lower) is a takeout double if your partner has not entered the auction and there are still two or three unbid suits. Takeout doubles in the balancing seat, takeout doubles of preemptive bids, and penalty doubles are covered in later chapters, but that still leaves us with a lot of room for discussion here. We still have to cover doubling an opponent's 1 NT response, doubling when the opponents have bid two suits, doubling when the opponents have shown great strength, doubling when you have made an earlier bid, and doubling when you have made an earlier pass.

Doubles of 1 NT and 2 NT Responses

If your left-hand opponent opens the bidding with a suit and your right-hand opponent responds in notrump, a double has the same meaning as when you double your right-hand opponent's opening suit bid; it is for takeout. For example:

Opp.	Partner	Opp.	You	
1 ◇	P	1 NT	DBL	♠ A 10 9 3
				♡ A Q 10 4
				◇ 7
				♣ K 8 6 2

Your double is takeout for the three unbid suits, but your partner may pass—convert the double into a penalty double—if he has a good hand with a strong holding in the diamond suit. If the bidding went 2 ◇ on your left (a weak two-bid) and 2 NT on your right, double would be correct with this hand.

Doubles When the Opponents Have Bid Two Suits

When your opponents have bid two suits, you may make a takeout double to ask your partner to bid one of the unbid suits. Since your partner has only two suits to choose between, it is doubtful to double unless you have at least four cards in each unbid suit. The minimum point-count requirement varies with the shape of your hand: with 4-4 in the unbid suits, you need a full opening bid to double; with 5-4 you should have at least 11 or 12 points; and with 5-5 you may double with as few as 9 or 10 points. You will note that the emphasis is more on distribution than on high cards, and therefore the vulnerability should have some influence on how daring you might be. Here are two examples:

Opp.	Partner	Opp.	You	
1 ♣	P	1 ♠	DBL	♠ A 2
				♡ J 10 8 6 3
				◇ K J 10 5 3
				♣ 4

With two fairly good five-card suits, this hand warrants a double regardless of the vulnerability.

Opp.	Partner	Opp.	You	♠ A Q 6 3
1 ♡	P	2 ♣	?	♡ A 9
				◊ J 8 6 5 4
				♣ 7 2

Your partner cannot have much with an opening bid on your left and a two-level response on your right. So with only nine cards in the unbid suits and a mediocre hand, take a chance and double if you are not vulnerable, but pass if you are vulnerable.

Doubles When the Opponents Have Shown Great Strength

When the opponents have shown that they have most of the high cards, you may still double for takeout if you have a highly distributional hand; you may have a good sacrifice, or in rare cases you may even be able to make a game. The most logical time for such a double is with favorable vulnerability, but with the right distribution you might take a chance with any vulnerability. For example:

Opp.	Partner	Opp.	You	♠ K J 10 9
1 ♡	P	3 ♡	DBL	♡ —
				◊ J 10 9 3 2
				♣ A Q 8 5

The ideal shape makes this double reasonable with any vulnerability; although not without risk, it is possible that both sides can make a game. If you do double it asks partner to bid one of the unbid suits.

Doubles When You Have Previously Acted

You may make a takeout double, or an overcall, and then double for takeout at your next turn to bid. For example:

Opp.	Partner	Opp.	You	♠ A Q 10 7
		1 ◊	DBL	♡ K Q 10 8
3 ◊	P	P	DBL	◊ 6
				♣ A K 9 2

Your second double is for takeout and shows a very strong hand; with a minimum double you would pass. Your partner is expected to bid one of the unbid suits, but he may pass 3 ◊ doubled if he has something good in diamonds. He may also jump to game with modest values; for example, he should bid 4 ♠ with ♠ K-X-X-X-X ♡ X-X-X ◊ X-X-X ♣ X-X.

Opp.	Partner	Opp.	You	♠ A Q 9 4
		1 ♡	DBL	♡ 3
2 ♣	P	P	DBL	◊ K Q J 6
				♣ A 9 8 5

Your second double still shows extra values, but partner may decide to pass for penalties because your first double implied that you had length in clubs. He must use his judgment to bid one of the unbid suits, or pass 2 ♣ doubled.

Opp.	Partner	Opp.	You	♠ 3
		1 ♠	2 ◊	♡ A 10 2
2 ♠	P	P	DBL	◊ A Q 10 7 4 2
				♣ K Q 8

Your double is for takeout showing extra values and some support for the two unbid suits (usually three-card support). Your partner should bid 3 ♣ or 3 ♡ with a five-card or longer suit, or else he may bid 3 ◊, bid 2 NT, or pass 2 ♠ doubled with strong spades.

NOTE: You may open the bidding and then later double for takeout, provided your partner has not entered the auction. This is covered in Chapter 15, which deals with competitive bidding by the opening bidder's side. See pages 169 and 170 for illustrations.

Doubles When You Have Previously Passed

We are concerned here with doubles of bids by your right-hand opponent— *direct doubles*. Doubles of bids by your left-hand opponent—*balancing doubles*—are explained in Chapter 13. There are two categories for doubling your right-hand opponent's bid when you have made an earlier pass: Either your pass was before the opponents opened the bidding, or your pass was after they opened the bidding. The meanings of the doubles are explained in the analysis of the following illustrations.

♠ K 10 8 2	You	Opp.	Partner	Opp.
♡ Q 10 9 4	P	P	P	1 ◊
◊ 7 6	DBL			
♣ A J 5				

Your double is for takeout, showing a maximum passed hand with support for the unbid suits.

Opp.	Partner	Opp.	You	♠ A 9 3
		1 ♠	P	♡ A Q 6 4
1 NT	P	2 ♣	DBL	◊ Q 9 8 7 2
				♣ 5

Your double is takeout for the two unbid suits. Note that you could not double the first time because you were not prepared for your partner to bid clubs.

Opp.	Partner	Opp.	You	♠ A Q 10 9
		1 ♠	P	♡ K Q 9 5
1 NT	P	2 ♠	DBL	◊ A J 7 2
				♣ 5

This time your double is for penalty. If you had support for the three unbid suits, you would have doubled the first time. If the opening bidder's rebid were 2 ♣— instead of 2 ♠—you should still double, but then your double would be for takeout.

12

Penalty Doubles, Lead-Directing Doubles, and Rescue Bids

♣　　♦　　♥　　♠　　♣　　♦　　♥　　♠

In this chapter you will find penalty doubles of overcalls, doubles of 1 NT opening bids, doubles of artificial bids, doubles of games bid in notrump, doubles of games bid in a suit, doubles of slams, and rescue bids, including the S-O-S redouble.

PENALTY DOUBLES OF OVERCALLS

If your partner opens the bidding and your right-hand opponent makes any bid, a double by you is for penalty.

NOTE: If you have adopted the modern convention of "negative doubles," doubles of overcalls are for takeout and the instructions that follow would not apply. However, a vast majority of players still play that doubles of overcalls are for penalty, and here is the way to do it.

If your partner opens the bidding and your right-hand opponent overcalls by bidding a suit at the one-level or two-level, the features in your hand that make a penalty double attractive are:

1. Length and strength in the opponent's suit, such as K-J-X-X or Q-10-X-X.
2. Shortness in your partner's suit; a singleton is ideal.
3. A reasonably strong hand, with at least one and one-half or two quick tricks. (You should be prepared to take further action if your double chases the opponents to another contract; you may double again, bid further, but do not allow the opponents to play another contract undoubled.)

When you are contemplating a double of an overcall at the one-level or two-level and your hand meets all three requirements, assume that your partner's hand will win three tricks and add that to the number of tricks you estimate your hand can win; if the estimate is enough to beat the contract, double. However, do not double an overcall of 2 ♡ or higher unless you are reasonably sure you can set the contract two tricks; if your opponent makes his contract, he will score a game.

Note that you may double at the higher levels of bidding anytime you think it will reward you with the biggest profit; it is not necessary that your hand meet all of these requirements.

You will score a bigger profit if you double and beat a vulnerable overcall than when you double and beat a nonvulnerable overcall. But on the other hand, the opponents are much more aggressive when they are not vulnerable, so big profits may be available by doubling a nonvulnerable overcall.

The average player does not double enough. If you do not occasionally double a contract you cannot beat, you are too conservative. In addition to the larger profits you will earn, your opponents will become more conservative when they learn that you are a "trigger doubler"; this will *not* work to their advantage. Anyway, your double is not the final word; your partner may take the double out if he chooses. Here are several illustrations:

Partner	*Opp.*	*You*	♠ K J 9 7
1 ♣	1 ♠	DBL	♡ K 4 3
			◇ A 9 8 6 2
			♣ 4

Many players never double at the one-level, and that can be a mistake. You should double here regardless of vulnerability. Remember, your partner will take the double out if he judges a bigger profit can be made elsewhere.

Partner	*Opp.*	*You*	♠ 5 3
1 ♠	2 ♣	P	♡ 7 4 2
			◇ 10 8 5
			♣ K Q 10 9 6

Do not double the only contract you can beat. If you double it is likely that your left-hand opponent will bid 2 ◇ or 2 ♡, and you are not prepared to take further action if he does. If 2 ♣ undoubled becomes the final contract, you should be delighted.

Partner	*Opp.*	*You*	♠ 9 2
1 ♡	2 ♣	2 ♡	♡ K 7 4
			◇ 10 8 5 4
			♣ A Q 8 3

With a reasonably good fit in partner's heart suit, it is wiser to support hearts than to double the 2 ♣ bid. If partner opened the bidding with 1 ♠, then doubling the 2 ♣ bid would be best.

Partner	*Opp.*	*You*	♠ 8 6
1 ♠	2 ◇	DBL	♡ A 9 7 5
			◇ A 9 7 5
			♣ J 6 3

You should estimate that your hand can win three tricks in defense (one for the four-card diamond suit). This is a very close double, since if partner can win three tricks it adds up to setting the contract by only one trick. Although your opponent will sometimes make his contract, partner's hand may be more productive and you might set him several tricks. The gambling double is in order, since if he makes his contract your loss will be a small one. If the overcall were 2 ♡ instead of 2 ◊, you should pass; if your opponent makes 2 ♡ doubled, he will score a game. Do not risk doubling the opponents into game unless you are reasonably sure you can set them two tricks.

Partner	*Opp.*	*You*	♠ A 10 7 5 2
1 ♣	4 ♡	DBL	♡ K 3
			◊ 9 4
			♣ 9 8 7 6

The double is best regardless of vulnerability. Although you may have a game your way, it would be highly speculative to bid over 4 ♡; if partner has the wrong hand you could be doubled and suffer a severe penalty. The purpose of the 4 ♡ bid (a preemptive bid) was to deprive you of bidding space, so you will not be able to explore for your best contract; it has done its job and you really have no choice but to double and take a reasonably sure profit, although it may be a small one.

If, after you have opened the bidding, your partner doubles an overcall at the one-level or two-level, you should leave the double in (that is, pass) unless:

1. You are void in the opponent's suit.
2. You have one small card in the opponent's suit and fewer than three defensive tricks (quick tricks).
3. You have a singleton honor or two or more cards in the opponent's suit, but, because you have a highly distributional hand, you are reasonably sure a bigger profit can be made by bidding and making a game or a slam.

These three guidelines are not rules; they are only meant to aid your judgment. If there is any doubt in your mind it is probably better to pass—your partner is usually happier when you trust his bidding. Also note that these guidelines apply to the one-level and two-level. If your partner doubles an overcall at the three-level or higher, you should be much more inclined to leave it in. For example:

♠ K 9 7 6 2	*You*	*Opp.*	*Partner*	*Opp.*
♡ A 8 6	1 ♠	2 ♣	DBL	P
◊ A Q 9 6 3	2 ◊			
♣ —				

If the overcall was at the one-level or two-level, always take the double out if you are void in the enemy suit.

♠ K 7 5 3 2	*You*	*Opp.*	*Partner*	*Opp.*
♡ A K Q 6	1 ♠	2 ♣	DBL	P
◊ 8 7 2	2 ♡			
♣ 6				

To pass the double with only one small card in the enemy suit, you should have at least three defensive tricks; you have only two and one-half (the ♠ K and the ♡ A-K).

```
♠ A K 5 3 2      You      Opp.      Partner   Opp.
♡ A J 9 5        1 ♠      2 ♣       DBL       P
◊ 8 7 3          P
♣ 4
```

With three defensive tricks and one small card in the enemy suit, you should
pass your partner's double.

```
♠ K Q J 10 9 6 4   You      Opp.      Partner   Opp.
♡ A Q J            1 ♠      2 ♣       DBL       P
◊ 2                4 ♠
♣ 7 5
```

It is rarely right to take the double out with two cards in the enemy suit, but with
this tremendous spade suit and limited defensive values it appears that 4 ♠ will
be the most profitable contract.

If your right-hand opponent rescues his partner from a doubled contract by bidding a new
suit, you should double his bid with at least three strong trumps, or else pass and give your
partner a chance to double. However, with a highly distributional hand it might be right to
bid. If you double, partner should take it out if he is very short in the trump suit. If you pass,
partner is required to bid again. Here is one example:

```
♠ A Q 10         You      Opp.      Partner   Opp.
♡ A K 9 5 2      1 ♡      2 ♣       DBL       2 ♠
◊ 8 7 6          DBL
♣ 5 3
```

Your partner should take the double out with a singleton or a void in spades. If
your right-hand opponent bid 2 ◊ instead of 2 ♠, you should pass and give
partner a chance to double; he may not pass 2 ◊.

If your partner's opening bid is 1 NT (showing 16 to 18 points), you should double an
opposing overcall with a smattering of high cards (usually 7 high-card points or more) and a
potent holding in the enemy's suit (such as J-9-X-X, or K-10-X); but doubling with fewer
than four trumps is questionable. For example:

```
Partner   Opp.    You      ♠ A J 9
1 NT      2 ♡     DBL      ♡ K 9 7 4
                           ◊ 6 2
                           ♣ 10 8 5 3
```

You have 8 points and your heart holding is adequate for the double. The
opponents have at most 16 high-card points between them, and it is highly
probable that doubling will provide the maximum result for your side. If the
overcall were 2 ♠ instead of 2 ♡, many players would still favor a double; but
with only three spades 2 NT is also a reasonable bid.

If your right-hand opponent makes an overcall of 1 NT, you should double with 9 high-
card points or more. It seems that your side has most of the high cards and therefore should
be able to win most of the tricks if the hand is played in notrump. Here is one example:

Partner	Opp.	You	♠ 5 3
1 ♠	1 NT	DBL	♡ K 10 7 4
			◇ A Q 9 8
			♣ 8 7 6

If everyone passes 1 NT doubled, you should lead the ♠ 5. On rare occasions your partner will have a poor opening bid and, because of the favorable location of the cards, the declarer will make his bid; but far more often you will set the contract two or three tricks. Even if they do make 1 NT doubled, your loss will be a small one.

If your right-hand opponent makes a takeout double, a good profit from a penalty double may be available. For example:

Opp.	Partner	Opp.	You	♠ 7
	1 ♠	DBL	RDBL	♡ A J 8 5
P	P	2 ♡	DBL	◇ K 10 6 3
				♣ K 9 5 2

It appears that 2 ♡ doubled will be a lucrative result. With this marvelous defensive hand, you should double anything the opponents bid.

The opening bidder, also, may make a penalty double, provided his partner has been in the bidding. For example:

♠ K 10 7	You	Opp.	Partner	Opp.
♡ 4	1 ◇	P	1 ♡	2 ♣
◇ A Q 9 7 3	DBL			
♣ A J 9 2				

Since your partner has already bid, your double is for penalty. If your partner has a reasonable hand, the opponents are in trouble and your double should pay off handsomely.

DIRECT DOUBLES OF 1 NT OPENING BIDS

A double of your right-hand opponent's opening 1 NT bid is a penalty double, and your partner is expected to pass unless he has a worthless hand and a long suit. You may double with as few as 14 or 15 high-card points if you have a very good suit to lead. It seldom pays to double without a good safe lead; you may have to lead away from a treacherous holding and give away a trick, and the knowledge that you have all the missing high cards may enable the declarer to play the hand better. However, you should double without a good suit to lead if you have a very strong hand, say 18 high-card points or more. Here are three examples:

Opp.	You	♠ A 6 4
1 NT	DBL	♡ K Q J 10 9 3
		◇ 8
		♣ A J 2

If everyone passes you are almost certain to beat 1 NT and if partner can contribute anything to the defense you may beat it two or three tricks. If your left-hand opponent runs—for example, he bids 2 ◇—you can bid hearts at your next turn.

Opp.	You	♠ Q 9 7
1 NT	P	♡ K J 6 3
		◇ A J 10
		♣ A J 5

Assuming the 1 NT opening bid shows 16 to 18 high-card points, it is a wild gamble to double with this hand, and it would be a losing proposition in the long run. If we take the best of it and give the 1 NT bidder 16 points there are only 8 points missing. If your partner has most of those points, a double would be successful, while if your left-hand opponent has most of the points, you would be in serious trouble; if the 8 points are evenly divided between your partner and left-hand opponent, a double would work against you because the declarer may play better knowing that you have a big hand and you may give away a trick on the opening lead.

Opp.	You	♠ K Q 9
1 NT	DBL	♡ A J 10 7
		◇ A J 4
		♣ K 3 2

With 18 high-card points the double is recommended, but you again have no good lead and the double might show the declarer how to make his bid.

When your partner doubles an opening 1 NT bid, he is making a penalty double and you should pass unless you have a worthless hand and a long suit. For example:

Opp.	Partner	Opp.	You	♠ 10 7 5
1 NT	DBL	P	P	♡ 7 6 4
				◇ J 9 3 2
				♣ 8 7 3

Your hand will be a disappointment to your partner and you may not beat 1 NT, but you figure to get into deeper trouble if you bid.

Opp.	Partner	Opp.	You	♠ 7
1 NT	DBL	P	2 ◇	♡ 8 3 2
				◇ 10 9 6 4 3 2
				♣ 7 5 2

Your partner's strong hand should be useful in helping you make 2 ◇, while your hand would contribute nothing to the defense of 1 NT doubled.

Opp.	Partner	Opp.	You	♠ K 2
1 NT	DBL	P	P	♡ Q J 10 7 4
				◇ J 5 3
				♣ 10 8 7

With 7 high-card points, you have about as much as your partner could hope for. Your opponents will not make 1 NT doubled.

DOUBLES OF ARTIFICIAL BIDS

When one of your opponents makes an artificial bid, such as a Stayman two-club bid, a control-showing bid, or a response to Blackwood, a double by you indicates a strong enough holding in that suit to beat the contract if the double is left in. But the purpose of your double is to tell your partner that you want him to lead that suit, not that you expect to defend that contract, and most certainly not that you want your partner to bid. A double of any artificial bid is always for penalty, for lead-directing purposes. Here are five examples:

Opp.	Partner	Opp.	You	♠ 6 5 2
1 NT	P	2 ♣	DBL	♡ A 3
				◊ 9 7 6
				♣ K Q J 10 9

In all probability your left-hand opponent will become declarer in hearts, spades, or notrump, and your double asks for a club lead. Note that if the opponents elect to play the contract 2 ♣ doubled (or redoubled), you have five tricks and are well prepared to defend.

Opp.	Partner	Opp.	You	♠ 10 4 2
1 ♣	P	1 ♡	P	♡ 9 8 6 5
1 ♠	P	2 ◊	DBL	◊ A Q J 9 7
				♣ 3

It is not unlikely that your left-hand opponent's next bid will be in notrump, and you certainly want a diamond lead. Although the 2 ◊ bid is technically not an artificial bid, the double could have no meaning other than asking for a diamond lead, since the opponents have bid all four suits.

Opp.	Partner	Opp.	You	♠ A Q J 9
1 ◊	P	3 ◊	P	♡ 7 2
3 ♡	P	3 ♠	DBL	◊ Q J 5
				♣ 8 7 6 4

Your right-hand opponent would have bid spades the first time if he had a real suit, so his 3 ♠ bid is artificial, to show a stopper, obviously the ♠ K. It is imperative that you make a lead-directing double to get your partner to lead a spade, or your left-hand opponent may bid 3 NT and make it with a different lead.

Opp.	Partner	Opp.	You	♠ 5 4 2
1 ♠	P	3 ♠	P	♡ J 10 9 7 6
4 ♣	P	4 ◊	DBL	◊ K Q 10
				♣ 5 2

The 4 ◊ bid is a control-showing bid, and your double asks partner to lead a diamond against the expected spade contract. If your right-hand opponent had bid 4 ♡ instead of 4 ◊, you should pass; your partner should conclude that your heart holding is not strong, and this may influence him to lead the unbid suit, diamonds.

Opp.	Partner	Opp.	You	♠ Q 9 7 5
1 ♡	P	3 ♡	P	♡ 7
4 NT	P	5 ◊	DBL	◊ K J 10 3
				♣ 8 6 5 2

Another opportunity for a lead-directing double is when an opponent responds to Blackwood. Here your double calls for a diamond lead.

DOUBLES OF GAMES BID IN NOTRUMP

If you double an opposing 3 NT contract when you have the opening lead you will most likely regret it if your double was based on a generally strong hand without a good opening lead. For example:

Opp.	Partner	Opp.	You	
		1 NT	P	♠ K J 4
2 NT	P	3 NT	P	♡ K 9 8
				◇ A J 7
				♣ K 10 7 5

Since you have 15 high-card points and the opponents have bid 3 NT, your partner obviously has nothing. If you double 3 NT you "tip your hand"; knowing where all the missing high cards are, the declarer should have no trouble making his contract.

When you have the opening lead, a double of 3 NT may be right with a moderate number of high cards, provided (1) your opponents have bid sluggishly, an indication that they had barely enough to bid game; (2) your high cards are favorably located, that is, in the suit or suits bid by your right-hand opponent; and (3) you have an attractive suit to lead. For example:

Opp.	Partner	Opp.	You	
		1 ♡	P	♠ 7
1 ♠	P	1 NT	P	♡ A Q 10
2 NT	P	3 NT	DBL	◇ Q J 10 9 2
				♣ 8 6 5 3

With a good lead (the ◇ Q), well-located honor cards (the ♡ A-Q-10 behind the heart bidder), and sluggish bidding (an indication that they have barely enough high cards to venture a game bid), the double is a good gamble.

If you double 3 NT when your partner has the opening lead, your double is a lead director, calling for a specific suit to be led. If neither you nor your partner has bid, it says *lead the first suit bid by the dummy* (provided the suit was not rebid or supported). If you have bid a suit, your double says *lead my suit*. Here are three examples:

Opp.	Partner	Opp.	You	
1 ♣	P	1 ♠	P	♠ K Q J 10 9
1 NT	P	3 NT	DBL	♡ 7 5 4
				◇ 8 4 3
				♣ A 2

Double to get the spade lead, by all means. With a spade lead the contract will surely be set, while with another lead there is little hope.

Opp.	Partner	Opp.	You	
1 ♣	P	1 ♠	P	♠ K Q 10 9
1 NT	P	2 NT	P	♡ 7
3 NT	P	P	DBL	◇ 9 8 6 4 2
				♣ A 7 4

The last hand was too good to be true, so here is a more realistic example. The spade lead will give you an excellent chance to beat the contract. If you do not double you can expect your partner to lead a heart, and that will not only lose the timing but may give the declarer an extra heart trick. If you change the bidding so that your right-hand opponent jumps to 3 NT—instead of bidding 2 NT—doubling 3 NT becomes a doubtful action; the opponents may have extra values, in which case they may redouble and make their contract in spite of the spade lead.

Opp.	Partner	Opp.	You	
			1 ◇	♠ 6 3
				♡ J 9 7 4
DBL	P	3 ♣	P	◇ A Q J 10 9
3 NT	P	P	DBL	♣ A 2

Your double commands your partner to lead a diamond, which will almost surely beat 3 NT.

If your partner (the opening leader) has bid a suit, or if both you and your partner have bid a suit, your double of a 3 NT contract *asks* your partner to lead his own suit if it will not jeopardize a trick. With holdings such as A-Q-J-X-X he should not lead his own suit, he should try to get you on lead so that you can play through declarer's known honor card or cards.

DOUBLES OF GAMES BID IN A SUIT

Lead-directing doubles are not used when the opponents bid game in a suit. You can usually increase your profit by doubling an opposing suit game provided you have a long, strong, and *safe* holding in their trump suit and you are reasonably sure they cannot escape to a better contract. Also, if you have a close decision, sluggish bidding by your opponents should influence you to make an aggressive double.

Be wary of doubling when your opponents voluntarily bid a suit game and your holding in their trump suit is unprotected, such as Q-X-X, Q-10-X-X, A-J-X-X, etc. Your double will show declarer a way to make his contract by finessing through you for a missing trump honor.

You should also be reluctant to double an opposing suit game when holding three or four quick tricks but no trump tricks. When your opponents bid game voluntarily with few high cards, it means they have compensating values in the form of excellent distribution and a very substantial trump suit. Of course, if it is apparent that the opponents are sacrificing, you should double without a trump trick anytime you think it is the most profitable action.

Here are three examples:

Opp.	Partner	Opp.	You	
		1 ♠	P	♠ Q J 10 9
				♡ A 4
2 ♠	P	4 ♠	DBL	◇ A J 7
				♣ 8 7 5 3

It appears that you can set the contract one trick, and if your partner can contribute anything you may beat them more than one.

Opp.	Partner	Opp.	You	
				♠ 7 4
1 ♡	P	1 ♠	P	♡ Q J 10 9 5
3 ♡	P	3 ♠	P	◇ A J 6
4 ♡	P	P	P	♣ 8 3 2

If you make the mistake of doubling 4 ♡ , they may run to 4 ♠ and make it.

Opp.	Partner	Opp.	You	♠ Q 10 7 4
		1 ♠	P	♡ A J 10 8
2 ♠	P	4 ♠	P	◇ A 6 5
				♣ 3 2

It would be risky to double 4 ♠. You may show the declarer how to make his contract by an unusual line of play.

DOUBLES OF SLAMS

If your opponents bid a slam voluntarily and you have the opening lead, do not double unless you are sure you can beat the contract and the opponents cannot escape to a different slam contract that you cannot beat. You are giving big odds when you double an opposing slam if you have the opening lead; if you beat the contract one trick your double will gain you an extra 50 or 100 points, while if your opponents make their slam because of your double (and they may redouble) it will cost you a bundle. Here are three examples of when not to double:

Opp.	Partner	Opp.	You	♠ 7 5 2
		1 ♡	P	♡ 6 3
3 ♡	P	6 ♡	P	◇ A K 10 5
				♣ A 9 7 6

Predictably, the declarer is void in diamonds; otherwise he would have used Blackwood, or a control-showing bid, to make sure he would not lose the first two tricks. Even if you could set the contract one trick, a double would gain only an extra 50 or 100 points. If the contract is makable and you double, it would cost you an extra 590 points if they redouble.

Opp.	Partner	Opp.	You	♠ Q J 10 9
		1 ♠	P	♡ 9 6 4 2
2 NT	P	3 ♠	P	◇ 10 7 5
4 ♠	P	6 ♠	P	♣ Q 3

Although you can surely beat this 6 ♠ contract, it would be wrong to double. You may chase the opponents into a 6 NT contract, which may be unbeatable. If this happened against vulnerable opponents, your double would cost you 1540 points: 750 for slam bonus, 500 for game bonus, 190 for tricks, and 100 you would have won for beating 6 ♠ undoubled one trick.

Opp.	Partner	Opp.	Expert	♠ 9 5 2
		2 NT	P	♡ A K 8
6 NT	P	P	DBL	◇ 8 7 6 4 3
7 ♣	P	P	DBL	♣ 10 5

   This is a true story. It happened to one of the world's best players many years ago. He was on lead against 6 NT and could win the first two tricks with the ace and king of hearts. His opponents were two young men he had never seen before, so he took a chance and doubled. His left-hand opponent realized the expert must have the first two tricks to double 6 NT (probably A-K in a suit), so he bid 7 ♣. Our expert doubled again, but now his partner had the opening lead and had to choose between leading a diamond, heart, or spade. He chose to lead a diamond, and 7 ♣ doubled was made. Here is the full deal:

NORTH
♠ A Q 10 4
♡ Q J 5
◊ A K Q
♣ K 7 6

WEST
♠ 8 7 6 3
♡ 9 6 4 2
◊ J 10 9
♣ 3 2

EAST
♠ 9 5 2
♡ A K 8
◊ 8 7 6 4 3
♣ 10 5

SOUTH
♠ K J
♡ 10 7 3
◊ 5 2
♣ A Q J 9 8 4

As you can see, with a diamond lead South could win all thirteen tricks and score up 2330 points for making 7 ♣ doubled. If our unlucky expert had passed 6 NT he would have won 100 points, so his double cost him 2430 points. Incidentally, the South player's choice to bid 6 NT is a pretty good one; that contract should succeed most of the time.

If you double a slam when your partner has the opening lead, your double calls for an "unusual lead." The odds are very much in your favor when you double a slam for a lead. If the lead you direct beats the slam, you will save over 1000 points if the opponents are not vulnerable and over 1500 points if they are vulnerable, while the extra amount you lose if they make their slam is moderate by comparison. Note that the reason for a lead-directing double of a slam is not to increase the amount you will win, but rather to increase your chances of beating the contract.

If neither you nor your partner has bid a suit, a double of a suit slam asks your partner to lead a suit—other than the trump suit—that was bid by either opponent. When two suits have been bid by the opponents, your partner must decide which to lead. In a vast majority of cases the lead-directing slam double is used when you have a void suit you want led so you can trump the first trick. So when your partner must decide between two suits to lead, he should generally lead the longer suit. You may also double a suit slam with honor strength in the suit you want led, but be wary of such doubles, as one of your opponents may be void in that suit, or have a singleton. For example:

Opp.	Partner	Opp.	You	
		1 ♠	P	♠ —
2 ♡	P	4 ♡	P	♡ 6 4 2
4 NT	P	5 ♡	P	◊ K 10 7 3
7 ♡	P	P	DBL	♣ 9 8 6 5 4 2

Since the only suit the opponents have bid other than hearts is spades, your double calls for a spade lead.

Opp.	Partner	Opp.	You	
1 ♠	P	2 ◊	P	♠ —
2 ♡	P	4 NT	P	♡ A 4
5 ♡	P	6 ♡	DBL	◊ 10 8 7 3 2
				♣ 9 8 6 5 4 2

This time the opponents have bid two suits other than their trump suit, spades and diamonds. Since the lead-directing slam double is usually based on a void suit, your partner must choose between the two and lead his *longer* suit, which will surely be spades.

An interesting problem here would be whether you should double 6 ♡ without the ♡ A (say your heart holding is ♡ 4-2). The answer is yes, you should double to get the spade lead and hope your partner can take a trick to set the contract. This is, of course, a gambling double, but the odds are good; if you beat the slam you prevent a huge loss, while the extra amount you lose if they make the slam is small by comparison.

You may use a lead-directing double of a suit slam even when the opponents have not bid any side suits. Your double implies that you have a void suit and you want your partner to lead his longest suit. For example:

Opp.	Partner	Opp.	You	
1 ♡	P	3 ♡	P	♠ J 10 9 7 2
6 ♡	P	P	DBL	♡ A 9 4
				♢ 10 8 6 5 3
				♣ —

Almost surely your partner's longest suit will be clubs, and a club lead will beat the 6 ♡ contract.

If you have bid a suit and your partner is on lead against a slam, the normal expectation is that he will lead your suit. So if you double the slam, you are telling your partner not to lead your suit; he must lead one of the other suits, and it might be an unbid suit, or a suit bid by an opponent. For example:

Opp.	Partner	Opp.	You	
		1 ♠	2 ♢	♠ 9 7 3
2 ♡	P	4 ♡	P	♡ 5 4
6 ♡	P	P	DBL	♢ K 10 9 8 6 2
				♣ A K

Your double commands your partner not to lead a diamond. He must guess whether to lead a spade or a club, but should generally lead the longer suit as you may be doubling with a void suit.

Doubling for a lead against a suit slam is dangerous unless you have a void suit. For example:

Opp.	Partner	Opp.	You	
1 ♡	P	2 ♣	P	♠ 8 4 2
3 ♡	P	4 NT	P	♡ 7 3
5 ♡	P	6 ♡	P	♢ 10 9 6 5
				♣ A K 10 9

If you double 6 ♡ it would call for a club lead, but your left-hand opponent may have a void suit or a singleton in clubs, so the double is too risky. If the declarer happens to have more than one club in his hand, you may beat the contract without a club lead, or your partner may have a singleton club and lead the suit anyway.

If your partner is on lead against a notrump slam, a double by you calls for the dummy's first-bid suit to be led, the same as when you double a 3 NT bid. For example:

Opp.	Partner	Opp.	You	♠ A K 3
1 ◊	P	1 ♠	P	♡ 9 7 4 3 2
2 NT	P	3 ♣	P	◊ 6 4
3 NT	P	6 NT	DBL	♣ 10 8 5

Your double calls for a spade lead, the first suit bid by the dummy.

When your opponents bid a slam as a sacrifice bid, lead-directing doubles do not apply. For example:

Opp.	Partner	Opp.	You	♠ 7
			1 ♡	♡ A K Q 9 8
1 ♠	2 ◊	4 ♠	5 ◊	◊ A Q 5 3
5 ♠	6 ◊	6 ♠	DBL	♣ 7 4 2

The opponents are obviously sacrificing against a slam they think you can make. Your double of 6 ♠ is simply because you do not think your side should bid any higher and you expect to beat the contract, possibly several tricks; it is *not* a lead-directing double.

RESCUE BIDS AND THE S-O-S REDOUBLE

When Partner's Overcall Has Been Doubled for Penalty

When your partner's overcall gets doubled for penalty and you are short in his suit, you may bid your own suit provided your suit is very substantial (such as K-Q-J-10-X, or Q-10-9-X-X-X). Do not rescue without a good suit, especially if you have to raise the level of bidding to bid it. For example:

Opp.	Partner	Opp.	You	♠ Q 9 6 5 2
1 ♠	2 ♣	DBL	P	♡ 7 3
				◊ K J 8 7 4
				♣ 6

Although it looks like your partner is in trouble at 2 ♣ doubled, your diamond suit is too weak to rescue him.

Opp.	Partner	Opp.	You	♠ 8 5 2
1 ♠	2 ◊	DBL	2 ♡	♡ Q 10 9 7 4 3
				◊ 4
				♣ 6 5 3

This time your suit is sufficiently strong and you should rescue your partner. If you exchange your hearts and clubs (so you have ♡ 6-5-3 and ♣ Q-10-9-7-4-3), a pass is recommended; you need an even stronger suit to rescue your partner when you must raise the level of bidding.

When your partner's overcall gets doubled for penalty and you have extreme length (at least 5-5) in the two unbid suits, you may rescue by redoubling; this is the S-O-S redouble, and your partner must bid one of the two unbid suits. (This is a very risky bid unless you trust your partner to understand its meaning; if he passes, the redoubled penalty may read like a telephone number.) For example:

Opp.	Partner	Opp.	You	♠ Q 9 8 7 5
1 ♡	2 ♣	DBL	RDBL	♡ 6 3
				◊ 10 9 7 6 4 2
				♣ —

Your partner is expected to bid whichever of the two unbid suits (diamonds or spades) he prefers. Suppose you are on the other side of the table:

Opp.	Partner	Opp.	You	♠ K 6 3
		1 ♡	2 ♣	♡ K 10 8
DBL	RDBL	P	2 ♠	◊ J
				♣ A Q 10 7 5 2

Your partner's redouble asks you to choose between diamonds and spades, so you *must* bid 2 ♠. Note that if you get doubled in 2 ♠, you will fare much better than you would in 2 ♣ doubled, or redoubled.

When an Opponent Has Passed His Partner's Takeout Double

If you get doubled for *penalty* in a suit at the one-level or two-level, it is wrong to redouble if you think you can make your contract; you will get a good score if you pass and make it, but you will give the opponents a chance to run to another contract if you redouble. Therefore the redouble is used as a distress signal, asking your partner to rescue you by bidding another suit. So the S-O-S redouble is used not only when your side has been doubled in an overcall, but also when an opponent has passed his partner's takeout double.

If your right-hand opponent has passed his partner's takeout double, you have in effect been doubled for penalty. Logically your right-hand opponent must have a very powerful holding in your suit to pass, because he expects to beat you at the one-level and collect a sizable penalty. If you have a long and strong suit—very unlikely—you should, of course, pass, but if you have a weak suit you should run to a safer contract. If your cards in the other suits are evenly divided—you do not know which suit to run to—you may redouble and ask your partner to bid his longest unbid suit. For example:

♠ 9 8 6 5	You	Opp.	Partner	Opp.
♡ A Q 3	1 ♣	DBL	P	P
◊ A 5 4	RDBL			
♣ A 6 2				

If you pass, the final contract is 1 ♣ doubled, and that will not be good, so here is the perfect situation to redouble and ask your partner to rescue you by bidding his longest suit. If you do not trust your partner to understand the meaning of your S-O-S redouble, this is not recommended; if he passes 1 ♣ redoubled you may suffer a 2200-point penalty instead of 1100. The best way to handle this bidding if you do not trust your partner is to bid 1 ◊; if they double that, run to 1 ♠. You are in trouble and should be happy to play any contract undoubled. If the worst happens you will probably wind up in 1 NT doubled, but what usually develops is that an opponent bids someplace along the line and lets you off the hook, or your partner wakes up and bids a long suit if he has one. Suppose you are on the other side of the table:

Opp.	Partner	Opp.	You	♠ 8 7 4
	1 ♣	DBL	P	♡ 10 9 8 7 2
P	RDBL	P	1 ♡	◊ 9 7 6 3
				♣ 3

You must be alert to the meaning of your partner's redouble and bid your longest suit. As you can see, 1 ♡ is a cozy contract, but if you play 1 ♣ redoubled it will be a disaster. Do not pass your partner's S-O-S redouble, not even when you must bid a four-card suit and have a few cards in the redoubled suit.

When you redouble a takeout double it shows a strong hand; it is *not* the S-O-S redouble. For example:

♠ A K 5 2	You	Opp.	Partner	Opp.
♡ A J 6	1 ♣	P	P	DBL
◊ 4	RDBL			
♣ A K J 10 9				

Your redouble here shows a strong hand and says you can make your 1 ♣ contract, although you do not expect your opponents to let you play it. The purpose of the redouble is to prepare for a competitive auction, to encourage your partner to enter the bidding even though he is known to have a very poor hand.

It may be necessary for the responder to do the rescuing. For example:

Opp.	Partner	Opp.	You	♠ 8 7 4
	1 ♣	P	P	♡ 10 9 8 7 2
DBL	P	P	1 ♡	◊ 9 7 6 3
				♣ 3

Your partner's pass does not mean he has a good hand or a good club suit. If you pass your partner will be left to play 1 ♣ doubled, so it is obviously right to bid 1 ♡ and rescue him. If you take away one of your little hearts and add a little spade, so you have four cards in each of the unbid suits, your proper action would be to redouble—an S-O-S redouble to ask your partner to bid his longest and strongest unbid suit.

13

Balancing

♣   ♦   ♥   ♠   ♣   ♦   ♥   ♠

You are in the balancing seat when you and your partner have never entered the auction and the last bid was made by your left-hand opponent; if you pass, the bidding is over. When you are in the balancing seat and your opponents have stopped bidding below game, it sometimes pays to overcall or double with a weaker hand than is required when you are in the "direct seat."

How much weaker might your hand be to enter the bidding when you are in the balancing seat? Provided the auction is right, a good rule of thumb is to overbid by 3 points; pretend that you have an extra king in your hand and bid accordingly for the rest of the auction. The logic to this scheme will be explained as we go along.

WHEN ONE OF A SUIT IS PASSED

It is not always safe to bid with shaded values in the balancing seat, depending on the auction. One of the best times is when your right-hand opponent passes his partner in a suit bid of one, because the bidding is still very low and you will be able to play the hand better with the knowledge that one defender has most of the missing high cards. The vulnerability might influence how daring you might be, but the following illustrations assume that the recommended bid would be correct regardless of the vulnerability unless a specific vulnerability is stated:

Opp.	Partner	Opp.	You	
1 ♠	P	P	2 ♡	♠ 7 2
				♡ A Q 10 8 2
				◇ K J 5
				♣ 9 7 4

This hand is clearly too weak for a 2 ♡ overcall in the direct seat, but in the balancing seat the requirements are not so strict.

Opp.	Partner	Opp.	You	♠ A Q J 9 3
1 ◊	P	P	DBL	♡ 7 2
				◊ 8 4
				♣ A K Q 5

You must overbid your strong hands too. An overcall shows about 9 to 17 points, so in the direct seat the right bid is 1 ♠. When you add 3 points this hand becomes worth 20 points; it is too strong for an overcall in the balancing seat, so you must double first with the intention of bidding your long suit later.

Opp.	Partner	Opp.	You	♠ 9 5 4
1 ♡	P	P	1 NT	♡ K 10 2
				◊ A Q 10 6
				♣ K J 8

You should pass this 13-point hand in the direct seat, because a 1 NT overcall would show 16 to 18 points. If you follow the rule that you should overbid by 3 points in the balancing seat, the requirement for a 1 NT overcall would be 13 to 15 points; but most experts prefer to overcall 1 NT in the balancing seat with even weaker hands, as low as 11 or 12 points. My recommendation is you play 1 NT overcalls in the balancing seat to show 12 to 15 points and, of course, at least one stopper in the opponent's suit.

Opp.	Partner	Opp.	You	♠ A 6 3
1 ♡	P	P	DBL	♡ Q J 5
				◊ K Q 10
				♣ A J 9 4

This 17-point hand is perfect for a 1 NT overcall in the direct seat. In the balancing seat you must overbid by 3 points; so double first and bid notrump at your next turn to show an actual 16 to 18 points, or a mythical 19 to 21.

Opp.	Partner	Opp.	You	♠ A J 10
1 ♠	P	P	2 NT	♡ K 4 2
				◊ A Q J 8
				♣ K Q 5

In the direct seat you should double with this 20-point hand and plan to bid notrump later; a direct 2 NT overcall would be the "unusual notrump." The unusual 2 NT overcall is not used in the balancing position; the 2 NT bid shows a balanced hand with 19 to 21 points.

Opp.	Partner	Opp.	You	♠ 3
1 ♡	P	P	2 ◊	♡ 5 2
				◊ A K J 9 8
				♣ Q J 10 5 4

Since the unusual notrump is not played in the balancing seat, the only logical bid is the higher-ranking of your two five-card suits.

Opp.	Partner	Opp.	You	♠ A J 6
1 ◊	P	P	DBL	♡ A 9 4
				◊ 7 3 2
				♣ Q 10 7 5

Doubling with this mediocre hand in the direct seat is unthinkable; but doubling in the balancing seat with only 11 points and 4-3-3-3 distribution is okay. The opponents have advertised weakness, so it is safe to enter the bidding, and your partner will take into account that your double may be 3 points weaker.

Opp.	Partner	Opp.	You	♠ A 10 7
1 ♣	P	P	P	♡ K 5
				◊ 7 6 3
				♣ K Q J 9 8

You will probably beat the 1 ♣ contract, and this is your best chance for a profit. A bid of 1 NT is conceivable, but a double is out, as that would be for takeout. You should pass in the direct seat also.

Opp.	Partner	Opp.	You	♠ 10 7 3
1 ♠	P	P	P	♡ 9 5
				◊ K 8 6 3 2
				♣ A 10 4

You do not always bid in the balancing seat. Even after you add the 3 imaginary points, this hand does not qualify for any bid.

When your partner overcalls or doubles in the balancing seat, you must be aware that he is consistently overbidding by about 3 points. As a corrective measure, you, the responder, must underbid by about 3 points. For example:

Opp.	Partner	Opp.	You	♠ A Q 3
		1 ♡	P	♡ A 9 8
P	1 ♠	P	2 ♠	◊ 10 4 3
				♣ Q 7 6 4

If partner overcalled 1 ♠ in the direct seat, a raise to 2 ♠ would show 7 to 11 points and a jump to 3 ♠ would show 12 to 14, so the right bid with this hand would be 3 ♠. Since partner is in the balancing seat, you must underbid by 3 points.

Opp.	Partner	Opp.	You	♠ 9 6 4
		1 ♠	P	♡ K J 10
P	1 NT	P	P	◊ 8 5 3
				♣ A Q 5 2

If partner overcalled 1 NT in the direct seat, showing 16 to 18 points, your normal response would be 3 NT with 10 points. His 1 NT overcall in the balancing seat shows 12 to 15 points, so your hand is too weak to try for game.

Opp.	Partner	Opp.	You	♠ 7 2
		1 ♠	P	♡ A Q 9
P	1 NT	P	2 NT	◇ A 8 6 3
				♣ Q 5 4 2

Your partner's 1 NT bid shows 12 to 15 points, so your 2 NT bid is right with 11 or 12 points. Your partner should pass with 12 or 13 points, or bid 3 NT with 14 or 15.

Opp.	Partner	Opp.	You	♠ K Q 7 4
		1 ◇	P	♡ J 8 5
P	DBL	P	1 ♠	◇ 9 6 4
				♣ A J 2

If partner doubled in the direct seat, you should bid 2 ♠; with 10 to 12 points you must jump the bidding. Since partner is in the balancing seat you must underbid by 3 points, hence the nonjump 1 ♠ bid.

Opp.	Partner	Opp.	You	♠ Q 10 7 2
		1 ♡	P	♡ 6 4 3
P	DBL	P	2 ♠	◇ A K
				♣ A 8 5 2

Here you have 13 points, so even after you deduct 3 points you have a 10-point hand and must jump the bidding. If partner had doubled in the direct seat, your proper bid would be a cue-bid of 2 ♡; with this good-looking 13-point hand you should insist on reaching game. Note that it was right to pass over 1 ♡ with this hand, holding only two diamonds.

Opp.	Partner	Opp.	You	♠ K 7
		1 ♣	P	♡ K 10 6
P	DBL	P	P	◇ 4 3 2
				♣ A Q 10 8 5

You could not have hoped for a better auction. If your left-hand opponent passes 1 ♣ doubled, you will reap a handsome profit.

Once you have overcalled or doubled in the balancing seat, you must continue to overbid by 3 points in your subsequent bidding. Compare the two following auctions:

Opp.	Partner	Opp.	You	♠ J 8 6 4
		1 ◇	DBL	♡ A K J 4
P	1 ♠	P	P	◇ 7 2
				♣ A 9 3

With a minimum double, 14 points, you must pass. You need 16 to 18 points to bid 2 ♠.

Opp.	Partner	Opp.	You	♠ J 8 6 4
1 ◇	P	P	DBL	♡ A K J 4
P	1 ♠	P	2 ♠	◇ 7 2
				♣ A 9 3

Since you have doubled in the balancing seat, you must treat your hand as being worth 17 points.

WHEN THE OPPONENTS HAVE SHOWN A FIT

Another "green-light auction" for balancing is when the opponents agree on a trump suit and then stop bidding at the two-level. For example:

Opp.	Partner	Opp.	You	♠ 10 8 6 5 3
		1 ♡	P	♡ 7 4 2
2 ♡	P	P	2 ♠	◇ A Q 8
				♣ Q 3

If you pass this hand, the bidding is over and the final contract will be 2 ♡. If you analyze why the opponents stopped bidding at 2 ♡, the obvious answer is that they did not have the 26 points needed to bid a game. They are counting about 3 or 4 points for distribution (both partners count points for short suits, as well as for high cards and long suits, when they discover a good trump fit) and therefore are unlikely to have more than about 20 high-card points between them. You have 8 high-card points and your opponents have about 20, so your partner has the balance, about 12 high-card points. Although your hand was too weak to bid 1 ♠ over 1 ♡, it is worthy of a 2 ♠ bid after this auction.

Opp.	Partner	Opp.	You	♠ K J 8 3
		1 ♡	P	♡ 7
2 ♡	P	P	DBL	◇ Q 10 5 2
				♣ K 9 7 3

This hand is too weak to double 1 ♡; if your partner had a poor hand you might be in trouble, or partner would expect a better hand and bid too much. To the contrary, it is much safer to double in the balancing seat because your partner is known to have values and he will not bid too much because he knows you were not good enough to double the first time.

Opp.	Partner	Opp.	You	♠ A 2
		1 ♡	P	♡ 6 4
2 ♡	P	P	2 NT	◇ K 10 8 7
				♣ Q 10 9 5 4

Here your 2 NT bid is unusual, asking partner to bid one of the minor suits; since you passed the first time, you cannot have a strong notrump-type hand. It would have been outlandish to make an unusual 2 NT bid directly over 1 ♡ with only nine cards in the minor suits, but the requirements are eased considerably after this auction.

The following three hands demonstrate how the responder should bid in the three preceding auctions:

Opp.	Partner	Opp.	You	♠ A 9 7
1 ♡	P	2 ♡	P	♡ J 8
P	2 ♠	P	P	◇ K 9 7 6
				♣ K 10 9 2

It should be clear that your partner was too weak to bid over 1 ♡, so there is no hope for game. It gets interesting if an opponent bids 3 ♡ over partner's 2 ♠ bid. It is tempting to bid 3 ♠, and it could be right, but you really should pass; it is unlikely that you can make 3 ♠, and you may set 3 ♡.

Opp.	Partner	Opp.	You	♠ Q 2
1 ♡	P	2 ♡	P	♡ J 10 3
P	DBL	P	3 ♢	♢ A K J 8 6
				♣ 6 5 4

Your partner's double is for takeout, so your 3 ♢ bid is routine. If the opponents bid 3 ♡ you should pass and hope to set them; it is very unlikely that you can make 4 ♢.

Opp.	Partner	Opp.	You	♠ K 10 7 3
1 ♡	P	2 ♡	P	♡ J 8 5
P	2 NT	P	3 ♢	♢ A Q 9 3
				♣ J 2

Your partner's 2 NT bid is unusual, asking you to choose between the two minor suits. So, once again, a 3 ♢ bid is routine.

Provided the auction is right, aggressive bidding in the balancing seat is a winning style. It may be that you and your partner can make a part-score or a game, but neither of you can bid, because your hand is slightly too weak to overcall or double. So you pass and wait. If the opponents bid strongly, you simply pass throughout. If they stop bidding at a low level and you find yourself in the balancing seat, it means they do not have the points needed to bid game and your partner has the balance of the points.

Some players are so elated when their opponents have stopped bidding in a part-score—instead of bidding a game or a slam—that they always pass; they are afraid if they reopen the bidding the opponents will change their minds and bid a game. But you should compete readily in these auctions, in the hope that you can push your opponents higher and set them, or outbid them and make a contract. Do not underrate the value of a part-score and give up too quickly when your opponents stop bidding below game. You may even occasionally push them into a game they can make, but the odds are heavily against them; you can expect them to fail if they bid game.

WHEN THE OPPONENTS HAVE NOT SHOWN A FIT

It is sometimes wrong, or at least risky, to bid with shaded values in the balancing seat. If the opponents' bidding implies that they have a misfit, or in some auction where notrump has been bid, you should not enter the bidding unless you have a sound hand. For example:

Opp.	Partner	Opp.	You	♠ 8 5 4
1 ♣	P	1 ♡	P	♡ Q 9
2 ♣	P	P	P	♢ K 10 7 3 2
				♣ A J 5

This bidding suggests that the opponents may have a misfit, and mathematical common sense suggests that both sides have a fit or both sides have a misfit. Also, the opponents do not count points for short suits when they have a misfit; they may have 23 or 24 high-card points between them, leaving only 16 or 17 for you and your partner. If you venture a 2 ♢ bid with this hand, you are asking for trouble.

Opp.	Partner	Opp.	You	♠ Q J 9 6 2
1 NT	P	P	P	♡ 7 6 4
				◊ A 5 3
				♣ K 10

The opening bidder has indicated 16 to 18 high-card points and his partner may pass with as many as 7, so your partner is apt to have a very weak hand. It is extremely dangerous to bid 2 ♠ here; if partner has a good hand you may make 2 ♠ and win 60 points, but if he has a bad hand you may get doubled and suffer a huge penalty.

Opp.	Partner	Opp.	You	♠ A 9 7 2
1 NT	P	P	?	♡ J 10 6
				◊ A K 5
				♣ Q 9 3

If you double a 1 NT opening bid in the balancing seat, your partner is supposed to pass if he can contribute something to the defense, or bid if he has a long suit and a weak hand; but what if he has a weak hand and no long suit? Many experts would elect to double with this hand and hope they get lucky, but at least they know they will be skillful in the subsequent bidding. My advice to you is to pass with this kind of hand; leave the hair-raising doubles of 1 NT to the experts.

Opp.	Partner	Opp.	You	♠ A 9 7 2
1 NT	P	P	P	♡ 8
				◊ A Q 6 2
				♣ K J 4 3

If you double with this hand your partner will bid hearts, or he will pass 1 NT doubled and lead a heart. Both roads lead to disaster.

Opp.	Partner	Opp.	You	♠ 10 9 7 2
		1 NT	P	♡ 8
2 ♡	P	P	DBL	◊ A Q 6 2
				♣ K J 4 3

This is the same hand as the preceding illustration, except I have replaced the ♠ A with the ♠ 10, and yet a takeout double of 2 ♡ is clearly right on this auction. Your partner knows you want him to bid a suit other than hearts, and your left-hand opponent has revealed that he has a weak hand—0 to 7 points. It sounds like the opponents have about 20 high-card points between them, about 17 on the right and about 3 on the left. The time to bid with shaded values is when you have the right type of hand for an overcall or a takeout double and the opponents have sent out a weakness signal.

14

Bidding Over Preemptive Bids

♣   ♦   ♥   ♠   ♣   ♦   ♥   ♠

When an opponent opens the bidding with a preemptive bid, you and your partner may have to do some helter-skelter bidding in an effort to get to your best contract. Deprived of so much bidding space, scientific bidding is minimized considerably; you must rely heavily on good judgment (and good luck) to achieve the maximum result.

Balancing plays an important part in the strategy for bidding over preemptive bids. If your right-hand opponent opens the bidding with a preemptive bid, do not enter the bidding unless you have sound values, especially if you are vulnerable. If your left-hand opponent opens the bidding with a preemptive bid *below the game level* and it is passed around to you, you should often bid with doubtful values; here is where you do your gambling.

The vulnerability may sometimes influence your decision whether or not to enter the bidding over an opening preemptive bid, but, unless otherwise stated, the actions in the following illustrations are recommended regardless of the vulnerability. To get started, here is how to decide when you should, and when you should not, overcall in a suit.

SUIT OVERCALLS OF PREEMPTIVE BIDS

Opp.	You	
		♠ A Q 10 8 5
3 ♡	P	♡ 7 2
		◇ A Q 4
		♣ 9 5 2

You would, of course, overcall a 1 ♡ opening bid with 1 ♠, but your suit is too weak to venture a bid at the three-level. If you are unlucky and find your left-hand opponent with good spades and a strong hand, he would double 3 ♠ and you would probably be set several tricks. Also, your partner might bid game on hands where even 3 ♠ would fail; he would expect your hand to have more offensive strength.

Opp.	*Partner*	*Opp.*	*You*	♠ A Q 10 8 5
3 ♡	P	P	3 ♠	♡ 7 2
				◊ A Q 4
				♣ 9 5 2

Your right-hand opponent's pass of 3 ♡ indicates that his hand is limited, so your partner is marked with at least a fairly good hand. Also, if your partner is short in spades, you will not encounter a trump stack *behind* you. Another reason for bidding is that partner will not bid game unless he has a strong hand; he knows you might be bidding with shaky values in the balancing seat. As was stated earlier, bid soundly in the direct seat and do your gambling in the balancing seat.

Opp.	*You*	♠ A Q 9 8 5 2
3 ◊	3 ♠	♡ 9 3
		◊ 5
		♣ A K J 3

You have a good spade suit and excellent distribution. There is not much chance that you will be doubled and set, and if partner bids a game (or a slam) you should make it easily; he will not be disappointed with this hand.

If the bidding went opponent 3 ◊ , partner P, opponent P, you are in the balancing seat and should bid 4 ♠ ; you must gamble that partner has the meager values needed to make a game. If you bid only 3 ♠ , he will expect a weaker hand and may pass with sufficient values to make game.

Opp.	*You*	♠ A Q J 10 9 2
3 ♡	3 ♠	♡ 4
		◊ K J 4
		♣ 7 6 5

This hand qualifies for an overcall at the three-level by virtue of its strong suit. Your partner may expect a better hand and bid game without the values you need to make it. Then again, he may have the values to bid a makable game. Another thought is that your defensive strength is limited and the opponents may be able to make 4 ♡ ; there may be a double game swing, or you may have a good sacrifice.

Opp.	*You*	♠ 4
3 ♠	P	♡ A Q J 10 9 2
		◊ K J 4
		♣ 7 6 5

Logically, you need a better hand to bid at the four-level than at the three-level, but a 4 ♡ bid is conceivable here with favorable vulnerability. If you had a seven-card heart suit in the same hand, a 4 ♡ bid would be good with any vulnerability.

The strategy for bidding in the balancing seat with shaded values applies when the opponents have stopped bidding *below* game, because you can then predict that your partner has values. *The balancing theory does not work over opening preemptive bids at the game level;* the requirements to bid in the balancing seat are about the same as in the direct seat. However, the *location* of honor cards might influence you to gamble a bit more in the balancing seat. For example:

Opp.	Partner	Opp.	You	
4 ♠	P	P	5 ♡	♠ 7
				♡ A Q 10 6 4 3
				◇ A 10 5 3
				♣ 8 2

If you are lucky, you may make 5 ♡, get doubled in 5 ♡ and find that it is a good sacrifice against a makable 4 ♠ contract, or push the opponents to 5 ♠ and set them. If you are unlucky you may get doubled and be set a few tricks. The 5 ♡ bid is a better gamble in the balancing seat than it would be in the direct seat because if the trumps are stacked against you, the missing heart honors will be in front of—instead of behind—your A-Q-10.

A cue-bid of the opening preemptive bidder's suit shows a powerhouse, just as it does over an opening one-bid. The responder is expected to bid one of the unbid suits, and he needs very little to bid a slam. For example:

Opp.	You	
3 ♠	4 ♠	♠ —
		♡ A Q 10 2
		◇ A Q 7 4 3
		♣ A K J 10

If your partner bids 5 ♣, 5 ◇, or 5 ♡, you should pass, as he may have a very poor hand. If a slam can be made, it is up to your partner to bid it.

If your partner overcalls a preemptive bid in the direct seat, he has a sound hand, especially when he is vulnerable. If your partner overcalls a preemptive bid below game in the balancing seat, he may be bidding with shaky values, especially when he is not vulnerable. As a responder, you must take these factors into account. For example:

Opp.	Partner	Opp.	You	
3 ♡	3 ♠	P	4 ♠	♠ K 8
				♡ 5 4 2
				◇ 10 9 7 6 3
				♣ A Q 4

The 4 ♠ bid is recommended regardless of the vulnerability, but you should feel more comfortable doing so when your side is vulnerable, as partner can be relied upon to have a substantial trump suit.

Opp.	Partner	Opp.	You	
		3 ♡	P	♠ K 8
P	3 ♠	P	P	♡ 5 4 2
				◇ 10 9 7 6 3
				♣ A Q 4

You must give your partner leeway, as he may bid with a relatively weak hand in the balancing seat. It is not unlikely that he will be set in 3 ♠.

NOTRUMP OVERCALLS OF PREEMPTIVE BIDS

The point-count requirements to overcall an opening three-bid with 3 NT are hard to define; it depends on how much of a gambler you are. My suggestion for the minimum requirements is at least 18 or 19 points in the direct seat and at least 15 or 16 points in the balancing seat. You may also overcall an opening three-bid in the direct or balancing seat with 25 or 26 points, so your partner may have a difficult time figuring out whether or not to bid a slam. In all cases you must, of course, have at least one stopper in the enemy's suit. Here are three examples:

Opp.	Partner	Opp.	You	
3 ♡	P	P	3 NT	♠ K 4 2
				♡ A J 10
				◊ K J 10 7
				♣ K 10 5

This is a brash bid with only 15 points, but the fact that you have three tens should help; you should be able to make a game more often than not.

In the direct seat, you should pass this hand. It is too weak for 3 NT and the wrong kind of hand for any other bid.

Opp.	You	
3 ♡	3 NT	♠ K 9
		♡ A J 8
		◊ A K J 7 3
		♣ K 10 2

This hand is simply too strong to pass, and 3 NT is the most sensible bid. You have 20 points and it is reasonable to gamble that your partner can contribute about 6 points—with luck the right points.

You should also bid 3 NT in the balancing seat.

Opp.	You	
3 ♡	3 NT	♠ A J
		♡ A J 6
		◊ A K Q J 3
		♣ K J 2

You have 25 points and it may seem that you should make a stronger bid than 3 NT, but if you bid anything else you may get yourself beyond the reaches of a makable game. Since your partner will not expect such a strong hand, it is not unlikely that he will pass 3 NT when you can make a slam.

You should also bid 3 NT in the balancing seat.

Over an opening bid of 3 ♡ or 3 ♠, you may bid 4 NT with two very long and strong minor suits. This is another version of the "unusual notrump overcall." For example:

Opp.	You	
3 ♡	4 NT	♠ 7 3
		♡ —
		◊ A K J 9 2
		♣ A J 10 8 5 4

Your 4 NT bid asks your partner to choose between clubs and diamonds. Note that you need a very substantial hand to force your partner to bid at such a high level You should make the same 4 NT bid over a 3 ♠ opening bid.

A 4 NT overcall of an opening 4 ♡ or 4 ♠ bid is for takeout. A 4 NT overcall of 4 ♡ is takeout for the *two minor suits* (the unusual notrump), but a 4 NT overcall of 4 ♠ is takeout for *the three unbid suits*. For example:

Opp.	*You*	♠ 7
4 ♡	4 NT	♡ 3
		◊ A Q J 7 6 4
		♣ K Q J 10 2

Your 4 NT bid over the 4 ♡ opening bid asks your partner to choose between the two minor suits.

   If the opening bid were 4 ♣, you should simply bid 5 ◊; a bid of 4 NT would show support for hearts as well as clubs and diamonds.

Opp.	*You*	♠ —
4 ♠	4 NT	♡ A Q 10 6
		◊ A K 9 4
		♣ K 9 7 3 2

This is the kind of hand you show when you bid 4 NT over 4 ♠, support for all three unbid suits; it is like a takeout double. Note that you need a strong hand with excellent distribution to force your partner to bid at such a high level.

Here are two hands to show you the responder's action when his partner makes a 4 NT overcall:

Opp.	*Partner*	*Opp.*	*You*	♠ 10 8 7
4 ♠	4 NT	P	5 ♡	♡ 9 7 5 4 3
				◊ 8 2
				♣ A 6 4

Partner has shown a very strong hand, so, with a five-card suit and an ace, you would be unlucky to go down in 5 ♡. If you had another useful high card (for example, your heart suit was K-7-5-4-3), you would be justified in bidding 6 ♡.

Opp.	*Partner*	*Opp.*	*You*	♠ K Q 9 4 3
4 ♡	4 NT	P	5 ◊	♡ 7 6 5
				◊ 10 8 3
				♣ 8 2

Your partner will need an excellent hand if you are going to make 5 ◊, but you have no choice but to bid it once he bids 4 NT.

DOUBLES OF PREEMPTIVE BIDS

This subject must be divided into two parts: doubles of preemptive bids *below* the game level, and doubles of preemptive bids *at* the game level. There is a huge difference in the meanings of the doubles.

Below the Game Level

A double of an opening preemptive bid below the game level is a *takeout double*. The requirements are similar to those for doubles of opening suit bids of one, but since you will be forcing your partner to bid at the three-level or four-level you need a better hand. As with overcalls, doubling preemptive bids requires sounder values in the direct seat than in the balancing seat. Here are three hands to illustrate the minimum requirements:

Opp.	*You*	♠ K 10 5 3
3 ♡	P	♡ 8 3
		♢ A J 10
		♣ K J 6 2

It would be right to double an opening bid of one heart with this hand, but with 4-4-3 in the unbid suits you need a stronger hand to force your partner to bid at the three-level or four-level.

Consistent with the theory that you may bid with shaded values in the balancing seat, if the bidding went opponent 3 ♡, partner P, opponent P, you should double with this hand.

Opp.	*You*	♠ A J 7 4
3 ♡	DBL	♡ 5
		♢ A 10 6 2
		♣ K J 10 9

With 4-4-4 in the unbid suits, it is okay to double with just 13 points.

Opp.	*You*	♠ A Q 6
3 ♡	P	♡ 7 4 3
		♢ A 8
		♣ K Q 9 3 2

When your hand does not fit the pattern for a takeout double and your long suit is too weak to bid, it may be wise to pass with a strong hand. It is very likely that you will get into serious trouble if you bid with this hand.

If you are in the balancing seat, take a chance and double. The double could turn out to be a disaster (for example, partner may bid 4 ♢ with a mediocre suit), but then you could easily miss a game if you pass. The key is to take chances in the balancing seat, lest both you and your partner pass with good hands.

Since any double of an opening preemptive bid below game is for takeout, you have no choice but to pass with many hands that you would like to double for penalty. For example:

Opp.	*You*	♠ K J 9 8
3 ♣	P	♡ 4 3
		♢ A Q 6
		♣ A 10 7 2

Although it appears that the best result for your side would be to play 3 ♣ doubled, you have no choice but to pass. However, there is still a chance to play 3 ♣ doubled; if partner makes a takeout double in the balancing seat, you will pass.

When your partner doubles an opening preemptive bid below the game level, it is a takeout double; you *must* bid unless you have length and strength in the opponent's suit and judge that a pass will give you the most profitable result. For example:

Opp.	Partner	Opp.	You	♠ 8 2
		3 ♡	P	♡ K 10 9 7
P	DBL	P	P	◇ K J 4
				♣ 9 7 5 2

The only conceivable bid with this hand is 3 NT, but it is unlikely that you would make it; partner may have doubled with shaky values in the balancing seat, and you will need a strong dummy to make 3 NT. The surest profit, and possibly the biggest profit, is the amount you will win for beating 3 ♡ doubled.

Opp.	Partner	Opp.	You	♠ 9 7 5 4
3 ♡	DBL	P	3 ♠	♡ Q 6
				◇ Q 8 5 2
				♣ 10 6 4

You may be in trouble if you get doubled in 3 ♠ and your partner has a minimum double, but you must *not* pass from fright. If you pass, the opponents will score a game unless your partner has a powerhouse; and if your partner has a powerhouse, you will not get into trouble if you bid 3 ♠.

Opp.	Partner	Opp.	You	♠ A Q 10 4
3 ♡	DBL	P	4 ♠	♡ 8 2
				◇ J 9 8 3
				♣ Q 7 5

As you learned in Chapter 11, Takeout Doubles, if your partner doubles an opening suit bid of one and you have from 10 to 12 points, you must jump the bidding. When your partner doubles an opening suit bid of three he must have a stronger hand, so you should jump the bidding with a weaker hand, as few as 8 or 9 points. If you bid just 3 ♠, how is your partner to judge whether you have this hand, which is pretty good, or the preceding hand, which is terrible?

   If your partner had doubled 3 ♡ in the balancing seat, you should bid only 3 ♠; since he may have a weaker hand, you should underbid to compensate.

   When you double a preemptive bid and your partner dutifully bids a suit, he may have absolutely nothing, so you should not bid again unless you have a powerful hand. For example:

Opp.	Partner	Opp.	You	♠ K J 6 2
		3 ♡	DBL	♡ 7 3
P	3 ♠	P	P	◇ K Q 10 4
				♣ A K 8

To bid 4 ♠ with this hand would be a big mistake. If you look back to the two preceding examples, you will see that your partner would have bid 4 ♠ if you could make it. You need a much more substantial hand than this one to bid again over 3 ♠.

At the Game Level

A double of an opening 5 ♣ or 5 ◇ bid is for penalty; to this nearly everyone agrees. But the double of an opening 4 ♡ or 4 ♠ bid is controversial; the authorities do not agree whether the double should be for penalty, for takeout, or "optional." One popular method is to play a double of 4 ♡ as takeout and a double of 4 ♠ as penalty; to begin with I do not think this is a good way to play, but more important, these doubles are rare and most partnerships have no agreement or one of the players may forget. Here is an actual hand to demonstrate my point:

Bill Root	Opp.	♠ A 10 9 4 2
4 ♠	DBL	♡ J 7 6
		◊ 3
		♣ A Q 8 4

This was my left-hand opponent's hand; they were vulnerable and we were not. My right-hand opponent was void in spades and held ◊ Q-J-10-9-X-X-X, so instead of passing his partner's double he bid 5 ◊. My partner doubled 5 ◊ and we set them 1100 points, while 4 ♠ doubled would have been set one trick. The opponents had no agreement as to the meaning of the double—this is usually the case—so who is to blame?

The most important thing is to avoid a disastrous partnership misunderstanding, so my suggestion is: Never double an opening 4 ♡ or 4 ♠ bid unless you are prepared for your partner to bid or pass—the optional double. If you decide to play this way, the requirements to double an opening 4 ♡ or 4 ♠ bid are that you have at least three and a half quick tricks (high cards that will win tricks for your partner in case he bids, or against the opponent's contract in case he passes) and no singletons or voids in any of the unbid suits. Also, over a 4 ♡ opening bid, it is a good idea to have at least three cards in the spade suit. Here are three examples:

Opp.	You	♠ A 3
4 ♠	DBL	♡ 9 4
		◊ A Q 8 7 2
		♣ A K 10 2

If your partner passes, it looks like you have the tickets to beat 4 ♠ doubled. If your partner bids 5 ♡ he must have a good suit, as your double did not promise more than two cards in any suit (it was *not* a takeout double); even so he will be disappointed with your poor heart support, but he will be delighted with your four and a half quick tricks.

Opp.	You	♠ J 10 8
4 ♡	DBL	♡ A 5 3
		◊ K 7
		♣ A K 6 4 3

With three and a half quick tricks, no voids or singletons in the unbid suits, and three cards in the spade suit, it is okay to double.

Opp.	You	♠ K J 9 2
4 ♠	P	♡ A 8 7 3
		◊ A J 6
		♣ J 7

As I said earlier, do not double an opening 4 ♡ or 4 ♠ bid unless you do not care whether your partner bids or not; here you certainly do not want him to bid. If you double with this kind of hand, you can usually expect your partner to bid; he is obviously very short in spades (maybe void) and probably has a long suit.

If the *responder* makes a preemptive bid by raising his partner's opening 1 ♡ bid to 4 ♡, or 1 ♠ to 4 ♠, your double would be primarily for takeout; it shows good support for the three unbid suits and asks your partner to bid. For example:

Opp.	Partner	Opp.	You	
1 ♡	P	4 ♡	DBL	♠ K 10 8 2
				♡ 8
				◇ A K J 5
				♣ K J 10 4

Your partner should picture that you have this distribution and bid his longest suit—possibly a four-card suit—but since the bidding is so high, he may pass if he judges that defending 4 ♡ doubled will bring your side the best result. The meaning of your double would be the same if the opening bid were 2 ♡—a weak two-bid—or 3 ♡ instead of 1 ♡.

When your partner doubles a 4 ♡ or 4 ♠ opening bid his double is optional; the onus is on you to decide whether bidding or passing will bring the best result. If you just follow your instincts you will be right most of the time; bid when you feel like bidding, and pass when you feel like passing. Although the vulnerability may sometimes influence your decision, the bids in the following illustrations are recommended regardless of the vulnerability:

Opp.	Partner	Opp.	You	
4 ♡	DBL	P	P	♠ J 9 6 2
				♡ 8 2
				◇ A 8 5 4
				♣ 8 7 3

It is possible that you can make a game, but partner's double promises only three spades and two diamonds—not nearly enough trump support for you to chance bidding a four-card suit.

If partner doubled a 3 ♡ opening bid, his double is for takeout and it would be right to bid your four-card spade suit.

Opp.	Partner	Opp.	You	
4 ♡	DBL	P	4 ♠	♠ Q 10 7 6 2
				♡ 8 7 3
				◇ 3
				♣ 10 9 8 4

With a decent five-card suit and good distribution, there is a fair chance you can make a game in spades. Also, since you have no defensive tricks, it is not unlikely that the opponents would make 4 ♡ doubled if you pass.

Opp.	Partner	Opp.	You	
4 ♠	DBL	P	P	♠ 7 2
				♡ 6 5
				◇ A J 10 9 8 3
				♣ 10 7 4

You have an ace, so you should beat 4 ♠ doubled a trick or two. It would be optimistic to bid 5 ◇, because your partner cannot be expected to have the enormous hand you need to make it.

Opp.	Partner	Opp.	You	♠ 2
4 ♠	DBL	P	5 ◇	♡ 6 5
				◇ A J 10 9 8 3
				♣ Q 10 7 4

This hand with 6-4-2-1 distribution is much better than the last. Your partner has three-and-a-half or more useful quick tricks, so you should have a good chance to make 5 ◇ even if partner's trump support is not very good.

BIDDING OVER WEAK TWO-BIDS

If your opponents are playing weak two-bids, an opening bid of 2 ◇, 2 ♡, or 2 ♠ shows a hand with 5 to 11 high-card points and usually a good six-card suit (see page 87). A weak two-bid is sort of a "mini-preempt."

The requirements to overcall or double a weak two-bid are about the same as the requirements to overcall or double an opening suit bid of one, if you take into account the bidding is one level higher. Also, you may bid in the balancing seat with a weaker hand than in the direct seat, the same strategy as is used over any other opening suit bid below the game-level. Here are three examples:

Opp.	You	♠ A J 8 6 3
2 ♡	?	♡ 7 2
		◇ A J 8 5
		♣ 4 2

This is a close decision. My judgment is to bid 2 ♠ with favorable vulnerability, but to pass with equal or unfavorable. If you are in the balancing seat (the bidding has gone opponent 2 ♡, partner P, opponent P), you should definitely bid 2 ♠ regardless of the vulnerability. Also, if the opening bid were 1 ♡, you should overcall 1 ♠ in the direct seat regardless of the vulnerability.

Opp.	You	♠ K Q 10
2 ♠	2 NT	♡ A 4 3
		◇ A J 8
		♣ K Q 10 7

The point-count requirement to overcall a weak two-bid with 2 NT is 16 to 19. You must, of course, have at least one stopper in the opponent's suit. (Note that the "unusual 2 NT overcall" is not played over weak two-bids.)

In the balancing seat you should add 3 points to your actual point count and bid accordingly. Since this 19-point hand becomes worth 22, you should gamble and bid 3 NT.

Opp.	You	♠ K J 7 2
2 ◇	?	♡ A Q 9
		◇ 5 4
		♣ Q 10 8 3

Here is another close decision. My judgment is to double with favorable vulnerability, but to pass with equal or unfavorable. If the 2 ◇ bid is passed around to you in the balancing seat, you should double regardless of the vulnerability. Also, if the opening bid were 1 ◇, you should double in the direct seat regardless of the vulnerability.

15

Responses and Rebids in Competitive Auctions

♣   ♦   ♥   ♠   ♣   ♦   ♥   ♠

We are concerned here with the responses and rebids that take place after the opponents intervene with an overcall or a takeout double. You will often find that the same bid is available as in a noncompetitive auction and it will have the same meaning, while at other times the opponent's intervention deprives you of a bid or changes the meaning of a bid entirely. Other bids become possible after the opponents bid, such as a double, a redouble, or a strategic pass with a good hand when your right-hand opponent has made the last bid.

In some cases an opposing overcall or double will complicate your action; you must accept that and loosen up your bidding. It may be necessary to make a bid with a point or two less than is required in a noncompetitive auction, or to pass with a reasonably good hand.

It is not all bad news when the opponents bid. Sometimes you get information to help you get to the optimum contract, or to make a contract because their bidding revealed something about the location of the missing cards.

How to handle yourself in competitive auctions is described in great detail in the following pages.

RESPONSES AFTER AN OPPONENT OVERCALLS

If your partner opens the bidding with a suit bid of one and your right-hand opponent overcalls, any response by you is voluntary and called a "free bid." You are not required to keep the bidding open with 6 points, as partner will get another chance to bid even if you pass; in some cases it is right to pass with as many as 9 or 10 points. The requirements for the various free bids (and passes) are described by the following categories: raising partner's suit, responses at the one-level, responses in a suit at the two-level, responses in a suit at the three-level, 2 NT and 3 NT responses, the jump-shift response, cue-bidding the overcaller's suit, and responses after a 1 NT overcall. Penalty doubles of overcalls are omitted in this chapter; they can be found in Chapter 12, page 130.

Raising Partner's Suit

A single raise of your partner's suit shows 6 to 10 points and adequate trump support—at least three trumps to raise a major suit and at least four trumps to raise a minor suit. For example:

Partner	Opp.	You	
1 ◇	1 ♠	2 ◇	♠ 8 3
			♡ Q 6 2
			◇ Q 9 6 4
			♣ A 10 7 2

If your partner opened the bidding with 1 ♡, you should bid 2 ♡. The meaning of a single raise is virtually unaffected by an opponent's nonjump overcall.

The requirements to jump-raise an opening suit bid of one to the three-level are 13 to 16 points and at least four-card support, but over an intervening overcall it is sometimes necessary to shade the point-count requirement slightly or jump-raise with three strong trumps. For example:

Partner	Opp.	You	
1 ♡	2 ◇	3 ♡	♠ K Q 10
			♡ Q J 2
			◇ 9 8 5
			♣ A 7 6 4

The usual way to bid this 12-point hand if your right-hand opponent passed is to bid 2 ♣ first, with the intention of raising hearts later. But you cannot bid 2 ♣ over 2 ◇, and a bid of 3 ♣ would be misleading and a waste of time; you cannot stop below game once you bid 3 ♣. The 3 ♡ bid is forcing.

(NOTE: It is my suggestion that you play all jump bids by responder as forcing to game, except when responder is a passed hand. But a very popular variation is to play the jump raise in competition as a "limit raise," showing about 10 to 12 points; the opening bidder may pass with a minimum opening bid. If you play limit raises, the usual way to bid with a game-forcing hand is to make a forcing bid in a new suit, or cue-bid the opponent's suit. The accepted procedure in standard bidding is to play that all jump bids by responder are forcing to game; so if you decide to play limit raises in competition, be sure that you have an agreement with your partner to that effect.)

When your opponent makes a jump overcall it changes the nature and meaning of the responder's bid. Take careful note of the following three illustrations:

Partner	Opp.	You	♠ 6 2
1 ♡	2 ♠	3 ♡	♡ J 9 5
			◇ 10 7 4 3
			♣ A Q J 8

Your 3 ♡ bid shows 7 to 10 (or 11) points and three or more trumps. In other words you are telling your partner you would have bid 2 ♡ if you could, but did not want to be shut out of the bidding over the jump overcall.

Partner	Opp.	You	♠ A 6
1 ♡	3 ◇	4 ♡	♡ K 8 4 3
			◇ 9 8 7
			♣ A J 9 2

If your opponent had passed or made a nonjump overcall, the correct bid with this 13-point hand would be a forcing 3 ♡ bid; a bid of 4 ♡ would be preemptive. But after the jump overcall your 4 ♡ bid becomes a *single-jump* bid and shows a strong hand.

Partner	Opp.	You	♠ 7 2
1 ♡	3 ◇	3 ♡	♡ K 10 9 8 4
			◇ 6
			♣ J 10 7 5 3

If your opponent had passed or made a nonjump overcall, the correct bid with this distributional hand would be 4 ♡; a 3 ♡ bid would show a strong hand. Since the jump overcall changes the meaning and 4 ♡ becomes a strong bid, you are left with a choice of bidding 3 ♡ or nothing.

Responses at the One-Level

A new-suit response at the one-level over an intervening overcall shows 8 or more points and a four-card or longer suit (or maybe 7 points with a very good suit). A 1 NT response over an intervening overcall shows a balanced hand with 8 to 10 (or 11) high-card points and a stopper in the opponent's suit. With 7 points or fewer, you should pass; your hand is too weak for a free bid at the one-level. For example:

Partner	Opp.	You	♠ Q 5 3 2
1 ♣	1 ◇	P	♡ K 6 4
			◇ J 8 7
			♣ J 4 2

If your right-hand opponent passed over partner's 1 ♣ bid, your right bid would be 1 ♠. After the 1 ◇ bid you must pass with 7 junky points.

Partner	Opp.	You	♠ A Q 10 9 5
1 ◇	1 ♡	1 ♠	♡ 7 4
			◇ 7 5
			♣ 9 8 6 2

Although you have only 7 points, the free bid is recommended with this quality suit.

Partner	Opp.	You	♠ 6 4 2
1 ♣	1 ♡	P	♡ K 10 7 5
			◊ 8 4 3
			♣ K 9 7

It is tempting to bid 1 NT, but that would show 8 to 10 high-card points. If you add a queen someplace, you should bid 1 NT.

Partner	Opp.	You	♠ K 10 3
1 ◊	1 ♡	P	♡ 9 7 5
			◊ A J 2
			♣ 8 6 4 3

You must not bid 1 NT without a stopper in the opponent's suit and it is not desirable to raise your partner's minor suit with only three trumps, so a pass is right even though you have 8 points. If the overcall were 1 ♠ instead of 1 ♡, then 1 NT would be a good bid.

Partner	Opp.	You	♠ Q 7 3 2
1 ◊	1 ♡	1 ♠	♡ K 10 8
			◊ 8 5
			♣ A 10 9 3

Although it is tempting to bid 1 NT, 1 ♠ is a better bid. You should not respond 1 NT if you have a four-card major suit that can be bid at the one-level.

Responses in a Suit at the Two-Level

In a noncompetitive auction, a two-over-one response shows at least 11 points and the responder promises to bid again unless his partner bids game. After an opposing overcall, you may shade this requirement and bid at the two-level with 10 points, or a good 9 points, if you have a good five-card or longer suit to bid; your bid is, of course, forcing. Since a two-over-one response after an opposing overcall does not guarantee at least 11 points, it does not promise another bid as it does in a noncompetitive auction; if the opener wants to force the responder to bid again, he must bid a new suit or jump the bidding. For example:

Partner	Opp.	You	♠ 8 2
1 ♠	2 ♣	2 ◊	♡ K 6 4
			◊ A Q 7 5 2
			♣ 9 7 4

You have only 10 points, and if your right-hand opponent had passed, 1 NT would be the right response. After the 2 ♣ overcall, a free bid of 2 ◊ is okay with 10 points and a reasonably good five-card suit. If your partner's next bid is 2 ♠, 2 NT, or 3 ◊, his bid is not forcing and you should pass with only 10 points; if his next bid is 2 ♡ (a new suit) or if he jumps the bidding below game, you must bid again.

Partner	Opp.	You	♠ 8 3
1 ◊	1 ♡	P	♡ 6 4 2
			◊ 9 5
			♣ A Q 10 9 8 7

You have a great suit, but with only 8 points you are too weak to bid 2 ♣. If your right-hand opponent had passed, the correct bid would be 1 NT.

Responses in a Suit at the Three-Level

If an opposing overcall makes it impossible for you to bid your suit at the two-level, it may be wise to pass with as many as 10 or 11 points. For example:

Partner	Opp.	You	
1 ♠	2 ♡	P	♠ 7
			♡ 8 5 3
			♢ A Q 8 6 5 2
			♣ K 8 4

You have 11 points. If you bid 3 ♢ your partner is forced to bid again, and if he has a minimum opening with shortness in your suit, you could be in trouble. If the overcall were 2 ♣ instead of 2 ♡, it would be right to bid 2 ♢.

Partner	Opp.	You	
1 ♡	2 ♢	3 ♣	♠ 9 6 3
			♡ 4
			♢ 7 4 3
			♣ A K Q 10 9 5

Although you have only 11 points, you should bid 3 ♣ because your fabulous suit offers a good chance to make a game and makes it unlikely that you will get doubled and set.

2 NT and 3 NT Responses

A 2 NT response to an opening suit bid of one in a noncompetitive auction shows a balanced hand with 13, 14, or 15 high-card points and stoppers in all three unbid suits. The requirements to jump to 2 NT over an opposing overcall are a little more flexible; you may bid 2 NT with 12 high-card points—as well as with 13, 14, or 15—and without a stopper in an unbid suit, but your bid is still forcing to game. For example:

Partner	Opp.	You	
1 ♣	1 ♡	2 NT	♠ 10 6 3
			♡ A Q 8
			♢ Q 6 5 4
			♣ K J 2

After the 1 ♡ overcall, 2 NT is the only sensible bid, even though you have only 12 points and no stopper in the spade suit. If your opponent had passed, the right response would be 1 ♢. If your opponent had bid 1 ♠, you would be in an awkward position; the only logical thing to do is to make a temporizing bid of 2 ♢ with this dreadful suit.

Partner	Opp.	You	
1 ♢	1 ♡	2 ♣	♠ A Q 2
			♡ 8 5 4
			♢ K 8 6
			♣ A 10 9 7

Although you have a balanced hand and 13 high-card points, you may not bid 2 NT without a stopper in the opponent's suit. Your 2 ♣ bid is forcing and you and your partner must exchange more information to decide the best contract.

(NOTE: A popular deviation from standard bidding is to play that the jump to 2 NT in competitive auctions is invitational rather than forcing to game; it shows a balanced hand with 11 or 12 high-card points and at least one stopper in the opponent's suit. With stronger hands the procedure is to jump directly to 3 NT, or bid a new suit. This method has merit, but you must come to an agreement with your partner before using it. Without an agreement, *all jump bids by responder are forcing to game*, unless he is a passed hand.)

The requirements for a *nonjump* response of 2 NT are a balanced hand with 10 to 12 high-card points and at least one stopper in the opponent's suit; your bid is not forcing, so with a stronger hand you must jump to 3 NT. For example:

Partner	Opp.	You	
1 ◇	2 ♣	2 NT	♠ 10 9 7
			♡ A Q 8
			◇ 6 5 3 2
			♣ K Q 6

If you add the ♠ Q to this hand, to build the point count up to 13, the right response would be 3 NT.

The Jump-Shift Response

The requirements to jump the bidding in a new suit are the same in a competitive auction as they are in a noncompetitive auction: 17 to 19 points and a fit in partner's suit or an independent suit of your own. (A jump shift is not recommended with 20 points or more; see page 37.) For example:

Partner	Opp.	You	
1 ♡	1 ♠	3 ◇	♠ 8 6
			♡ A 10 6
			◇ A J 9 3 2
			♣ A K 8

Your plan should be to bid 4 ♡ at your next turn to bid. Your partner will then know your point count is 17 to 19 and he will be in a good position to decide whether or not to bid a slam.

Cue-Bidding the Overcaller's Suit

The cue-bid of an overcalled suit is forcing to game and alerts partner to slam possibilities. The cue-bid shows 17 points or more, support for partner's suit, and control of the opponent's suit—ace, void suit, or singleton. For example:

Partner	Opp.	You	
1 ♠	2 ♡	3 ♡	♠ A J 7 3
			♡ 2
			◇ A K Q J
			♣ 10 8 7 2

With 17 quality points this hand is too good to jump to 3 ♠, so the cue-bid followed by a raise to 4 ♠ describes the hand accurately.

Responses After a 1 NT Overcall

If your right-hand opponent overcalls your partner's opening bid with 1 NT, you should double with 9 high-card points or more (see page 134 for an illustration). So any suit bid that you make at the two-level would show fewer than 9 high-card points. With 5 to 8 high-card points, you may raise your partner's suit with adequate trump support, or bid a strong five-card or longer suit; with no support for partner and no good suit of your own, you should pass. For example:

Partner	Opp.	You	
1 ♠	1 NT	2 ♠	♠ J 4 2
			♡ A Q 8 6
			◇ 9 4
			♣ 9 6 5 3

Your 2 ♠ bid shows at least three-card support and 6 to 10 points, but at most 8 high-card points.

Partner	Opp.	You	
1 ♠	1 NT	2 ♡	♠ 7 4
			♡ K Q J 9 3
			◇ 8 7 6 5 2
			♣ 7

Your 2 ♡ bid shows a *good* five-card suit or any six-card suit and about 5 to 8 high-card points. If your opponent passed over partner's 1 ♠ bid, your right response would be 1 NT; you do not have the 11 points needed to bid a new suit at the two-level, and you must not pass with 6 or more high-card points.

Partner	Opp.	You	
1 ♡	1 NT	P	♠ A 10 6 3
			♡ 7 2
			◇ K 9 8 3
			♣ 8 7 4

With no support for partner's suit and no long suit of your own, you must pass with only 7 points. However, you have good defensive values and there is a good chance that you will beat 1 NT.

REBIDS BY THE OPENING BIDDER AFTER AN OPPONENT OVERCALLS

If Left-Hand Opponent Overcalls and Partner and Right-Hand Opponent Pass

You should be reluctant to pass unless you have a minimum opening bid and three or more cards in the enemy suit. Your partner may have passed a fairly good hand—as many as 9 or 10 points—because his hand did not meet the requirements for a free bid, and the fact that your right-hand opponent passed is an indication that your partner does have values.

If you do decide to bid again with a minimum opening bid, you may rebid a six-card or longer suit, bid a new four-card or longer suit provided you do not bid higher than two of your first suit (a reverse bid would show extra values), or double with support for the two unbid suits. With a balanced hand, or with length in the opponent's suit, it is usually right to pass unless you have a very good opening bid. For example:

♠ 4 3	You	Opp.	Partner	Opp.
♡ A K J 9 7 4	1 ♡	2 ♣	P	P
◇ K Q 2	2 ♡			
♣ 5 2				

There is a good chance you can fulfill a contract your way, or push the opponents higher and set them, so you must not pass with this excellent heart suit. If you had a stronger hand (for example, change your diamond holding to ◇ A-K-Q), you should jump to 3 ♡ to encourage your partner to bid game with modest values.

♠ 7 2	You	Opp.	Partner	Opp.
♡ A Q J 10 4	1 ♡	2 ♣	P	P
◇ A Q 10 5	2 ◇			
♣ 3 2				

With a two-suited hand, bidding again with a minimum opening bid is desirable. It would be wrong to rebid 2 ♡ and ignore the four-card suit.

♠ 3	You	Opp.	Partner	Opp.
♡ A 9 6 4	1 ◇	1 ♠	P	P
◇ A Q 10 9 2	DBL			
♣ K 10 9				

A double by the opening bidder of any suit bid below the game level is for takeout, provided his partner has not entered the auction. Your double shows support for the unbid suits—especially the unbid major suit—but does not promise extra strength. (Note that you must not bid 2 ♡ with this minimum opening; you need a strong hand to reverse the bidding.) Your partner should answer your double by bidding hearts with a four-card or longer suit, or else he may bid clubs, bid notrump, or raise diamonds; he may not pass unless he has a *powerful* spade holding and judges that the biggest profit will come from defending 1 ♠ doubled.

♠ A Q J 9 4	You	Opp.	Partner	Opp.
♡ K 10 8	1 ♠	2 ♡	P	P
◇ K 5 3	P			
♣ 7 2				

Your ♡ K is in front of the heart bidder and may be useless. That, together with your poor distribution, should discourage you from competing further.

♠ A K 6	You	Opp.	Partner	Opp.
♡ K 8 3	1 ♣	1 ♠	P	P
◇ K 9 5	P			
♣ J 10 4 2				

You have no choice but to pass with this minimum balanced hand. The only bid that would make any sense is 1 NT, and that would show a strong hand, about 19 high-card points; you are far too weak for that bid.

If Left-Hand Opponent and Partner Pass and Right-Hand Opponent Overcalls

You should be very reluctant to bid again unless you have a strong hand *and* good distribution. Your partner has indicated a maximum of 5 points, and he may have none; it is very dangerous to bid again with doubtful values, especially if you are vulnerable.

With a strong hand and the right distribution, you may rebid your own long and strong suit, bid a new four-card or longer suit, or double with support for the two unbid suits. With the wrong distribution you should not bid again even with a strong hand. Here are three examples:

	You	Opp.	Partner	Opp.
♠ A J 8 6 3	You	Opp.	Partner	Opp.
♡ A 5	1 ♠	P	P	2 ♣
◊ A K 10 7 2	2 ◊			
♣ 9				

You have 18 points and two five-card suits, so this hand qualifies for another bid. If partner has four small diamonds and a doubleton spade, you can make two or three diamonds, even if he has no high-card points. On your lucky day he might have five diamonds to the queen and a singleton spade, in which case you will probably make a game.

	You	Opp.	Partner	Opp.
♠ A Q 10 2	You	Opp.	Partner	Opp.
♡ A J 5 4 2	1 ♡	P	P	2 ♣
◊ A K 6	DBL			
♣ 7				

With 19 points and support for the unbid suits, you should double—a takeout double. There is a good chance you can make a part-score in one of the suits or even a game if partner has a long spade suit, while the risk of being doubled and penalized is remote.

	You	Opp.	Partner	Opp.
♠ A 5	You	Opp.	Partner	Opp.
♡ K J 7	1 ◊	P	P	2 ♣
◊ K J 8 3 2	P			
♣ A K 4				

You have the wrong distribution for any bid. Even with 19 high-card points it would be foolish to bid again with this balanced hand; you may get doubled and be set three or four tricks if partner has absolutely nothing. It is true that if you find partner with something like ♡ Q-10-X-X-X you might be able to make a part-score; but is it wise to make a bid when if you are right you win a cow, but if you are wrong you lose the farm? When your partner passes you out in a one-bid, do not bid again unless you have a strong hand *and* good distribution.

If Partner Responds and Right-Hand Opponent Overcalls

You should usually make your normal bid, but you may also pass with a minimum opening and nothing useful to say. For example:

	You	Opp.	Partner	Opp.
♠ A 7 3	1 ◊	P	1 ♡	1 ♠
♡ K 6 3	P			
◊ A J 5 4				
♣ J 8 2				

Your partner's 1 ♡ bid is forcing and you should rebid 1 NT if your right-hand opponent passed. After the 1 ♠ bid you may pass, as partner will get another chance to bid. The pass is often a good way to tell your partner that you have a minimum opening bid and mediocre distribution.

	You	Opp.	Partner	Opp.
♠ K J 3	1 ◊	P	1 ♡	1 ♠
♡ K 10 6	1 NT			
◊ A J 10 4				
♣ J 8 2				

You have 13 points, just as in the preceding hand, but this one is potentially much better; you have what looks to be two spade stoppers (instead of one) and two ten-spots. Although 1 NT is not a strong bid, it does imply that you have something extra.

	You	Opp.	Partner	Opp.
♠ A 7 3	1 ◊	P	1 ♡	1 ♠
♡ K 6 3 2	2 ♡			
◊ A J 5 4				
♣ J 8				

Even though you have a bare minimum opening, it is vitally important to raise your partner's suit with four-card support.

	You	Opp.	Partner	Opp.
♠ A 3	1 ◊	P	1 ♡	1 ♠
♡ 4	2 ♣			
◊ K 10 9 5 2				
♣ A J 8 6 3				

Although you have a minimum opening bid, it is right to bid 2 ♣ with such good distribution. If the overcall were 2 ♠ instead of 1 ♠, it would be wiser to pass, as a bid of 3 ♣ would show extra values.

REBIDS BY THE RESPONDER AFTER AN OPPONENT OVERCALLS

If the responder passed at his first turn to bid, he rebids as follows:

Opp.	Partner	Opp.	You	
	1 ◊	2 ♣	P	♠ K 8 5 3
P	DBL	P	2 ♠	♡ 7 4 2
				◊ 10 9
				♣ 8 7 6 3

Your partner's double is for takeout, and he is prepared for you to bid either of the unbid suits. You have no choice but to bid 2 ♠ with your four-card suit.

Opp.	Partner	Opp.	You	♠ K 8 5 3 2
	1 ◇	2 ♣	P	♡ K 8 7
P	DBL	P	3 ♠	◇ Q 5
				♣ 10 9 6

You have 9 points, not enough to make a free bid of 2 ♠ directly over the 2 ♣ bid. When partner doubles, you must jump to 3 ♠ to tell him you have maximum values for your previous pass, about 8 or 9 points. This will encourage your partner to bid on to game with a little extra, but he may pass with a minimum opening bid.

Opp.	Partner	Opp.	You	♠ 5 3
	1 ♠	2 ♣	P	♡ 7 4 2
P	DBL	P	P	◇ 10 8 5
				♣ K Q 10 9 6

Although partner's double is for takeout, you must pass for penalties. If 2 ♣ doubled is the final contract, you will show a big profit.

Opp.	Partner	Opp.	You	♠ 8 6 4 2
	1 ♣	P	P	♡ 10 5
1 ◇	1 ♡	P	2 ♣	◇ 9 6 5
				♣ 10 9 7 3

Although you had no intentions of bidding with this hand, you must take partner back to clubs with four clubs and only two hearts. If partner is allowed to play a club contract he should not be displeased with your hand, while if you pass 1 ♡ you may find he is one unhappy fellow.

Opp.	Partner	Opp.	You	♠ 5
	1 ♠	P	P	♡ 9 8 7 2
2 ♣	2 ◇	P	3 ◇	◇ Q 9 6 5 3
				♣ 6 4 3

Your partner has a strong hand with good distribution, so a 3 ◇ contract will be safe and he should be able to make a game if he bids it. Note that partner heard you pass his 1 ♠ bid, so he knows you are very weak and your 3 ◇ bid is based on good trump support and distribution. (See a possible hand for partner's bidding on page 170.)

Opp.	Partner	Opp.	You	♠ J 9 7 4 3
	1 ♡	P	P	♡ 5
2 ♣	DBL	P	2 ♠	◇ 10 8 5 4
				♣ 8 5 3

This time your partner is advertising a strong hand with support for the unbid suits; he must have three or four spades for his takeout double. Your hand is actually not so bad on this bidding—you could have only four spades—and if partner raises to 3 ♠, you would be justified in bidding a game. (See a possible hand for partner's bidding on page 170.)

RESPONSES AFTER AN OPPONENT DOUBLES FOR TAKEOUT

When your right-hand opponent doubles your partner's opening suit bid of one, the usual actions are:

> With 0 to 5 points, pass.
> With 6 to 9 points, bid something.
> With 10 or more *high-card* points, redouble.

These guidelines are subject to occasional deviations, as explained in the following pages, but they are accurate enough so that you should depend on them anytime you are in a doubtful bidding situation.

Responses with from 0 to 5 Points

As was stated above, you should generally pass with fewer than 6 points. However, if you have 5 points (or a good 4 points), you may raise partner's suit with good trump support, or bid a new suit at the one-level provided it is reasonably strong. For example:

Partner	Opp.	You	
1 ♣	DBL	P	♠ 8 5 4
			♡ 10 9 8 7 2
			◇ 9 7 6 5
			♣ 3

Some players would be petrified at the thought of passing this hand for fear that partner may have a poor club suit and be left to play a contract of 1 ♣ doubled, but this is erroneous thinking. If the doubler's partner passes he reveals to all that he has a powerful club holding and it is up to your partner to rescue himself if he has a poor club suit. It would be a grave error if you bid over the double.

Partner	Opp.	You	
1 ◇	DBL	2 ◇	♠ 8 7 5
			♡ 9 7 3
			◇ K J 10 9
			♣ 6 4 2

The raise to 2 ◇ is right with four strong trumps and 4 points, but only over an intervening double.

Partner	Opp.	You	
1 ♣	DBL	1 ♡	♠ 6 2
			♡ K J 10 4 3
			◇ 5 3 2
			♣ 9 7 6

Although you have only 5 points, it is okay to bid 1 ♡ with this strong suit. If partner's opening bid were 1 ♠, you should definitely pass; you must not bid at the two-level with such a weak hand.

Responses with from 6 to 9 Points

When your right-hand opponent doubles your partner's opening suit bid of one and you have 6 to 9 points, you should try very hard to find some bid. If you do pass you may find it impossible, or at least very awkward, to bid at your next turn. If you bid and show your partner that you have a fair hand, he can compete intelligently in the subsequent bidding. For example:

Partner	Opp.	You	♠ A 8 3
1 ◊	DBL	1 NT	♡ 7 4 2
			◊ Q 10 7
			♣ Q 9 5 2

Your 1 NT bid shows 6 to 9 high-card points and a relatively balanced hand; your partner can now bid again with the assurance that you have some values for him. Another bonus for bidding is that your opponents might be able to make a part-score in a major suit and they may not venture a bid over 1 NT, while they would have an easy time getting together if you passed.

Partner	Opp.	You	♠ A 8 3
1 ◊	DBL	1 ♡	♡ Q 10 7 3
			◊ 6 4
			♣ Q 9 5 2

It may seem wrong to bid a four-card major because the doubler implies that he has the major suits, but it is right to bid 1 ♡ because the doubler may have three hearts and your partner may have four hearts. Although your 1 ♡ bid is not forcing in standard bidding (it shows at most 9 high-card points), your partner will bid again unless he has a weak hand with at least three-card trump support.

Partner	Opp.	You	♠ 10 4
1 ♠	DBL	2 ◊	♡ 7 2
			◊ A Q 9 8 6 5
			♣ 8 4 3

When you bid a new suit at the two-level you show a strong five-card suit, or a six-card suit, and from 6 to 9 points. Note that if your right-hand opponent had passed, your proper bid would be 1 NT; you need at least 11 points to go to the two-level.

You may jump the bidding with fewer than 10 points. For example:

Partner	Opp.	You	♠ K 6 5 3
1 ♠	DBL	3 ♠	♡ 6
			◊ K 10 4 2
			♣ 8 7 6 2

If your right-hand opponent passed, your right bid would be 2 ♠. But over the double both the single raise and the jump raise show modest values in high cards; the jump raise is recommended when you have especially good trump support and/or distribution. If you replace the ♠ 3 with the ♡ 3 in this hand, 2 ♠ would be a better bid.

Partner	Opp.	You	♠ 7 6
1 ◊	DBL	3 ◊	♡ 8 5
			◊ Q J 9 6 4
			♣ Q 10 3 2

The jump raise of a minor suit over a double is also weak, but it is a risky bid unless you have at least five-card trump support. Replace the ◊ 4 with the ♡ 4 and you should bid only 2 ◊.

Partner	Opp.	You	♠ 7 3
1 ♣	DBL	2 ♡	♡ K J 10 9 8 4
			◊ 9 6 5
			♣ K 2

If your right-hand opponent passed, you should respond 1 ♡ with this hand and then rebid the suit if the bidding does not get too high; a jump to 2 ♡ would be out of the question, as it shows a powerful hand. After the intervening double the only strong action is to redouble, so even a jump shift shows fewer than 10 high-card points. The 2 ♡ bid is desirable because it makes it harder for the opponents to bid and it describes your hand accurately for your partner; the 2 ♡ bid says that you have the kind of hand with which you would normally bid 1 ♡ and then rebid 2 ♡.

Responses with 10 Points or More

If your partner opens the bidding with a suit bid of one and your right-hand opponent doubles, the standard procedure is to redouble anytime your hand has 10 high-card points or more, regardless of your distribution. (Experts make an exception to this rule, which I will point out later.) Your redouble is a request for your partner to pass at his next turn to bid, so that you will have a chance to double the opponent's bid. However, your partner is free to double an opposing bid himself, or to make a bid to describe a highly distributional hand. The redouble creates a "forcing auction," which means that you and your partner must outbid the opponents or double them; it is "your hand" and you must not allow the opponents to play any contract undoubled. Here are several examples:

Partner	Opp.	You	♠ A Q 7
1 ♣	DBL	RDBL	♡ 7 4 2
			◊ A 9 8 6
			♣ 5 3 2

You have 10 high-card points, so the normal action is to redouble.

Partner	Opp.	You	♠ A Q 10 9
1 ♡	DBL	RDBL	♡ 7
			◊ Q 10 8 3
			♣ K J 3 2

Your opponents appear to be in trouble. If your partner is allowed to play 1 ♡ redoubled, he should have no problems making it; he will score a game. If the opponents bid, you will double whatever they say; the penalty should be sizable, especially if they are vulnerable.

Unless your partner has a highly distributional hand, he should stay out of the bidding and give you a chance to double; your redouble is a request (not a command) for partner to pass at his next turn. It would be disappointing if your partner made a bid such as 2 ♡, letting the opponents off the hook.

Partner	Opp.	You	♠ K 9 6 4
1 ♡	DBL	RDBL	♡ K J 10 8
			◊ A Q 7
			♣ 7 2

If your right-hand opponent did not double, your correct bid would be to jump to 3 ♡. After the double, 3 ♡ is a weak bid, so you must redouble first and support hearts vigorously later.

Partner	*Opp.*	*You*	♠ 7
1 ♡	DBL	4 ♡	♡ K J 10 6 3
			◊ A J 9 8 4
			♣ 5 2

If your right-hand opponent did not double, your correct bid would be to jump to 3 ♡ with this strong 14-point hand. After the double, 3 ♡ is a weak bid, so you must decide whether to redouble or bid 4 ♡. The opponents may be able to make 4 ♠, or have a good sacrifice, and your 4 ♡ bid may keep them out of the bidding while a redouble would not. Your 4 ♡ bid misleads your partner into thinking you have a weak hand and you could miss a slam, but this is unlikely after the double. So the 4 ♡ bid should work out better in the long run.

Partner	*Opp.*	*You*	♠ 7
1 ♡	DBL	RDBL	♡ K J 10 6 3
			◊ A J 9 8 4
			♣ K 2

Now that the ♣ K has been added you have 17 points and the prospect of slam outweighs trying to keep the opponents out of the bidding. If the opponents do bid up to 4 ♠, you will just have to bid 5 ♡; but with this strong dummy, your partner should have no trouble making it.

Partner	*Opp.*	*You*	♠ A Q 9 7 4
1 ♣	DBL	RDBL	♡ A 8 6
			◊ Q 5 4 2
			♣ 2

It is nerve-racking to redouble with a singleton in your partner's minor suit, fearing that partner has a poor suit and everyone will pass. But if your left-hand opponent passes, it does not mean that he thinks he can beat the 1 ♣ contract; so if the doubler's partner does not bid, the doubler will—that is, if he knows what he is doing.

Partner	*Opp.*	*You*	♠ 3
1 ♣	DBL	RDBL	♡ K J 9 8 4
			◊ J 7 5
			♣ A Q 10 2

With 11 high-card points your first step is to redouble, planning to bid hearts at your next turn to bid. However, the bidding may be so high before it gets back to you—the opponents may bid up to 2 ♠, 3 ♠, or even 4 ♠—that you will not be able to describe your distribution. Still, the standard procedure is to redouble.

If you think that redoubling in the last two examples is wrong, so do the experts. Most experts play that *a new-suit bid at the one-level is forcing for one round;* you may bid a new suit at the *one-level only* with a strong hand without fear that your partner will pass. If this method is adopted, you should respond 1 ♠ and 1 ♡ respectively with the two previous examples. This is contrary to the way most players play, so you must make an agreement with your partner in advance if you decide to play this way. Then all subsequent bidding after a one-level suit response is the same as if there had been no double.

REBIDS BY THE OPENING BIDDER AFTER AN OPPONENT DOUBLES FOR TAKEOUT

Suppose that your left-hand opponent doubles your opening suit bid of one. If your partner passes, you should assume that he has 0 to 5 points, and you should not bid again unless you have extra values. If your partner makes any bid, he has at most 9 high-card points (unless he bids a new suit at the one-level and you have an agreement with your partner to play it as forcing), so you may pass, bid to a better part-score contract, or make a strong bid with extra values if you think there may be a game. If your partner redoubles, he has at least 10 high-card points and expects you to pass at your next turn unless you have a highly distributional hand, or unless you can double an opposing bid for penalty. For example:

	You	Opp.	Partner	Opp.
♠ K 7	*You*	*Opp.*	*Partner*	*Opp.*
♡ A K J 7 5	1 ♡	DBL	3 ♡	P
◊ K 10 8	P			
♣ 6 4 2				

Your partner has a relatively weak hand; he has a normal 2 ♡ bid. You should most emphatically pass with this minimum opening, and do not be surprised if you go down in 3 ♡. You should also pass if partner makes a jump bid in a new suit, such as 2 ♠.

	You	Opp.	Partner	Opp.
♠ 6 2	*You*	*Opp.*	*Partner*	*Opp.*
♡ A Q 8	1 ♣	DBL	1 ♠	P
◊ K 10 7	1 NT			
♣ A J 9 5 4				

In standard bidding the 1 ♠ response is not forcing, but you must not pass because partner may have a four-card suit. Your 1 NT bid shows a balanced hand with 13 to 15 points, just as it would in a noncompetitive auction.

	You	Opp.	Partner	Opp.
♠ A 8 5	*You*	*Opp.*	*Partner*	*Opp.*
♡ A Q 9 7 4	1 ♡	DBL	2 ♣	P
◊ K 10 3	P			
♣ 6 2				

Your partner's 2 ♣ bid shows a strong five-card suit, or a six-card suit, and a maximum of 9 high-card points. You must not rebid 2 ♡ because partner may have a singleton heart and pass. You must not bid 2 NT because that would show extra values. It is right to pass the 2 ♣ bid (even with a singleton) if there appears to be no better contract.

	You	Opp.	Partner	Opp.
♠ A 8 5	*You*	*Opp.*	*Partner*	*Opp.*
♡ A Q 9 7 4	1 ♡	DBL	2 ◊	2 ♠
◊ K 10 3	3 ◊			
♣ 6 2				

Your 3 ◊ bid does not show extra values—with a stronger hand you should bid 4 ◊—and it is important to compete in these auctions when you have good support for your partner's suit. It is likely that your partner can make 3 ◊, while if you passed the opponents could make 2 ♠.

♠ A 3	You	Opp.	Partner	Opp.
♡ A Q 10 9 4	1 ♡	DBL	RDBL	2 ♣
◊ K 10 6 2	P			
♣ 8 5				

Your pass gives your partner a chance to double the opponents, or to make some other bid to describe his hand; he will not pass and allow the opponents to play a contract of 2 ♣ undoubled. If your right-hand opponent had bid 2 ◊ instead of 2 ♣, you should double him; your partner should take the double out if he is very short in diamonds.

♠ A K 8	You	Opp.	Partner	Opp.
♡ 7 5 3 2	1 ♣	DBL	RDBL	P
◊ K 5 4	P			
♣ A 10 8				

Your partner's redouble does not promise trump support and passing here may worry you; suppose partner is short in clubs, the doubler passes, and you are left to play 1 ♣ redoubled. The normal meaning of your right-hand opponent's pass is that he has no clear-cut choice of suits to bid (he expects the doubler to bid his best suit, not to pass), it does not mean he has a potent club holding and wants to play 1 ♣ redoubled. Of course, an inexperienced player may not know all this and pass; but this rarely happens, and if it does you will probably win seven tricks anyway.

♠ 7	You	Opp.	Partner	Opp.
♡ A J 10 8 5 2	1 ♡	DBL	RDBL	1 ♠
◊ 6	2 ♣			
♣ A Q J 7 4				

Although you should normally pass in this situation and give your partner a chance to double the opponents, you must bid *now* with this highly distributional hand. For one thing, you are not interested in playing a contract of 1 ♠ doubled; but more important, you may not get the chance to describe your distribution if you pass. Your 2 ♣ bid tells your partner that you have great distribution (at least 5–5), and he must take this into consideration in his subsequent bidding.

REBIDS BY THE RESPONDER AFTER HE HAS REDOUBLED

Opp.	Partner	Opp.	You	
	1 ♣	DBL	RDBL	♠ K 4
P	P	2 ◊	2 ♡	♡ A K 10 7 3
				◊ 8 2
				♣ J 9 5 2

Your bidding shows a five-card or longer heart suit and at least 10 high-card points; the 2 ♡ bid is forcing. You could not bid 2 ♡ over the double, as that would show a maximum of 9 high-card points and your bid would not be forcing.

Opp.	Partner	Opp.	You	♠ 9 3
	1 ♠	DBL	RDBL	♡ 8 7 2
P	P	2 ♡	P	◊ A J 9 4
				♣ A Q 10 5

Your pass is *forcing* and says that you have no clear-cut action; you do not have a strong enough holding in the opponent's suit to double them, you do not have a long suit to bid, and you do not have trump support for your partner's suit. Your partner should double the opponents with a strong holding in their suit or make any other bid to describe his hand, but he may not pass. If one of your opponents had bid 2 ♣ or 2 ◊ instead of 2 ♡, you should double for penalty.

16
Sacrifice Bids

♣　　　♦　　　♥　　　♠　　　♣　　　♦　　　♥　　　♠

When your opponents have bid a game or slam contract that you are confident they can make, it sometimes pays to bid to a higher contract that you cannot make. If you get doubled and set, the penalty—you hope, at least—will cost less than you would lose if you allowed your opponents to play and make their contract.

The vulnerability is of the utmost importance. With favorable vulnerability you should be very daring with your sacrifice bids, with equal vulnerability you should take the middle road, and with unfavorable vulnerability it rarely pays to sacrifice.

Although it is not advisable to sacrifice when you think it will be too expensive if you get doubled, it is downright foolish to sacrifice when you think you may beat the opponent's contract. Beware the "phantom sacrifice." There is nothing quite so frustrating as to be doubled and set in a sacrifice bid and, when the smoke clears, find you could have beaten the opponent's contract.

As you can see, good judgment is required to be successful at sacrifice bidding.

USING YOUR JUDGMENT

In the following four hands, assume the vulnerability is favorable:

Opp.	Partner	Opp.	You	♠ 7 6 4
		1 ♠	2 ♡	♡ K Q J 8 6 3
2 ♠	3 ♡	4 ♠	5 ♡	◇ A 2
				♣ 7 4

It is reasonable to estimate that, if your 5 ♡ contract gets doubled, you will be set about two tricks. Your partner should have one useful high card for his bid—such as the ♡ A—and since you hold three spades, the bidding suggests he has a singleton. If this analysis is correct, you will lose two clubs, one diamond, and one spade; down two tricks at 5 ♡ doubled.

If you allow the opponents to play 4 ♠, they would almost surely make it. You have only one defensive trick—your ♡ K-Q are useless after your partner has raised your suit—and partner has indicated meager values by his "weakish" 3 ♡ bid.

So, if you bid 5 ♡ and get doubled, you can expect to lose about 300 points. If you allowed the opponents to play and make 4 ♠, you would lose 620 points—500 bonus for game and 120 trick score. (NOTE: The 500-point bonus for game applies to "Chicago bridge" and duplicate bridge. In old-fashioned rubber bridge, the effective value of the second game with this vulnerability is about 350, not 500. So the amount you save would be less at rubber bridge.)

Opp.	Partner	Opp.	You	
		1 ♠	2 ♡	♠ 8 6
2 ♠	3 ♡	4 ♠	P	♡ A J 10 9 5 2
				◇ 4 3
				♣ A 7 4

With two aces there is some chance that you can beat the 4 ♠ contract; while if you bid 5 ♡ and get doubled, you may be set three or four tricks. So passing is the right decision, but note that the bidding is not over; your partner still has a bid coming **and** will have the opportunity to pass or sacrifice.

Opp.	Partner	Opp.	You	
1 ♠	2 ♡	2 ♠	3 ♡	♠ 7
4 ♠	P	P	5 ♡	♡ K 8 7 3
				◇ 9 8 7 2
				♣ K 8 6 5

Since the only defensive value in your hand is the ♣ K, it is very unlikely that you can beat 4 ♠. Your good trump support and singleton spade suggest that playing 5 ♡ doubled would not be as expensive as letting the opponents play and make 4 ♠. Note that if your partner held the previous hand, you would be set two tricks at 5 ♡ doubled, while the opponents would have no trouble making 4 ♠.

Opp.	Partner	Opp.	You	
1 ♠	2 ♡	2 ♠	3 ♡	♠ 7 4
4 ♠	P	P	P	♡ Q 8 3
				◇ A 9 8 7
				♣ K 6 5 2

This time your hand may take two tricks defensively, so there is a good chance you can beat 4 ♠. Note that if your partner held the hand before the previous one, the opponents figure to be set in 4 ♠, while a contract of 5 ♡ doubled would be set two or three tricks.

It sometimes pays to sacrifice before the opponents reach their obvious game contract. This is actually a preemptive bid, and its purpose is to jam the opponents' bidding—to make it more difficult for them to decide whether to double you or to bid further. For example, with favorable vulnerability:

Opp.	Partner	Opp.	You	
1 ♡	1 ♠	3 ♡	4 ♠	♠ Q 10 8 5
				♡ 7 6 4
				◇ A 10 9 7
				♣ 3 2

The opponents are going to bid 4 ♡ if you let them, and your hand calls for a sacrifice bid. Your jump to 4 ♠ is better than bidding 3 ♠ followed by 4 ♠, as it robs your opponents of bidding space; it will be harder for them to make the winning decision whether to double you or bid 5 ♡.

When you have made a sacrifice bid, your opponents sometimes greedily bid again rather than double your contract. If they do bid again, you should generally pass; it is bad technique to sacrifice against that bid, or to double them. You should be very satisfied to push your opponents one trick higher than they wanted to bid and then set them.

Suppose, with favorable vulnerability, you again hold the hand above and the bidding continues:

Opp.	Partner	Opp.	You	
1 ♡	1 ♠	3 ♡	4 ♠	♠ Q 10 8 5
5 ♡	P	P	P	♡ 7 6 4
				◇ A 10 9 7
				♣ 3 2

Although the opponents may be able to make 5 ♡, you should not bid 5 ♠; it may be a phantom sacrifice and/or 5 ♠ doubled may be too costly.

It is sometimes necessary to put in a bid with shaky values, to set the stage for a possible sacrifice. For example, with equal vulnerability:

Opp.	Partner	Opp.	You	
1 ♡	1 ♠	3 ♡	3 ♠	♠ J 9 3
				♡ 8 4
				◇ K J 10
				♣ 9 8 6 5 2

With this hand, it is not clear that a sacrifice bid of 4 ♠ will be profitable. But you should definitely bid 3 ♠, so your partner will be in an intelligent position to decide whether or not to sacrifice; with the right hand, it is even conceivable that he can make 4 ♠.

A sacrifice bid is most apt to pay off when your partner has been in the bidding and you have found a good trump suit. When your partner passes throughout the auction it is harder to judge when a sacrifice is desirable, so you should tend to be more conservative. However, if you are reasonably sure the opponents can make their contract and it will not be too expensive if they double you, or if you have hope of making your contract, you should bid. For example, with favorable vulnerability:

Opp.	Partner	Opp.	You	
		1 ♠	2 ♡	♠ 3
2 ♠	P	4 ♠	5 ◇	♡ K Q J 9 7 4
				◇ A K J 10 2
				♣ 5

You would be very unlucky to go down more than one trick in 5 ◇ or 5 ♡ doubled, and you may even make your contract if partner should have an ace. Although there is no way to know whether the opponents can make 4 ♠ or not, it is a good gamble to bid 5 ◇.

AFTER YOUR SIDE HAS MADE A PREEMPTIVE BID

When your partner has made a preemptive bid and you have support for his suit, it usually pays to bid whether you have a good hand or not; you bid to make, to jam the opponent's bidding, or to sacrifice. Also, it is surprisingly easy to tell how many tricks each side is likely to win. In the following four hands, assume that the vulnerability is favorable.

Partner	*Opp.*	*You*	♠ A 7 5
3 ♠	4 ♡	4 ♠	♡ 9 6 2
			◇ K 9 5
			♣ A 8 6 3

When your partner opens the bidding with a preemptive bid, you should assume that his hand can win at most one trick defensively. Your hand appears to be capable of winning two or three tricks, so it is unlikely (but possible) that you could beat a 4 ♡ contract. You must take out insurance and bid 4 ♠, which figures to be set one or two tricks. The 4 ♠ bid is recommended regardless of the vulnerability, because with equal or unfavorable vulnerability your partner must have a sounder hand; he may even make 4 ♠.

Partner	*Opp.*	*You*	♠ 6 4 2
3 ♡	3 ♠	5 ♡	♡ K 10 8
			◇ A 9 6 5 3
			♣ 7 2

If your partner can take one trick defensively, the opponents can make 5 ♠; they surely can make 4 ♠ and maybe 6 ♠. Your 5 ♡ bid should give them a headache; and if they double your 5 ♡ bid, it should be a good sacrifice.

Partner	*Opp.*	*You*	♠ J 8 5
3 ♠	P	P	♡ 7 3 2
			◇ A K 9 4
			♣ 10 9 6

It is very possible that the opponents can make a game—probably 4 ♡, but maybe 3 NT—and that 4 ♠ doubled would be a good sacrifice; but the opponents' high cards may be evenly divided and they may let you play 3 ♠ undoubled. If they do bid 4 ♡, you can bid 4 ♠ as a sacrifice later.

Note that if your right-hand opponent bid 4 ♡ or doubled over your partner's 3 ♠ bid, you should bid 4 ♠. If after you have bid 4 ♠ your opponents bid 5 ♡, you should pass and hope to set them.

Partner	*Opp.*	*You*	♠ K 8 7 5
3 ♠	P	?	♡ 6
			◇ J 10 9 7 3
			♣ 6 5 2

Unless your partner can take a trick, the opponents can make a grand slam. If they bid 7 ♡ and make it you will lose 2210 points, and if they bid 6 ♡ and make it you will lose 1430 points; so this is clearly a sacrificing situation. The question is what to bid—and *any* bid under 7 NT has merit. You might bid 4 ♠ (5 ♠ or 6 ♠), or 4 ♡ as a psychic bid; when you get doubled you will of course run back to spades.

If, over whatever you choose to bid, they bid 6 ♡, you must bid 6 ♠; and if they bid 7 ♡ and your partner does not double them, you should bid 7 ♠. Your partner should be able to win about eight or nine tricks playing in spades, so 7 ♠ doubled would cost 700 or 900 points. Of course, you may be doubled in a lower contract and get away with a cheaper sacrifice.

When your partner's preemptive bid is an overcall, you should employ the same tactics. For example, with favorable vulnerability:

Opp.	Partner	Opp.	You	♠ K 7 3
1 ♡	4 ♠	4 NT	?	♡ J 9 2
				◊ 6 4
				♣ Q J 10 6 2

Your right-hand opponent thinks he can make a slam, and from the looks of your hand he can. The question is whether to bid 5 ♠ or 6 ♠, and either bid might work out right; but if you do bid 5 ♠ and they bid 6 ♡, you should sacrifice.

The best time to sacrifice is when you have support for your partner's suit, or when your partner has raised your suit. It seldom pays to sacrifice alone, and this is most emphatically true when you have opened with a preemptive bid. Here is an actual hand from a rubber-bridge game that shows my partner taking a phantom sacrifice:

♠ K Q J 10 9 7 6	Partner	Opp.	Bill Root	Opp.
♡ —	3 ♠	P	P	4 ♡
◊ 7 5 4	4 ♠	DBL		
♣ Q 3 2				

With favorable vulnerability, my partner judged that 4 ♠ doubled with 100 honors would be less expensive than the cost of a vulnerable game. The result was down two for a score of minus 200, but my hand was ♠ 4-2 ♡ A-Q-J-9-8 ◊ J-10 ♣ A-7-6-4. The decision to bid 4 ♠, pass, or double 4 ♡ should have been mine. As you can see, I would have doubled and we probably would have set them three tricks for a profit of 800 points. Note that it would have been perfectly okay for my partner to open the bidding with 4 ♠ if he chose; but once he bid 3 ♠, he should not bid again.

GETTING YOUR SIDE INTO THE BIDDING

Many a good sacrifice is missed because players do not have the courage to enter the bidding when their opponents have indicated great strength. For example, with favorable vulnerability:

Opp.	You	♠ K J 10 6 3
2 ♣	2 ♠	♡ 7 4 2
		◊ Q J 7 5
		♣ 8

Your hand does not meet the normal requirements for an overcall at the two-level, but with favorable vulnerability the chance of being doubled in 2 ♠ and losing more for the penalty than the opponents could win by bidding and making a game or a slam is minimal. At the same time, your partner will recognize that your bid is setting the stage for a possible sacrifice; the opponents' strong bidding makes it obvious that you cannot have a strong hand. Suppose your partner has the following hand and the bidding continues as shown:

Opp.	You	Opp.	Partner	♠ Q 8 7 2
2 ♣	2 ♠	3 ♡	?	♡ 9
				◇ K 10 6 4
				♣ 10 6 5 3

Some bid to jam the opponents' bidding (such as 4 ♠, 5 ♠, or 6 ♠) is in order here. I would choose 5 ♠ to take Blackwood away from the opponents, but any of several bids might work as well or better. With a strong two-bid on his left and a positive response on his right, your partner should judge from his poor defensive hand that the opponents can probably make a small slam and maybe even a grand slam; against these two hands they can surely make a small slam and probably a grand slam in hearts or clubs (maybe even 7 NT). Almost any bid you choose will make it harder for the opponents to reach their optimum contract. If they should bid 7 ♡ or 7 ♣, it would be profitable for you or your partner to bid 7 ♠; minus 700 or 900 (the amount you figure to lose if doubled in 7 ♠) is a better score than minus 2210 or 2140 (the amount you lose if your opponents bid and make 7 ♡ or 7 ♣). If they get greedy and bid 7 NT, you may beat them.

Note that if you had not made your aggressive 2 ♠ bid, there would be no opportunity for a sacrifice and the opponents would have an easier time reaching their best slam contract.

THE UNUSUAL NOTRUMP

The "unusual 2 NT overcall" (see page 111) often sets the stage for a sacrifice bid. For example, with both sides vulnerable:

Opp.	Partner	Opp.	You	♠ 9 7 6
1 ♠	2 NT	4 ♠	5 ◇	♡ Q 7 4 3 2
				◇ A 10 8 5
				♣ 3

It looks like the opponents can make 4 ♠, and 5 ◇ doubled will be a good sacrifice; and if partner has the right hand (such as ♠ X ♡ X ◇ K-J-9-X-X ♣ A-Q-J-X-X-X), you may even make 5 ◇. If the opponents decide to bid 5 ♠, you should pass and hope to set them.

The "unusual 3 NT overcall" is almost unheard-of, but it is possible. For example, with favorable vulnerability:

Opp.	Partner	Opp.	You	♠ 7
1 ♠	P	3 ♠	3 NT	♡ 3
				◇ K J 10 8 6
				♣ Q J 9 5 4 2

Your partner can tell that your 3 NT overcall is unusual because of the opponents' strong bidding; there are not enough high cards in the deck for you to have a hand strong enough for a normal 3 NT overcall. In view of the bidding and the nature of your hand, it seems that the opponents can make a game or a slam and you may have a good sacrifice in a minor suit. However, your 3 NT bid has described your hand well, and the decision whether or not to sacrifice will be up to your partner. Suppose your partner holds the following hand and the bidding continues:

Opp.	You	Opp.	Partner	♠ A 4 2
		1 ♠	P	♡ Q 10 4 2
3 ♠	3 NT	4 ♠	5 ♣	◇ 9 5
				♣ K 8 7 3

Your partner should reason that his hand is not strong enough defensively to hope to beat 4 ♠ and, in view of the vulnerability, 5 ♣ doubled should be a good sacrifice. With these two hands it appears that the opponents would have no trouble making their 4 ♠ contract, while 5 ♣ doubled will be set one or two tricks, depending on the distribution of the diamond suit. If the opponents should bid 5 ♠, both you and your partner should most emphatically pass.

WHEN YOUR OPPONENTS HAVE MADE A SACRIFICE BID

When your opponents sacrifice against your bid, you and your partner are often faced with a difficult decision whether to double their contract or bid one higher. Since the vulnerability is usually unfavorable for your side when the opponents sacrifice, assume that this is the case in the three following examples:

♠ K 10 2	You	Opp.	Partner	Opp.
♡ A Q 9 7 4	1 ♡	1 ♠	3 ♡	4 ♠
◇ A 8	DBL			
♣ 6 5 3				

It is very unlikely that you can make 5 ♡ with your balanced minimum opening bid, especially since the bidding indicates that your partner has a singleton spade and the ♠ K will be useless for offense. To the contrary, your spade holding is good for defense against 4 ♠. You should set the opponents about two tricks (maybe three), so doubling should provide the biggest and surest profit.

♠ 6	You	Opp.	Partner	Opp.
♡ A K J 9 8 6	1 ♡	1 ♠	3 ♡	4 ♠
◇ K 10 9 4	5 ♡			
♣ 7 6				

There is no question that you should bid 5 ♡ with this excellent distributional hand. You would be very unlucky to fail in 5 ♡, while your poor defensive strength makes it very doubtful that you could beat 4 ♠.

♠ 7	You	Opp.	Partner	Opp.
♡ A Q J 8 6	1 ♡	1 ♠	3 ♡	4 ♠
◇ 5 3 2	P			
♣ A Q 10 9				

When the decision whether to bid or double is not obvious, you should pass and let your partner decide. If your partner has good defensive strength he will double, and if he has an offensive type hand he will bid higher; *he may not pass* 4 ♠. The bidding by you and your partner has been very strong, making it clear to both of you that it is "your hand," so you must either double the opponents or outbid them. Your pass is a "forcing pass."

Here is another hand to illustrate the use of the forcing pass. Once again, assume that the vulnerability is unfavorable:

♠ 6	*You*	*Opp.*	*Partner*	*Opp.*
♡ A Q J 7	2 ♣	2 ♠	P	4 ♠
◊ K Q J	P			
♣ A K Q 5 2				

No matter whether your 2 ♣ opening is a natural strong two-bid or an artificial strong two-bid, your pass is absolutely forcing. Although your partner has already shown a weak hand by his pass, it still may be better to compete further if partner has a long suit and maybe one useful high card such as the ♡ K or ◊ A. Your pass describes this kind of hand; you must double 4 ♠ to discourage your partner from bidding. Suppose your partner holds the following two hands:

Opp.	*You*	*Opp.*	*Partner*	♠ 7 3
	2 ♣	2 ♠	P	♡ K 10 8 6 2
4 ♠	P	P	5 ♡	◊ 9 5 4 2
				♣ J 4

The 5 ♡ contract is a big favorite to make, while 4 ♠ doubled figures to be set only one or two tricks; and they might even make it.

Opp.	*You*	*Opp.*	*Partner*	♠ 8 5
	2 ♣	2 ♠	P	♡ 10 9 5 3
4 ♠	P	P	DBL	◊ 9 7 4 2
				♣ 7 4 3

Without a long suit to bid, your partner must double; he may not pass.

17

Slam Bidding

♣   ♦   ♥   ♠   ♣   ♦   ♥   ♠

Slam bidding is the most challenging aspect of the game. To be good at it, you must adopt some of the popular slam-bidding conventions; natural bidding alone will not get the job done. The most common and useful aid for bidding slams is the "control-showing bid" (often called a "cue-bid"). Other helpful conventions covered in this chapter are the voluntary bid of five in a major suit, the Blackwood convention, the Gerber convention, the quantitative notrump raise, and the grand slam force. Before getting into these conventions, let us consider the requirements to bid slams and the right approach.

THE REQUIREMENTS TO BID SLAMS

The minimum requirement to bid six of a suit is 33 points (including distributional points), provided you have found a good trump suit and the opponents cannot win the first two tricks. This does not mean that, if the hands meet all of these requirements, you will make every slam you bid. But the proper odds for bidding a small slam are about fifty-fifty, so considerable chance-taking is in order.

The minimum requirement to bid seven of a suit is 37 points (including distributional points). When many of your points are being counted for distribution, it may be dangerous to bid a grand slam unless you are reasonably sure that thirteen tricks are available. You are giving about two-to-one odds when you bid a grand slam, so you should be more conservative than when you bid a small slam.

The minimum requirement to bid 6 NT is 33 high-card points, and to bid 7 NT is 37 high-card points. You may make a notrump slam with fewer high-card points if you have a long, strong suit and sufficient controls (aces and kings) in the side suits. However, it usually pays to seek a suit slam before deciding on a notrump slam; a suit slam rates to be easier, assuming there is a satisfactory trump suit.

THE RIGHT APPROACH TO SLAM BIDDING

1. Bid a slam directly if the combined hands meet all the requirements. For example:

   ♠ A J 8 6 3   *You*   *Partner*
   ♡ A Q 7 5 2   1 ♠   3 ♠
   ◇ A 7   6 ♠
   ♣ 4

   You have 20 points (15 for high cards, 2 for the two five-card suits, 2 for the singleton, and 1 for the doubleton), and your partner has shown 13 to 16 points. Since you have found a good trump suit and have first-round control of three suits and second-round control of the fourth suit, your hand meets all of the requirements to bid a slam directly, and you should bid 6 ♠. It would be wrong to bid your heart suit, or to make any other bid, since that would not help you in your quest for slam and would give your opponents information which may aid their defense.

2. Keep the bidding as low as possible when you do not know which trump suit to select, even when you know the combined hands have enough points to bid a slam. Avoid jump bids when you can make a nonjump bid that is forcing. Do not employ any of the slam-bidding conventions until you have decided which trump suit, or notrump, to play. For example:

   Partner   *You*   ♠ A K J 7 5
   1 ♡   1 ♠   ♡ A
                          ◇ 9 3 2
                          ♣ A K J 3

   It is obvious that you should bid at least a small slam with this powerful hand; but you must decide whether to play the hand in a suit or notrump, and whether to bid six or seven. You will need bidding room to exchange information with your partner, so the forcing 1 ♠ bid is better than jumping the bidding immediately.

3. Make a control-showing bid (a cue-bid) when you have agreed on a trump suit and want to exchange information about *which* controls (aces, kings, void suits, singletons) you and your partner hold. You may also use a control-showing bid when you are not quite sure the combined hands have the required strength to bid a slam, but do not bid beyond the game level if you think it may put your game contract in jeopardy.

4. Use Blackwood if your only problem is *how many* aces (and perhaps kings) your partner holds and you are confident that it is safe to bid at the five-level—that is, if you are reasonably sure the combined hands have at least 33 points.

THE CONTROL-SHOWING BID

The control-showing bid (also called a cue-bid) has two primary functions: (1) It is a way to find out which first-round controls (aces and void suits) and which second-round controls (kings and singletons) your partner has. (2) It is a quantitative probe to find out if your partner has extra values when you are not sure whether or not the combined hands have the required point count to bid a slam. The initial control-showing bid usually takes place below the game level, so you can still stop bidding at game if it becomes apparent that a slam should not be bid.

In a vast majority of cases, a control-showing bid takes place after you and your partner have agreed on a trump suit. The first control-showing bid informs your partner that you are interested in bidding a slam and you have first-round control in the suit you have bid. To get started, here are four hands in which you use a control-showing bid because you do not have first- or second-round control of one of the unbid suits:

	You	Partner
♠ A K 10 8 2		
♡ 7 3	1 ♠	3 ♠
◊ K 10 7 4	4 ♣	
♣ A K		

Your partner's 3 ♠ bid shows 13 to 16 points and at least four spades. After his raise, your hand becomes worth 20 points, so the combined hands have at least 33 points. Since it is possible that the opponents can win the first two heart tricks, it would be wrong to bid a slam directly, or to use Blackwood. Your 4 ♣ bid says you are interested in bidding a slam and have first-round control of clubs.

Partner	You	♠ A K 10 8 5 2
1 ◊	1 ♠	♡ 7 6 5 4
3 ♠	4 ♣	◊ K 9 8
		♣ —

A control-showing bid with a void suit is also correct. Your hand becomes worth 15 points after your suit has been raised and partner has shown 17 to 19, so this hand is certainly worth a try for slam.

	You	Partner
♠ A K J 8 5 2		
♡ 10 9 3	1 ♠	3 ♠
◊ A Q 7 3	4 ◊	
♣ —		

When there are two possible control-showing bids, show an ace before a void suit.

	You	Partner
♠ K Q J 8 6 3		
♡ A Q 10	1 ♠	3 ♠
◊ 7 2	4 ♣	
♣ A 4		

With two aces, it is usually better to bid the one that keeps the bidding lower first.

The control-showing bid is indispensable when you are uncertain whether or not the combined hands have the required point count to bid a slam and want to find out if partner has anything extra. For example:

♠ A 10 8	*You*	*Partner*
♡ A Q J 10 3	1 ♡	3 ♡
◇ A 7 6 2	3 ♠	
♣ 4		

Your hand becomes worth 18 points when you add 2 for the singleton and your partner's 3 ♡ bid shows 13 to 16. The combined total is therefore 31 to 34. Although you have adequate controls to bid a slam, your hand is not good enough to bid beyond the game level and too good to bid just 4 ♡. Your 3 ♠ bid is a "slam try." If partner's subsequent bidding is encouraging, you will bid a slam; if not, you will still be able to stop bidding at 4 ♡.

If your partner raises your major suit to the three-level or higher, a new suit bid by you is a control-showing bid. If your partner raises your minor suit to the three-level or higher, a new suit bid by you *at the four-level* or higher is a control-showing bid. Note the two following cases in which new-suit bids are not control-showing bids:

1. If your partner raises your *major suit* to the *two-level*, a new suit bid by you is a *game try*, not a slam try. (See page 53.)
2. If your partner raises your *minor suit* to the *two-level or three-level*, a new suit bid by you below 3 NT shows a *stopper;* it is not a slam try. (See pages 54 and 55.)

Sometimes you can make a control-showing bid *before* you or your partner have raised the other's suit. In addition to showing a strong hand with control of the bid suit, such a bid *promises very good support for your partner's bid suit.*

♠ K Q 9 2	*You*	*Partner*
♡ A 7	1 NT	3 ♠
◇ A Q 8 3	4 ◇	
♣ K 10 3		

The two normal actions for you to take after your partner's 3 ♠ bid are to raise to 4 ♠ or bid 3 NT; *you are barred from bidding beyond the game level* after opening 1 NT. Your 4 ◇ bid is a slam try, showing excellent spade support and a maximum 1 NT opening bid with a concentration of strength in diamonds; if your minor suits were reversed, you should bid 4 ♣. If you chose to bid 4 ♠ instead of 4 ◇, your partner would not visualize a slam unless he had at least 15 points; your 4 ◇ bid encourages him to bid a slam with a slightly weaker hand. Partner must bid 4 ♠ to sign off, or make any other bid if he thinks there may be a slam.

A control-showing bid in a suit bid by an opponent is called a cue-bid. Some forms of cue-bids are used to encourage your partner to bid a game, or force to game; they do not promise control of the opponent's suit and they are not slam tries (see Chapters 10, 11, 13, and 14). The cue-bids that are meant to be slam tries indicate good support for your partner's bid suit and an ace, void, or singleton in the opponent's bid suit; these cue-bids usually occur after an enemy preemptive opening bid, or when your side has opened the bidding. For example:

Opp.	Partner	Opp.	You	♠ K 10 7
3 ♣	3 ♠	P	4 ♣	♡ A K J 10 9
				◇ 9 8 5 2
				♣ 3

Your 4 ♣ bid shows good spade support and the ace, void, or singleton in clubs. If your partner has a mediocre spade overcall, he should bid 4 ♠ to sign off. With a sound overcall, he should make any other bid to try for slam.

Partner	Opp.	You	♠ A 7 6
1 ♡	1 ♠	2 ♠	♡ K J 4 2
			◇ A K Q
			♣ 9 5 3

This 17-point hand is slightly too strong for a jump to 3 ♡, so the 2 ♠ cue-bid is the logical choice with good heart support and the ♠ A.

The Bidding After a Control-Showing Bid

After your partner has made a control-showing bid, you may return to the agreed suit to discourage bidding a slam, or bid a new suit in which you have a first-round control. However, do not make a control-showing bid that carries the bidding beyond the game level with minimum values. For example:

Partner	You	♠ K Q 7 4
1 ♠	3 ♠	♡ 6 2
4 ♣	4 ◇	◇ A J 6 5
		♣ Q 9 8

You have a minimum 3 ♠ bid (13 points), but it is okay to cue-bid your ace when the bidding is still below the game level.

Partner	You	♠ K Q 7 4
1 ♠	3 ♠	♡ 6 2
4 ♡	4 ♠	◇ A J 6 5
		♣ Q 9 8

With minimum values, do not cue-bid beyond game; your 4 ♠ bid is to discourage your partner from bidding a slam.

Partner	You	♠ K Q 7 4
1 ♠	3 ♠	♡ 6 2
4 ♡	5 ◇	◇ A K 6 5
		♣ Q 9 8

You have a good-looking 15 points. Your 5 ◇ bid shows a maximum 3 ♠ bid (15 or 16 points) and first-round control in diamonds. Replacing the ◇ J with the ◇ K makes a big difference.

Partner	You	♠ K Q 7 4
1 ♠	3 ♠	♡ 6 2
4 ♡	4 ♠	◇ A J 6 5
5 ♣	5 ◇	♣ Q 9 8

On this auction you indicate a minimum 3 ♠ bid and first-round control in diamonds.

If you return the bidding to the agreed trump suit after you have made a control-showing bid, it means you do not want to bid a slam unless your partner has something extra; your slam try was a mild one. For example:

Partner	You	
		♠ 7 2
1 ♠	2 ♡	♡ A Q 10 9 8 7
3 ♡	4 ♣	◇ 9 4
4 ◇	4 ♡	♣ A K J

Your partner's bidding has indicated a minimum-range opening bid (13 to 16 points), and you have 18. If your partner has only 13 or 14 points or thinks he has the wrong hand, he should pass 4 ♡. If he has 15 or 16 points or thinks he has the right hand, he should bid again. The following two hands illustrate when your partner should pass and when he should bid again:

	Partner	You	
♠ Q J 10 8 3	1 ♠	2 ♡	♠ 7 2
♡ K 6 4	3 ♡	4 ♣	♡ A Q 10 9 8 7
◇ A K 2	4 ◇	4 ♡	◇ 9 4
♣ 10 5	P		♣ A K J

Your partner has minimum values for his previous bidding, including only two and one-half quick tricks. He should therefore reject your slam invitation and pass 4 ♡.

	Partner	You	
♠ A K 10 4 3	1 ♠	2 ♡	♠ 7 2
♡ K 6 4	3 ♡	4 ♣	♡ A Q 10 9 8 7
◇ A 8 3	4 ◇	4 ♡	◇ 9 4
♣ 7 6	6 ♡		♣ A K J

This hand has only 1 point more, but it does include three and one-half quick tricks; so your partner should accept your slam invitation and bid 6 ♡. As you can see from these two hands, good slam bidding often requires good judgment. In this case, the opening bidder has to judge that within the framework of his previous bidding, this hand is a good one, while the preceding hand is not.

Once a control-showing bid has been made, the partnership is committed to playing the hand in the agreed suit. This allows you to show controls in suits that have been bid naturally before the trump suit was agreed upon. For example:

Partner	You	
		♠ K J 8 4 2
1 ♡	1 ♠	♡ A 9
3 ♠	4 ♣	◇ 7 4 3
4 ◇	4 ♡	♣ A 10 7

Your 4 ♡ bid is a control-showing bid; it is not meant to show normal heart support and your partner *must not pass*. Since the heart suit was bid previously, it would be appropriate to bid 4 ♡ with the ♡ K, as well as with the ♡ A; but it is a doubtful maneuver to make a control-showing bid in your partner's suit with a void or a singleton.

Showing Second-Round Controls

A second control-showing bid in the same suit shows *second-round* control (king or singleton) in that suit. These bids are especially useful when investigating a grand slam. For example:

♠ A K 10 9 6 4	*Partner*	*You*	♠ Q J 8 2
♡ K 5	1 ♠	3 ♠	♡ A Q 10
◊ A Q 8 3 2	4 ◊	4 ♡	◊ K 4
♣ —	5 ♣	5 ◊	♣ Q 9 6 5
	7 ♠		

Your 5 ◊ bid shows second-round control, and provides valuable information to partner. Note that your partner could visualize a grand slam if you held two key cards, the ♡ A and ◊ K. He planned his bidding perfectly to give you a chance to show your hand. If you did not bid 4 ♡ followed by 5 ◊, he would have settled for a contract of 6 ♠.

Partner	*You*	♠ 9 2
2 ♡	3 ♡	♡ J 10 9 3
3 ♠	4 ♣	◊ 7 6 3
4 ◊	5 ♣	♣ A K 8 4

Your 4 ♣ bid showed first-round control, and your 5 ♣ bid shows second-round control of the club suit.

When an opponent doubles your partner's control-showing bid (as a lead director), you may redouble to show second-round control of that suit; it does not mean that you want to play that contract redoubled. For example:

♠ A K 10 6 3	*You*	*Opp.*	*Partner*	*Opp.*
♡ K 9 8	1 ♠	P	2 ♡	P
◊ Q 9 7 2	3 ♡	P	4 ♣	DBL
♣ 3	RDBL			

Your redouble shows second-round control of clubs. With no club control, you should pass to encourage your partner in his slam effort, or bid 4 ♡ to discourage him.

THE VOLUNTARY BID OF FIVE IN A MAJOR SUIT

When you and your partner have agreed to play in a major suit, a "voluntary" bid of five in that major asks your partner if he has first- or second-round control in a specified suit. Note that this convention does not apply if an opponent's bid forced you to bid at the five-level; it must have been possible for you to bid, or pass, four of the agreed major.

Here is how it works. If your side has bid all of the suits except one, a bid of five of the agreed major asks for control of the unbid suit. If an opponent has bid a suit, a bid of five of the agreed major asks for control of the opponent's suit. The responses are: (1) With first-round control in the specified suit, cue-bid the specified suit. (2) With second-round control of the specified suit, bid six of the agreed major. (3) With the guarded king in the specified suit, bid 5 NT. (4) With no control in the specified suit, pass. For example:

♠ A K 10 9 4	*You*	*Partner*
♡ 7 5	1 ♠	3 ♠
◇ K 4	4 ♣	4 ◇
♣ A K J 8	5 ♠	

Hearts is the specified suit. Your 5 ♠ bid tells partner to bid 6 ♡ with first-round control, 6 ♠ with second-round control, 5 NT with the guarded king, or to pass 5 ♠ with no first- or second-round control.

♠ A 10 9 5	*You*	*Opp.*	*Partner*	*Opp.*
♡ A K 10 7 4 2	1 ♡	2 ♣	2 ♠	P
◇ A	5 ♠			
♣ J 3				

Clubs is the specified suit. Your partner should bid 6 ♣ with first-round control, 6 ♠ with second-round control, 5 NT with the guarded king, or pass with no first- or second-round control.

THE BLACKWOOD CONVENTION

The Blackwood 4 NT bid is a way to ask your partner how many aces he holds. The responses are:

> 5 ♣ = no aces, or all four aces
> 5 ◇ = one ace
> 5 ♡ = two aces
> 5 ♠ = three aces

When to Use Blackwood

The average bridge player uses Blackwood on many hands with which a different approach should be used to search for a makable slam. All of the following conditions should be met before asking for aces. Do not use Blackwood unless:

1. You know the intended trump suit and are prepared to bid a slam if partner's response shows that one ace is missing.
2. Your hand does not contain a void suit. Partner's response will tell you *how many* aces he has, not *which*; if he holds the ace in your void suit, it may be worthless.
3. You do not have two quick losers in an unbid suit. Holdings in an unbid suit such as Q-J-X or X-X should rule out Blackwood.
4. You are reasonably sure the combined hands have at least 33 points. You will then be prepared to bid a slam if it develops that one ace is missing, and to play at the five-level if two aces are missing. Blackwood is not a *slam try*. It is simply a check back to make sure you have the required number of aces to bid a slam.

5. You hold at least two aces if clubs are to be trumps and at least one ace if diamonds are to be trumps. Then partner's response announcing that two aces are missing will not carry the bidding higher than five of the agreed suit. You should be aware of the danger of using Blackwood when you are shy of aces and partner's response might trap you, but this is a rule that may be broken as you shall see in one of the following illustrations.

Here are five examples:

Partner	You	♠ K 9 8 7 3
1 ♠	4 NT	♡ A K Q 9 5 2
		◊ 3
		♣ 6

This hand meets all of the requirements and is perfect for Blackwood. If partner bids 5 ◊, you will bid 5 ♠; if he bids 5 ♡, you will bid 6 ♠; and if he bids 5 ♠, you will bid 7 ♠. If he bids 5 ♣, sue Mr. Blackwood.

♠ A K Q 10 3	You	Partner
♡ K Q 2	2 ♠	3 ♠
◊ —	4 ♣	
♣ A K Q J 5		

If your partner has the ♡ A, you should bid 7 ♠; but if you use Blackwood and he shows one ace, you will not know which one. To find out which ace your partner has, use a *control-showing bid;* do not use Blackwood with a void suit.

Partner	You	♠ A Q 7 4 2
1 ♣	1 ♠	♡ 7 3
3 ♣	4 ◊	◊ A 10 9 8
		♣ K 2

It is very possible that your partner does not have any control in hearts. The first step toward finding out is to bid 4 ◊, a control-showing bid. Note that Blackwood would not give you the answer if partner shows only one ace. Do not use Blackwood with two quick losers in an unbid suit.

♠ K Q J 7 4 2	You	Partner
♡ K J 10	1 ♠	3 ♠
◊ 4	4 ♣	
♣ A 10 8		

Here you are only justified in making a *slam try* below the game level because the combined hands may not have 33 points; you have 18 and partner has shown 13 to 16. If your partner's next bid is 4 ◊ or 4 ♡, you will bid 4 ♠; partner should bid again if he has a maximum and likes his hand. If your hand were a little stronger (say your clubs were A-Q-10), it would be right to bid 4 NT (instead of 4 ♣) with the intention of bidding 6 ♠ if partner shows two aces.

Partner	You	♠ A K Q
1 ♡	2 ♣	♡ 5 2
2 ◊	4 ♣	◊ Q
4 ◊	4 NT	♣ K Q J 10 9 7 6
5 ◊	?	

Here is the trap that may occur if you use Blackwood when clubs is the intended trump suit and you have only one ace. It is so unlikely that partner has only one ace that you can hardly be blamed for bidding 4 NT. Off two aces, it seems that the only makable contract still available is 5 NT; but you must not bid it over 5 ◇ as that would ask for kings. However, there is an escape: If you bid five of an unplayable suit, in this case 5 ♠, it is a command for partner to bid 5 NT. This is a handy convention when the need arises, but you should always be wary about using Blackwood with fewer than two aces when clubs is the intended trump suit.

How to Ask for Kings

A bid of 5 NT asks for kings, *provided it follows a Blackwood 4 NT bid.* The responses to 5 NT are:

6 ♣ = no kings
6 ◇ = one king
6 ♡ = two kings
6 ♠ = three kings
6 NT = four kings

Since a 5 NT Blackwood bid commits the bidding to the six-level, it could not possibly have any purpose except to try for a grand slam. Therefore, never bid 5 NT if an ace is missing, or if partner's response may get you overboard. Here are two examples showing how asking for kings may help to reach a grand slam:

♠ A Q 10 8 7	*You*	*Partner*
♡ A Q 5 3	2 ♠	3 ♠
◇ A K	4 NT	5 ♣
♣ A K	5 NT	

Note that, even when you have all four aces, you must go through the routine of bidding 4 NT first, before you can ask for kings. If partner shows two kings, you should bid 7 ♠.

♠ K Q 10 3	*You*	*Partner*
♡ A 7 3	1 ◇	1 ♠
◇ K Q J 10 5	3 ♠	4 NT
♣ 2	5 ◇	5 NT
	7 ♠	

Your partner must have the three missing aces to bid 5 NT. It is up to you to bid the grand slam because you know the trumps are solid and partner will be able to discard any heart losers on your diamond suit.

How to Show a Void Suit

If your partner bids 4 NT (Blackwood) and you have a void suit, it is sometimes possible to show your void suit and tell your partner how many aces you have at the same time; but a void suit is never treated the same as an ace. The following method for showing a void suit is probably the best and it is practiced by many experts, but it is not commonly known in nonexpert circles; so do not use it unless you have a firm agreement with your partner in advance.

Provided a trump suit has been agreed upon and you have a void suit, answer your partner's 4 NT bid as follows:

1. With exactly one ace, bid six in your void suit if it ranks below the trump suit, or bid six of the trump suit if the void suit ranks higher than the trump suit. For example:

Partner	You	♠ Q 7 2
1 ♠	2 ♣	♡ —
2 ♡	3 ♠	◊ K 10 8 2
4 NT	6 ♡	♣ A Q 9 7 4 2

Your 6 ♡ bid shows exactly one ace and a void in hearts. If your void suit were diamonds, you would jump to 6 ◊.

♠ A K 7 4 2	You	Partner
♡ —	1 ♠	2 ◊
◊ K 10 5 3	3 ◊	4 NT
♣ Q 9 8 3	6 ◊	

Your 6 ◊ bid shows a void in a higher-ranking suit, which is obviously hearts. If your void suit were clubs, you would bid 6 ♣.

2. With exactly two aces and a void suit, always bid 5 NT. If the agreed trump suit is a minor, there is no way to tell your partner which of your suits is the void. But if the agreed suit is a major, the 4 NT bidder may follow with a bid of 6 ♣ to ask in which suit you are void; you then bid six of the void suit if it can be shown below six of the trump suit, or bid six of the trump suit if it cannot be shown. For example:

Partner	You	♠ A 10 8
1 ♠	2 ◊	♡ —
2 ♡	3 ♠	◊ A Q J 9 7 5
4 NT	5 NT	♣ 6 4 3 2
6 ♣	6 ♡	

Your 6 ♡ bid shows a void in hearts. If your void suit were clubs, you would bid 6 ♠.

3. With zero aces and a void suit, bid 5 ♣. With three aces and a void suit, bid 5 ♠. In other words, using this method, there is no way to show a void suit unless you hold one or two aces.

NOTE: Probably the most popular method for showing a void suit in response to a 4 NT Blackwood bid is: 6 ♣ = no aces and a void suit; 6 ◊ = one ace and a void suit, 6 ♡ = two aces and a void suit; and 6 ♠ = three aces and a void suit. This is not the best way to play because it does not indicate which suit is the void, and in some cases the response cannot be made because it would be higher than six of the agreed trump suit. Although playing this way is better than nothing, the method described above is far superior.

Blackwood Responses over Intervening Bids

When an adventurous opponent decides to bid after your partner's 4 NT bid (obviously heading for a sacrifice bid and trying to jam up your bidding), you need a different method to tell your partner about your aces. One popular method that is as good as any is "DOPI." If an opponent makes a bid at the five-level over your partner's 4 NT bid:

> Double = no aces
> Pass = one ace
> First bidding step = two aces
> Second bidding step = three aces
> Third bidding step = four aces

DOPI gets its name from "double-zero, pass-one." Here is one example:

Opp.	Partner	Opp.	You	
	1 ♠	2 ♡	3 ♠	♠ K 10 9 6
4 ♡	4 NT	5 ♡	5 ♠	♡ 6 4
				◊ A 8 7 6
				♣ A J 2

Your 5 ♠ bid is the first bidding step and shows two aces. With no aces you would double, with one ace you would pass, with three aces you would bid 5 NT, and with four aces you would bid 6 ♣.

THE GERBER CONVENTION

Gerber is a way to find out how many aces and kings your partner holds, as is Blackwood, but 4 ♣ is the asking bid for aces and 5 ♣ is the asking bid for kings.

A few players use Gerber instead of Blackwood because it keeps the bidding lower. However, 4 ♣ is too useful as a natural bid, or as a cue-bid, to give it up entirely to ask for aces. So the vast majority of players use Blackwood on the auctions where 4 NT would ask for aces, and use Gerber on many of the auctions where 4 NT would not ask for aces.

A bid of 4 ♣ asks for aces provided your partner's last bid was 1 NT or 2 NT, or provided your own last bid was a Stayman 2 ♣ bid. In all other cases, including when your partner's last bid was 3 NT, a bid of 4 ♣ is *not* Gerber; 4 ♣ *must be a jump bid to ask for aces.* (NOTE: Some players use Gerber in auctions not recommended here, so it is important that you and your partner are in accord as to when a 4 ♣ bid is Gerber and when it is not.)

The responses to a 4 ♣ Gerber bid are:

> 4 ◊ = no aces, or all four aces
> 4 ♡ = one ace
> 4 ♠ = two aces
> 4 NT = three aces

Here are two hands in which it would be appropriate to use Gerber:

Partner	You	
1 NT	4 ♣	♠ K Q J 7 6 4 2
		♡ 3
		◊ K Q J 9
		♣ 7

If partner responds 4 ♠ to show two aces, you will pass; if he bids 4 NT to show three aces, you will bid 6 ♠; if he by some miracle bids 4 ◊ to show four aces (he could not have zero aces), you will bid 7 NT.

Partner	You	♠ K Q 6
1 NT	2 ♣	♡ K Q 10 8
2 ♡	4 ♣	◊ A 7 4 3 2
		♣ 7

It is possible that two aces are missing, and Gerber is the way to find out. If partner responds 4 ♡, you will pass; if he responds 4 ♠ or 4 NT, you will bid 6 ♡.

Provided it follows a Gerber 4 ♣ bid, a bid of 5 ♣ asks for kings. The responses are:

  5 ◊ = no kings
  5 ♡ = one king
  5 ♠ = two kings
  5 NT = three kings
  6 ♣ = four kings

Here is one example:

♠ A Q J 3	You	Partner
♡ K 8	1 ◊	2 NT
◊ A Q J 10 7	4 ♣	4 ♠
♣ K 2	5 ♣	

Partner's 2 NT bid shows 13 to 15 high-card points. He has shown two aces, and it is possible that he has two kings. If he bids 5 ♠ you should bid 7 NT; if he bids 5 ◊ or 5 ♡, you should bid 6 NT.

WHEN IS A 4 NT BID NOT BLACKWOOD?

There are other important uses for a bid of 4 NT besides asking for aces, and this poses a grave problem for the average player. To my knowledge, there is no simple and efficient guideline spelling out exactly when 4 NT is or is not Blackwood. I propose that you make the following agreements with your favorite partners, although they would not be considered 100% accurate in expert circles.

Treat all 4 NT bids as Blackwood with the following exceptions:

1. If your partner's last bid was a natural 1 NT, 2 NT, or 3 NT, or if your own last bid was a 2 ♣ (Stayman) response to a 1 NT opening bid, 4 NT is not Blackwood; it is the "quantitative notrump raise," explained immediately following this section.
2. If your own last bid was 3 NT and no major suit has been agreed, 4 NT is not Blackwood; it means you wish to play a contract of 4 NT. For example:

♠ K Q 10	You	Partner
♡ A Q 7	1 ◊	3 ◊
◊ J 9 4 3	3 NT	4 ◊
♣ Q 10 2	4 NT	

Your bid says you wish to play 4 NT.

♠ A K J 9 2	You	Partner
♡ K 10 4	1 ♠	2 ♣
◊ A 8 3	3 NT	4 ♠
♣ K J	4 NT	

Since a major suit has been agreed, 4 NT is Blackwood. These situations are very rare.

3. If one or both of your opponents have bid but your partner has not, 4 NT is not Blackwood; it means you want your partner to bid a suit. Note the following example and then see "4 NT Overcalls," pages 114, 155 and 156.

♠ —	*You*	*Opp.*	*Partner*	*Opp.*
♡ A Q 7 4 2	1 ♡	1 ♠	P	4 ♠
◊ K Q 10 8	4 NT			
♣ A K J 3				

Your 4 NT bid is not Blackwood and it is not natural; it asks your partner to bid a suit.

The one remaining ambiguous case is: What does an opening bid of 4 NT mean? In yesteryear it showed a very strong balanced hand, about 28 to 30 high-card points, but this is not practiced by the experts today and is by no means the best way to play. It is my recommendation that you play an opening 4 NT bid as Blackwood. Here is a deal that actually took place in a rubber bridge game years ago, and it convinced me to use an opening 4 NT bid as Blackwood:

NORTH
♠ Q 8
♡ A 5 3
◊ 10 9 6 4 2
♣ 7 5 2

WEST
♠ A J 10 6 2
♡ 4
◊ K J 8 7
♣ J 9 3

EAST
♠ K 9 7 5 4
♡ 9 8 7 6 2
◊ Q 5 3
♣ —

SOUTH
♠ 3
♡ K Q J 10
◊ A
♣ A K Q 10 8 6 4

South	*West*	*North*	*East*
4 NT	P	5 ◊	P
6 ♣	P	P	P

North and South were two experts using a 4 NT opening bid as Blackwood. They were vulnerable versus nonvulnerable opponents. They of course made 6 ♣ with 100 honors and scored up 1470 points. If North and South had not been playing the 4 NT opening bid as Blackwood, the opening bid would probably have been 2 ♣. This would allow the nonvulnerable West player to overcall 2 ♠ and set the stage for an excellent sacrifice bid. When North and South eventually bid 6 ♣, East would bid 6 ♠, which would probably be set only one trick.

THE QUANTITATIVE NOTRUMP RAISE

If your partner's *last* bid was a natural 1 NT, 2 NT, or 3 NT, then a 4 NT bid by you is a "quantitative raise," asking partner to bid further (usually 6 NT) with maximum values, or to pass 4 NT with minimum values. The number of points you need to bid 4 NT depends on the number of points your partner has shown by his notrump bid. For example:

Partner	You	♠ A 10 2
1 NT	4 NT	♡ K 7 5
		◇ K 10 9 8
		♣ A J 4

Assuming partner's opening 1 NT bid shows 16 to 18 high-card points, your 4 NT bid shows 15 or 16. Your 4 NT bid *invites* slam. Partner should pass with only 16 points, bid 6 NT with 18 points, and use his judgment (sometimes a pure guess) with 17 points.

Partner	You	♠ K 10 8
2 NT	4 NT	♡ 7 6 3
		◇ K Q 7
		♣ K 9 5 2

Assuming partner's opening 2 NT bid shows 21 to 23 high-card points, your 4 NT bid shows 10 or 11. Your partner should pass 4 NT with only 21 points, bid 6 NT with 23 points, and use his judgment with 22 points.

When you know the combined total is 33 to 36 high-card points, do not bid 4 NT to invite a slam; bid the slam directly if you know where to play it. For example:

Partner	You	♠ 6 4 2
1 NT	6 NT	♡ A K 10
		◇ A J 7 5
		♣ K Q 8

You have 17 points and partner has 16 to 18, so the combined total is 33, 34, or 35. With 4-3-3-3 distribution, 6 NT is obviously the right contract. Your 6 NT bid shows 17 or 18 points, so *your partner must pass*.

A 4 NT bid is quantitative as long as your partner's *last* bid was 1 NT, 2 NT, or 3 NT; it does not necessarily have to be an opening bid. For example:

Partner	You	♠ A 10 7 2
1 ♣	1 ♡	♡ K Q 9 5
1 NT	4 NT	◇ A Q 3
		♣ K 10

Your 4 NT bid shows 18 or 19 high-card points. Your partner's 1 NT rebid shows a maximum of 15 high-card points. He should bid 6 NT with 15, pass 4 NT with 13, and use his judgment with 14.

	You	Partner
♠ A K Q 6 3	1 ♠	2 NT
♡ J 10	4 NT	
◇ A K J		
♣ 8 7 2		

Your 4 NT bid shows 18 or 19 high-card points. The 2 NT response shows 13, 14, or 15 high-card points. Your partner should bid 6 NT with 15, pass 4 NT with 13, and use his judgment with 14.

There is one case in which the quantitative 4 NT bid applies even though partner's last bid was a suit. This occurs when it immediately follows a Stayman bid of 2 ♣. For example:

Partner	You	♠ A Q J 7
1 NT	2 ♣	♡ K 5
2 ♡	4 NT	◊ A J 10 3
		♣ 10 9 2

Your 4 NT bid shows 15 or 16 high-card points. The purpose of the 2 ♣ bid was to find out if partner had a spade suit; a suit slam with a 4-4 fit is often a better contract than 6 NT. Now that partner has bid the wrong major, you bid 4 NT to invite him to pass 4 NT with a minimum, or to bid again with a maximum. If he does bid again, he should bid another four-card suit if he has one, or else 6 NT.

There is also a quantitative 5 NT bid, but it is not commonly known and should not be used unless you have a special partnership agreement. The quantitative 5 NT raise applies to any auction in which a quantitative 4 NT raise applies (partner's last bid was a natural 1 NT, 2 NT, or 3 NT). The 5 NT bid invites partner to bid 7 NT with a maximum and to bid 6 NT with a minimum; *he may not pass.* For example:

Partner	You	♠ A Q 7
1 NT	5 NT	♡ K Q 9
		◊ A 10 2
		♣ A 9 5 4

Your 5 NT bid shows 19 or 20 high-card points. Your partner should bid 6 NT with a minimum 1 NT opening, or bid 7 NT with a maximum.

THE GRAND SLAM FORCE

The grand slam force is a way to inquire about your partner's trump honors. A bid of 5 NT, not preceded by 4 NT, asks partner to bid a grand slam if he has two of the top three trump honors: A-K, A-Q, or K-Q. If he has none or one of the top three honors, he must bid six of the intended trump suit. For example:

♠ A K 7	You	Partner
♡ A J 9 8 3	1 ♡	3 ♡
◊ —	3 ♠	4 ♣
♣ K Q J 7 2	5 NT	

If your partner has the king and queen of hearts, he will bid 7 ♡; otherwise he must bid 6 ♡.

Partner	You	♠ 10 6 4
1 ♡	3 ♡	♡ K Q 7 2
3 ♠	4 ♣	◊ K 8 7 3
5 NT	7 ♡	♣ A 10

Now I have put you on the other side of the table. Holding the king and queen of hearts, you must bid 7 ♡. You can see by looking at the two hands that the grand slam can be made by discarding one of dummy's spades on the club suit.

When there is no agreed trump suit, a bid of 5 NT asks about the trump honors in partner's last-bid suit. For example:

    ♠ A 10 8   *You*   *Partner*

    ♡ A K Q J 6   1 ♡   2 ◊

    ◊ Q 9 7 6 3   5 NT

    ♣ —

If your partner has the ace and king of diamonds, he will bid 7 ◊ ; otherwise he must bid 6 ◊.

The above is the fundamental version of the grand slam force that has been around for half a century. Although much more is done in expert circles, I recommend that you make an agreement with your regular partners to play the following: The responses to 5 NT are altered so that you bid seven of the intended trump suit with two of the top three honors; six of the agreed trump suit with none of the top three honors; and 6 ♣ with one of the top three honors. Note that when clubs is the intended trump suit, you must bid 6 ♣ with either none or one of the top three honors. The following example illustrates how it can be important to find out whether partner has none or one of the top three honors:

    ♣ A Q 10 7 2   *You*   *Partner*

    ♡ K Q 9 3   2 ♣   3 ♠

    ◊ A K Q J   4 ◊   4 ♡

    ♣ —   5 NT

After finding out that partner has the ♡ A, you are prepared to bid a grand slam if he has the ♠ K. If partner's next bid is 6 ♣ to show one of the top three spade honors, you will bid 7 ♠. If he bids 6 ♣ to deny one of the top three spades, you will pass.

18

The Scoring and the Strategy

♣　　♦　　♥　　♠　　♣　　♦　　♥　　♠

The scoring method for old-fashioned rubber bridge and its successor, Chicago bridge, is "total points." The most common scoring method for duplicate bridge is "match points," but scoring by "international match points" (IMPs) is popular in team-of-four contests. The various scoring methods are explained at the end of this chapter, and it will certainly improve your game if you are familiar with the scoring for the game that you play.

The way a game is scored dictates the odds, so there are some differences in strategy. The first seventeen chapters of this book were written with total-point scoring in mind; but, as I look back, just about everything applies equally well to match points and IMPs. So the differences between scoring methods are not extraordinary; they are limited to special areas of bidding. "Part-scores" (partials) carry over from one deal to the next when playing total points, and part-scores have a heavy influence on the bidding strategy. So before getting into match-point strategy and how it differs from total-point strategy, note the two subtle differences between old-fashioned rubber bridge and Chicago bridge, and then how you should bid when a part-score is involved.

1. In the second or third deal at Chicago bridge (when your opponents are vulnerable and you are not), you should open the bidding very light in fourth seat to "take away their vulnerability." If you open with as few as 9 or 10 high-card points, the opponents are apt to outbid you; but since they are both passed hands, it is extremely unlikely that they will bid and make a game. If you pass in fourth seat, the deal is redealt with the same vulnerability; while either side may be lucky and pick up a big hand, the opponents are in a position to win much more because the scoring bonuses for vulnerable games and slams are bigger than the bonuses for nonvulnerable games and slams.
2. When your opponents are vulnerable and you are not, a sacrifice bid is more apt to be profitable at Chicago bridge than at rubber bridge. For example, suppose your opponents bid 4 ♠, which they can make, and you bid 5 ♦, expecting that you will be set two or three tricks. In Chicago bridge you save a clear 320 or 120 points—minus 300 or 500 instead of minus 620. In rubber bridge the fact that you lose a lesser amount is clouded because the opponents need only one more game to win the rubber while your side needs two games. While minus 300 is worthwhile at rubber bridge (especially to prolong the rubber if your current partner is better than the other players), minus 500 is not. Please note that this difference in strategy applies to favorable vulnerability; if both sides are vulnerable, there is no difference.

PART-SCORE BIDDING

The fact that one side or the other has a part-score can make a big difference in your bidding. This vital topic is rarely seen in bridge books or taught by bridge teachers, so most players are at a total loss as to what to do when a part-score is involved. Here is your chance to enlighten yourself about part-score bidding.

When Your Side Has a Part-Score

The requirements for overcalls and takeout doubles are the same as when there are no part-scores. A part-score of 20 or 30 makes little difference in the strategy, so you should open the bidding and respond to partner's opening bids in very much the same way as you do without a part-score. It is when your side opens the bidding and has a part-score of 40 or higher that there are some drastic changes. In some cases the size of your part-score (40, 60, 70, etc.) will affect the bidding. These differences in strategy will be explained in the analysis of the following illustrations.

♠ A 6 3
♡ A 7 2
◇ K J 10 5
♣ 9 4 2

You should pass this hand whether your side has a part-score or not. If you are wondering why I bothered to put this hand in, it is to squelch any ideas you might have about opening lighter just because you have a part-score.

♠ J 6 3 2
♡ A K J 7
◇ A 8 5
♣ 6 5

Open the bidding with 1 ♡ if you have a part-score. If your side did not have a part-score, the right opening bid would be 1 ◇; but with a part-score you should shy away from opening with a three-card suit. Even though you play "five-card majors," it is okay to open the bidding with a *strong* four-card major suit when you have a part-score.

♠ Q 6 4 2
♡ A K J
◇ A Q 5
♣ K 10 3

Open this 19-point hand with 1 NT if you have a part-score. Without a part-score you should open with 1 ♣; you need 16 to 18 points to open 1 NT. With a part-score the emphasis is more on showing your distribution than your point count; you may open 1 NT with a point more or less than is normally required.

Partner	Opp.	You	
1 ♡	P	?	♠ J 10 2
			♡ 4 2
			◇ K 10 8 6
			♣ 9 8 7 3

With a 70 part-score you should pass, as you would with no part-score. But with a part-score of 40 or 60, you should bid 1 NT. Do not pass your partner below game unless your hand is almost worthless; for example, if you take away the ◇ K (leaving only 1 high-card point), you should of course pass 1 ♡ whether you have a part-score or not.

Partner	Opp.	You	
1 ♡	P	?	♠ 6 4
			♡ Q 8 6
			◇ A J 9 8
			♣ 7 5 3 2

Bid 2 ♡, regardless of the part-score situation. If you had a 70 part-score you would be "bidding over score," but you would not be making a slam try. It is usually best to get your one little bid in early to discourage the opponents from bidding and to help your partner to compete intelligently in the subsequent bidding in case the opponents do bid. If your partner has a strong hand and bids over 2 ♡ to try for a slam, you can discourage him in the next round of bidding. Note that if partner's opening bid were 1 ♠, you should bid 1 NT regardless of the part-score situation, for all the same reasons.

Partner	*Opp.*	*You*	♠ A 10 4
1 ♡	P	?	♡ 5 2
			◇ K 8 7 6 2
			♣ K J 9

With a part-score *below* 60 you should bid 2 ◇ with your 12-point hand, as you would without a part-score. However, with a part-score of 60 or higher you should bid 1 NT. When your two-over-one response is enough for game, it is not forcing; your partner may pass with a worthless doubleton in your suit. A 2 ◇ contract here may be set if you get a bad trump break, while 1 NT seems much safer. When your response is enough for game, avoid bidding a weak suit at the two-level; bid the contract you are most anxious to play.

Partner	*Opp.*	*You*	♠ 4 2
1 ♡	P	?	♡ 7
			◇ K 9 8 2
			♣ Q J 10 9 6 3

With a part-score of 60 or higher, bid 2 ♣. When your bid is enough for game, you may bid a new suit at the two-level with fewer than the 11 points normally required, provided you have an excellent suit. With no part-score, or a part-score below 60, you should bid 1 NT with the thought that you may bid clubs later if you get another chance to bid and the bidding does not get too high.

Partner	*Opp.*	*You*	♠ A K Q 3
1 ♡	P	?	♡ 8 5
			◇ 9 4
			♣ A K 10 7 2

With no part-score, or with a part-score below 60, you should bid 2 ♣ with this 17-point hand; it is wrong to jump-shift right away when you have no idea which suit will be trump. Your 2 ♣ bid is forcing and you will show your strength later in the bidding. With a part-score of 60 or higher you should jump to 3 ♣ and *your bid is absolutely forcing for one round;* when a nonjump new-suit response completes a game (as a 2 ♣ bid would here), you should jump-shift with any hand containing 17 or more points.

Partner	*Opp.*	*You*	♠ 6 4
1 ♡	P	?	♡ K J 9 3
			◇ A Q 10
			♣ K 10 7 2

Bid 3 ♡ regardless of the part-score situation. If partner's opening bid were 1 ♠, you should bid 2 NT. The requirements for these strong jump responses are the same whether you have a part-score or not, except that with a part-score they are not forcing.

♠ A K J 8 4	You	Opp.	Partner	Opp.
♡ 9 7 5	1 ♠	P	2 ♣	P
◇ A J 2	?			
♣ 7 3				

With no part-score, or with a part-score below 60, you are forced to bid again and should bid 2 ♠. With a part-score of 60 or higher your partner must have a very good club suit but may have a relatively weak hand (his bid is not forcing), so you should pass; you should also pass with this minimum opening if partner's response were 2 ◇, 2 ♡, 2 NT, or 3 ♣, but you would be required to bid again if he made a jump shift such as 3 ♣.

♠ K 10 9 7	You	Opp.	Partner	Opp.
♡ 6 4 2	1 ◇	P	1 ♡	P
◇ A K 8 5	?			
♣ K 4				

When partner's response is a suit bid at the one-level, you should be reluctant to pass even with a part-score of 70 or higher. If your partner's hand is so weak that he can make only 1 ♡, the opponents will surely compete and drive you higher. The right rebid here is 1 ♠, to arrive at the most sensible contract, or to set the stage for an intelligent competitive auction. If partner responded 1 ♠ instead of 1 ♡, your normal rebid is 2 ♠ regardless of the part-score situation.

Partner	Opp.	You	♠ K J 8 3 2
1 NT	P	?	♡ 4
			◇ A Q 7
			♣ 7 6 5 2

Without a part-score, the normal response with this hand is 3 ♠ to force your partner to bid again and reach game. With a part-score of 40 or higher, the right bid is just 2 ♠. You are not going to bid a slam when partner opens the bidding with 1 NT; so why get to the three-level, which might put your game in jeopardy if you encounter bad breaks?

Partner	Opp.	You	♠ K Q 6 4
1 NT	P	?	♡ A 10 8 6
			◇ 5 3 2
			♣ 7 4

With no part-score or with a part-score below 60, the normal response with this hand is 2 ♣, Stayman. With a part-score of 60 or higher, the most sensible call is to pass.

When Your Opponents Have a Part-Score

The tactics are obvious; compete more aggressively than you would if they had no part-score, especially when the vulnerability is favorable. The best strategy is to get your side into the bidding as soon as possible in order to avoid making a risky bid later at a higher level of bidding. The most popular call with the following four hands would be to pass if no part-scores were involved; but if your opponents have a part-score, you should bid as follows:

♠ 6 3
♡ 9 5 2
◊ K Q 2
♣ A Q 10 7 4

As dealer, open the bidding with 1 ♣ regardless of the vulnerability; you avoid the risk of competing later at a higher level of bidding and taking a big set. Notice that it is more important to open the bidding with unfavorable vulnerability than with favorable vulnerability; if you pass and the opponents open the bidding, it would be much more dangerous to bid if your side is vulnerable.

Opp.	Partner	Opp.	You	
1 ♠	P	2 ♠	3 ◊	♠ 8 5
				♡ A Q 6
				◊ Q 9 7 5 4 2
				♣ 10 3

Bid 3 ◊ with favorable or equal vulnerability, but a pass is recommended with unfavorable. If you do bid 3 ◊, you may occasionally get doubled and suffer a big penalty; but often you will drive the opponents to a higher contract and set them, or outbid them, while if you passed they would score a game. If the opponents did not have a part-score, it would be foolish to bid with this hand regardless of the vulnerability; you might get doubled and take a big set on occasions when the opponents cannot make a game, or your partner will expect you to have a better hand and bid too much.

Opp.	You	
1 ♠	?	♠ 8 3
		♡ J 9 3 2
		◊ A Q 10
		♣ K 10 6 4

Double with favorable or equal vulnerability, but pass with unfavorable unless you feel lucky.

Opp.	You	
1 ♡	?	♠ Q J 7 3
		♡ 8 5 2
		◊ 7 4
		♣ A K 9 5

Bid 1 ♠ with favorable vulnerability, or possibly with equal vulnerability, but pass with unfavorable. Overcalling with such a weak four-card suit would be unthinkable if the opponents did not have a part-score.

MATCH-POINT STRATEGY

Match-point scoring is the method used in most duplicate bridge games. The object at match points is to get a better score than the other pairs on each deal; the amount by which you beat them does not matter, since you can win only 1 match point for each pair that you beat whether you beat them by 10 points or 2000 points. Since the goal in total points is to win as many points as you can, while the goal in match points is to beat as many pairs as you can, there are obviously some differences in strategy. In the limited space allotted to the subject here, I will discuss the highlights of how match-point scoring affects the strategy for: (1) competitive bidding; (2) choosing the final contract; and (3) sacrifice bidding. (NOTE: The strategy for play and defense is ignored in this book on bidding.)

Competitive Bidding

You should use much more daring tactics in competitive bidding at match points than at total points, because the *frequency* with which your bid will win or lose is more important than the *amount* your bid will win or lose. The vulnerability is usually important in competitive situations; assume that both sides are vulnerable in the four following illustrations:

Opp.	You	
1 ♠	?	♠ 8 5
		♡ A Q 10 7 3
		◊ 9 6
		♣ K Q 4 2

Bid 2 ♡ at match points, but pass at total points. Once in a while you will get doubled and suffer a big penalty, but more often your 2 ♡ bid will improve your match-point score.

Opp.	Partner	Opp.	You	
		1 ♠	P	♠ 7 6 3
2 ♠	P	P	?	♡ A 10 8
				◊ K 9 3 2
				♣ K 10 2

You should double at match points; but since your double may lead to a big loss, a pass would be wiser at total points. Your partner will have to bid at the three-level, but aggressive competitive bidding in the balancing seat is a must at match points. If your partner has a good suit he may be able to make a part-score, or maybe the opponents will bid 3 ♠ and you will set them.

Opp.	Partner	Opp.	You	
	1 ♡	1 ♠	2 ♡	♠ A 10 6
2 ♠	P	P	3 ♡	♡ 9 7 4 2
P	P	3 ♠	?	◊ 8 7 2
				♣ A J 10

A double is a good gamble at match points, especially because the opponents are vulnerable; but pass at total points. If your opponents make 3 ♠, the doubled score is − 730 and the undoubled score is − 140. Your double would prove very costly at total points if they made their contract, but not at match points, as − 140 figures to be a below-average score anyway. On the good side, if you beat 3 ♡ one trick, the doubled score is + 200 and the undoubled score is + 100. If your side could make 3 ♡ for + 140, + 200 would be an excellent score while + 100 would be poor. When your side cannot make a game, + 200 at match points is a magic score, sometimes a top.

Opp.	Partner	Opp.	You	
	1 NT	2 ♡	2 ♠	♠ K 9 8 6 4
P	P	3 ♡	?	♡ 7 2
				◊ 8 4
				♣ A 5 3 2

Double at match points only. You and your partner have much the best of the high cards—at least 23 points between you—so you must try to win as much as possible. Although your double is technically a penalty double, your partner knows by your weak 2 ♠ bid that your hand is very limited; depending on his hand, he will pass or bid 3 ♠. At total points it would be wrong to double your opponents into a game they might make, when the extra amount your double will earn if you beat them one trick is 50 or 100 points.

Choosing the Final Contract

Here we are concerned with the *trick score;* that is, choosing among a major suit, a minor suit, or notrump. At total points it would not matter if you played a 4 ♠ contract and made it for a score of 420 points when you could also bid 3 NT and make four for a score of 430 points; but at match points it could be very costly. When you are playing match points and two contracts seem makable, you must bid the one that will provide the bigger trick score. Here is one example:

♠ 5	*You*	*Partner*
♡ A Q 4	1 ◊	2 NT
◊ A K Q 9 8 7	4 ♣ (Gerber)	4 ♡ (one ace)
♣ K 6 3	?	

> Even at the slam level, the trick score is important. You are off an ace, but have the values to bid a slam and the question is whether to bid 6 ◊ or 6 NT. At total points you should definitely bid 6 ◊ , the safer contract; but at match points a gambling bid of 6 NT is in order. Your partner has shown a hand with from 13 to 15 high-card points and you have 18, so the opponents have at most 9 high-card points. It is possible that the opponents have the ace and king of spades and, if they lead the suit, they can beat 6 NT while 6 ◊ would be made; but this is unlikely. If you bid 6 NT you are a big favorite to make it and the trick score of 190—instead of 120—will make a big difference in your match-point score.

Sacrifice Bidding

You should be more daring with your sacrifice bids at match points than at total points. If you are playing match points and your opponents bid a game you think they can make, it pays to get doubled and go down three tricks with favorable vulnerability (− 500 vs. − 600), go down two tricks with equal vulnerability (− 300 vs. − 400, or − 500 vs. − 600), and go down one trick with unfavorable vulnerability (− 200 vs. − 400); if you go down one trick too many, you may wind up with zero match points.

If you are sure that the opponents can make their contract, these calculations also would be accurate for Chicago bridge. But you usually are not sure whether the opponents can make their contract; and that is when more chance-taking at match points is desirable. For example, with both sides vulnerable:

♠ 7	*You*	*Opp.*	*Partner*	*Opp.*
♡ K Q J 8 2	1 ♡	DBL	2 ♣	4 ♠
◊ Q J 6	5 ♣			
♣ A 10 5 2				

> It sounds as though the opponents have bid to a normal contract that they think they can make. Partner's bidding suggests that he has a weak hand (something like ♣ K-Q-J-X-X and out), so 5 ♣ doubled figures to be down two tricks. As long as you think that 4 ♠ is a makable contract (which would cost you 620 points) and that 5 ♣ doubled will not be set more than two tricks (a minus score of 500 points), you should bid 5 ♣ when playing match points.
>
> At total points, the recommended call is to pass. It is wrong to make a bid that will gain you 120 points if you are right and cost you 600 points if you are wrong, unless you are quite sure you are right. At match points it is a question of how *often* you will be right or wrong; the *amount* that you win or lose is of less importance.

Another thought: At total points your opponents are likely to double your 5 ♠ bid and take a sure profit, even though it figures to be a lower score than they could get by making a game. At match points the opponents are more apt to bid 5 ♠ unless they think they can beat 5 ♠ doubled more than two tricks; +500 would be a poor match-point score if they could make 5 ♠ for +650. Your opponents are confronted with a difficult problem when you sacrifice, and they may decide to bid again rather than to double you; if you set that contract you have turned a big loss into a small profit. So aggressive sacrifice bidding is a winning style at match points.

If the vulnerability is favorable and you are playing match points, it pays to get doubled and go down seven tricks against a makable small slam (− 1300 vs. − 1370 or more); and it pays to get doubled and go down eleven tricks against a makable grand slam (− 2100 vs. − 2140 or more). A sacrifice bid will gain match points if the opponents can make their slam and *the other pairs are bidding it.* If you think that most of the other pairs will not bid the slam—which is usually the case if the field is weak and/or it is a tough slam to reach—a big penalty will gain you little or nothing, so pass and hope by some miracle you can beat the slam. Although the following example is unbelievable and may seem to violate the preceding words of caution, it could happen, and the sacrifice bid could earn match points. In any event, it should give you a chuckle. With favorable vulnerability:

Opp.	Partner	Opp.	You	
		1 ♠	P	♠ Q J 10 9
3 ◊	P	4 ◊	P	♡ 7 3 2
5 ♣	P	5 ♡	P	◊ 4 2
7 ◊	P	P	7 ♠	♣ J 9 8 5

If you pass and the opponents make their grand slam, you will lose 2140 points.

If you bid 7 ♠, you can be sure of taking two tricks; so 2100 points (down eleven tricks) is the most you can lose. For each other pair in the duplicate tournament that bid and made 7 ◊, you would earn 1 match point. If 7 ◊ could be set you will get zero match points for − 2100, but the jazzy bidding suggests the opponents know what they are doing.

Another thought is that the opponents may bid 7 NT (instead of doubling 7 ♠), but there is a good chance that contract will fail, and then you will have a top score.

RUBBER BRIDGE SCORING

Scoring Below the Line

TRICK SCORE: The only score entered below the line is the trick score. Points are awarded for each trick over six bid and made as follows: If trumps are clubs, 20; diamonds, 20; hearts, 30; spades, 30; notrump, 40 for the first trick and 30 for each additional trick. If the contract is doubled, multiply the trick score by two. If the contract is redoubled, multiply the trick score by four.

Scoring Above the Line

OVERTRICKS: For overtricks (tricks won in excess of the contract), if the contract is undoubled, the score is trick value, vulnerable or not; if the contract is doubled, the score not vulnerable is 100 per overtrick and the score vulnerable is 200 per overtrick; if the contract is redoubled, the doubled value of each overtrick is multiplied by two.

UNDERTRICKS: For undertricks (tricks by which declarer falls short of his contract), if the contract is not doubled, the score not vulnerable is 50 per undertrick and the score vulnerable is 100 per undertrick; if the contract is doubled, the score not vulnerable is 100 for the first undertrick and 200 for each additional undertrick, and the score vulnerable is 200 for the first undertrick and 300 for each additional undertrick; if the contract is redoubled, the doubled value of each undertrick is multiplied by two.

BONUSES:

For making any doubled or redoubled contract	50
For four trump honors (ace, king, queen, jack, or ten) in one hand	100
For all five trump honors in one hand	150
For all four aces at notrump in one hand	150
For a small slam (bidding and making twelve tricks)	
not vulnerable	500
vulnerable	750
For a GRAND SLAM (bidding and making thirteen tricks)	
not vulnerable	1000
vulnerable	1500
For winning the rubber when the opponents have no game	700
For winning the rubber when the opponents have scored a game	500

After the Rubber

After one side has won two games, the scores are totaled and the difference between the two scores is rounded to the nearest 100 (50 to the next higher 100). This difference is entered on the "back score" and then the players change partners for the next rubber.

CHICAGO BRIDGE SCORING (FOUR-DEAL BRIDGE)

Chicago bridge is a slightly higher-scoring game than rubber bridge and has been gaining in popularity, and today it has completely replaced rubber bridge in the leading bridge clubs. Rubber bridge is still popular with players who have not been exposed to Chicago bridge, plus a few diehards; but most experienced players prefer Chicago bridge for the following reasons:

1. In a cut-in game with five or six players, no player must stay out longer than four deals, about twenty minutes.
2. You can start the last rubber with the assurance that you will be finished in about twenty minutes.
3. The number of hands you play with each of the other players is nearer equal than in rubber bridge, at which a rubber may last two deals or twenty deals.

Procedure

A rubber consists of four deals, one by each player in rotation. On the first deal, neither side is vulnerable; on the second and third deals, the dealer's side is vulnerable and the other side is not; on the fourth deal, both sides are vulnerable. A deal passed out does not count; the same dealer deals again.

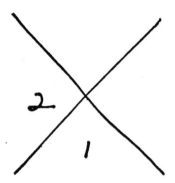

The Wheel

The "wheel" is used on the score sheet to keep track of who dealt first, the rotation of the deal, and the vulnerability. The scorekeeper draws a diagonal cross at the top of the score sheet and then writes the number 1 in the position of the first dealer, then successively 2, 3, and 4 as each successive dealer's turn comes up. In the diagram, the scorekeeper dealt first, the player on his left dealt second, and the scorekeeper will write 3 in the next space as it becomes the turn of his partner to deal.

Scoring

There is a bonus of 300 points for bidding and making a nonvulnerable game and 500 points for bidding and making a vulnerable game. These bonuses are entered on the score sheet at the time the game is made, and there is no further bonus for winning the rubber. (Note that it is possible to win from zero to four games in one rubber.)

On the fourth deal (only), there is a bonus of 100 points for making a part-score that does not complete a game. Part-scores made in the first three deals carry over to the next deal, but any game wipes out previous part-scores.

All scoring in Chicago bridge is the same as in rubber bridge with the exception of the game bonuses and the part-score bonus on the fourth deal.

After the Rubber

After four deals have been played, the scores are totaled and the difference is entered on the back score, as in rubber bridge, and then the players change partners for the next rubber.

DUPLICATE BRIDGE SCORING

At the end of each deal, the players in a duplicate game enter their score on a "traveling score slip" which accompanies each "duplicate board." The scoring is the same in duplicate bridge as it is in Chicago bridge, with two exceptions:

1. Honors do not count at duplicate bridge.
2. Part-scores do not carry over from one deal to the next in duplicate bridge; a bonus of 50 points is awarded for bidding and making any part-score.

The North player customarily does all of the scoring. After each deal has been completed, he enters on the traveling score slip:

> The contract (e.g., 3 H means the contract was three hearts); if the contract was doubled he adds an X (e.g., 2 C X for two clubs doubled); if the contract was redoubled he adds XX (e.g., 3 NT XX for three notrump doubled and redoubled)
> Who was declarer
> How many tricks declarer made or went down
> The North/South plus or minus score
> The East/West pair number

The E/W players should then check the score for errors. See the sample traveling score slip below.

Match-Point Scoring

The most popular form of duplicate bridge is a pair contest scored in match points. In this game you are actually competing against the pairs who hold the same cards as you and your partner, not the pairs you play against. Your score is compared with all of the other pairs who held your cards and you win 1 point for each pair that you beat and ½ point for each pair that you tie. The maximum possible score depends on how many times a board is played; if it is played twelve times, it would be possible to win 11 match points, so 11 is "top" and 5½ is "average."

The match-point scoring is done by the tournament director after all of the pairs who are going to play each board have done so. Although you are not required to do any match-point scoring, it is important that you know how it is done; remember, the scoring affects the strategy. Here is a sample traveling score slip for board #3, in which E/W are vulnerable and N/S are not:

N/S Pair	Contract & Declarer	Made	Down	Plus Score	Minus Score	E/W Pair	N/S Match Point Score
# 1	2 S by N	2		110		# 9	4
# 2	2 S by N	2		110		# 2	4
# 3	2 S by N	2		110		# 4	4
# 4	3 H by E		1	100		# 6	1 −
# 5	3 H by E		1	100		# 8	1 −
# 6	3 S by N		1		50	# 1	0
# 7	3 H XX by E		1	400		# 3	6
# 8	3 H X by E		2	500		# 5	7
# 9	3 S X by N	3		530		# 7	8

As you can see, board #3 was played nine times and it is possible to win from 0 to 8 match points. The tournament director match-points the N/S scores first, usually starting with the poorest score. Pair #6 did not beat or tie any pair and therefore gets a "zero," (a "bottom"). Pairs #4 and #5 beat #6 and tied each other for 1½ match points (" − " is the usual way the director indicates ½). Pairs #1, #2, and #3 beat three pairs and tied two to earn 4 match points. Pair #7 beat six pairs for 6 match points, pair #8 beat seven pairs for 7 match points, and pair #9 beat everybody for 8 match points.

The simplest way to figure out the E/W scores is by subtracting the score their opponents got from top on the board. Since top on the board here is 8, the scores for the E/W pairs are: #1 gets 8; #6 and #8 get 6½; #2, #4, and #9 get 4; #3 gets 2; #5 gets 1; and #7 gets 0.

After figuring the match-point scores on all of the traveling score slips, the director enters them on a "recap sheet" and totals them. In a "Mitchell Movement," the N/S and E/W rankings are determined separately to produce two winners, two runners-up, etc. In a "Howell Movement" (normally used when there are not enough players for a Mitchell), the N/S and E/W scores are jumbled together to produce one winner, one runner-up, etc.

This sample score slip shows that the duplicate game consisted of nine rounds. At the end of each round, the boards and the E/W players change tables. If two boards were played per round, the game was eighteen deals long. Since 4 match points is average for a board, 72 (4 x

18) is average for the session. A match-point score of 88 (two full boards above average, or a 61% game) would have a very good chance to win the tournament.

If you wish to test your ability at match-pointing, cover the match-point scores above and see if you can figure out the scores for all eighteen pairs. The nine N/S scores and the nine E/W scores must each total 36, or else you have made a mistake.

International Match-Point Scoring

IMP scoring is something in the middle, between total points and match points. The experts felt that total-point scoring gave too much credit to big swings (for example, if you lost 2000 points in one deal it would be hard to recover and win the match) and too little credit to part-scores, while match-point scoring did just the opposite. So IMPs were created to decrease the amount you win for big swings and increase the amount you win for smaller swings. This is done by transposing the difference between your score and your opponent's score into IMPs, as follows:

Difference in points	IMP	Difference in points	IMP
20–40	1	750–890	13
50–80	2	900–1090	14
90–120	3	1100–1290	15
130–160	4	1300–1490	16
170–210	5	1500–1740	17
220–260	6	1750–1990	18
270–310	7	2000–2240	19
320–360	8	2250–2490	20
370–420	9	2500–2990	21
430–490	10	3000–3490	22
500–590	11	3500–3990	23
600–740	12	4000 & up	24

The bidding strategy for IMP scoring is more in line with that for total points than with that for match points, but most experts are happy with this compromise scoring method.

IMPs are often used in team-of-four contests, rarely in pair games. Here is one example of how IMP scoring works: If you and your partner bid 4 ♠ and make it for a score of 620, while your opponents (holding the same cards against your teammates) bid 6 ♠ and go down two for a score of minus 200, your team wins by 820 total points; the 820 total points are converted into 13 IMPs.

Board-a-Match Scoring

This is simply match-point scoring in a team-of-four contest. Only 1 match point is at stake on each board. If your team gets a better score on a board than the team you are playing against (whether the difference is 10 points or 2000 points), you win 1 point; if the score is a tie, each team gets ½ point; if they beat you, you get 0.